THE CATHOLIC DIMENSION
IN HIGHER EDUCATION

By the same author:

TOWARDS A LIVING TRADITION
THE CHRISTIAN IMAGINATION

THE CATHOLIC
DIMENSION
IN HIGHER
EDUCATION

JUSTUS GEORGE LAWLER

With an Introduction
by Leo R. Ward, C.S.C.

THE NEWMAN PRESS
Westminster, Maryland, 1959

Nihil obstat: J. S. Considine, O.P.
                 Censor Librorum

Imprimatur: Albert G. Meyer, S.T.D., S.S.L.
                 Archbishop of Chicago
                 July 3, 1959

to John Nef

FOREWORD

THE SUB-TITLE ORIGINALLY CHOSEN FOR THIS BOOK WAS "An Essay in Criticism." Space limitations as well as the desire to avoid sounding too pretentious dictated its deletion. But I still hope that this book will be regarded as an *essay;* that is, as an attempt to treat the issues facing Catholic educators without being excessively definitive or conclusive—and, of course, without being too tentative. The thesis of the essay is, first, that the roots of our educational difficulties, from which stem the current confusion, are grounded in the spiritual order, and second, that they cannot be energized or invigorated save by infusing them with more balanced, less fractionary religious principles.

Too frequently the problems observable in Catholic education have been attributed to merely technical factors or historical conditioning, with the result that the solutions proffered have usually also been in the order of technique, in the order of methodic manipu-

lation, rather than of interior regeneration. It has
been suggested that the deficiencies evident in some
of our schools could be remedied by the creation of
outstanding centers for graduate study, by the introduction of more laymen into positions of authority,
by the unification of a number of small local colleges
into one larger system, by the augmentation of faculty
salaries, etc. It is not possible to discount the value
of these various correctives, but it is the thesis of the
present book that the real source of much of our bewilderment is to be found in the failure to accept the
Christian vocation as a commitment to examine afresh
in each age the relation of Christ and His teachings
to the world. This failure often takes the form of
identifying the Catholic intellectual tradition with
the culture of the Middle Ages, and of applying with
only slight modification the monistic spirituality of
that period to the issues of our time. In the educational order this results in rationalism of method, and
in the demeaning of the life of the mind and the work
of the world as profane activities not becoming to the
Christian.

However, if this book is an *essai à thèse,* it is not an
essai à clef. For, while I have necessarily had to draw
for illustration upon conditions and actions evident
in many schools and in many educators, I think it
would be a serious breach of good sense—as of charity
—to attempt to identify the different institutions and
educators that this work may happen to be criticizing.
In a review of *The Christian Imagination* in *The
Homiletic and Pastoral Review,* Brendan McGrath,
O.S.B., wrote:

Mr. Lawler, therefore, is, perhaps, prudent when he con-
fines his discussion more or less to generalities and typical
instances, without "naming names." The citation of more
pointed and particular illustrations of what he has in
mind would, perhaps, add interest and "spice" to his discussion, but, after all, it might also arouse a certain
amount of personal resentment and thereby weaken the
effect of his argument, which is unquestionably sound.
Everyone knows how hard most of us find it to listen
calmly to criticism of what is very dear to us—and it is
praiseworthy in religious to be devoted to the usages and
practices of their religious institute. But it is also good
when an "outsider" comes along and tells us that we are
in danger of failing to see the forest for the trees.

My examples in this book are more pertinent and explicit, not because I want to add "spice," nor even
because I am not now writing as an "outsider," but
because it has seemed necessary to exemplify my general assertions with facts—facts which it might not
have been incumbent upon me to bring out were it
not that there still seem to be many people to whom
the general contention of Msgr. Ellis' original essay
is simply incomprehensible. I have, however, as far as
possible tried to choose universally or, at least, commonly applicable examples. When I have cited an isolated instance which may be atypical, I have done so
only because it is possibly indicative of a tendency or
direction.

It would be an equally grave error in judgment to
assume that those conditions which I decry, or those
educators whom, in effect, I indict, are known to me
personally. To read this work as some kind of per-

sonal manifesto would be absurd. In point of fact, I
feel myself to have been fortunate in having taught
in schools where almost invariably the temper of the
institution and of its administration has been humane
and liberal. It is a fictional tradition, not without
its basis in history, ranging from the Mr. Brocklehurst
of *Jane Eyre* to the Mr. Pembroke of *The Longest
Journey*, that administrators are usually in conflict
with the working teacher. Instinctively, one applauds
Auden's "Reactionary Tract for the Times":

> Thou shalt not do as the dean pleases
> Thou shalt not write thy doctor's thesis
> On education,
> Thou shalt not worship projects nor
> Shalt thou or thine bow down before
> Administration.

Possibly if one were given to speculating on such matters, he might conceivably come up with an explanation of this traditional divergence of viewpoint between administration and faculty in terms of *being*
and *well-being:* the administration concerning itself
with the subsistence and maintenance of the school,
that is, with such things as endowments and buildings, while the faculty concerned itself with the
health, with the efflorescence and radiation of intellect
within the school. Or perhaps one might work out an
explanation in terms of a Hegelian triad—I leave all
such theorizing to those specialists who author books
bearing titles like, *Principles of Education, Organization and Curriculum,* etc. But whatever the source of
the conflict, it is not inevitable, and it is a pleasure to

be able to point to schools where what the dean pleases is what pleases the faculty also, and where the administration does not dominate the life of the institution.

And I am all the more delighted at being able to pay tribute to the administration of the school with which it is my privilege to be associated. Father Leo Ward in his recent book, *New Life in Catholic Schools,* has expressed what is the growing conviction of many Catholic educators that it is in such experiments as that of the Sisters of Mercy of Chicago, toward the development of a unified school system, that the hope of the future lies. It would not become me to re-echo such praise for a work toward the successful outcome of which I am contributing by my own efforts in the classroom. But it is fitting that I should publicly express my gratitude to the motive personality behind what has come to be known as the St. Xavier Program, to the vice-president of the college, Sister Mary Josetta, R.S.M., who has ever shown herself to be considerate in appraising my studies, critically appreciative of my teaching, and gently tolerant of whatever in my writings seemed to require amendment.

I owe a great debt also to many of my fellow teachers, at different schools throughout the Midwest, with whom I have discussed a number of topics treated in this book, and particularly to Brother Hilarian John, F.S.C., to Mr. Richard Nugent, whose critique of my first draft I have valued, to Mr. Jerome O'Mara, and to Mr. Thomas McMahon. I am deeply grateful also to Father Leo Ward for reading the manuscript and

for placing the work in the perspective of recent discussion on Catholic education by his kind Introduction. This book also has profited by the criticism of
Sister Josetta, R.S.M., Yves M.-J. Congar, O.P., and
Gerald Vann, O.P. Of course, in no instance is this
work to be taken as necessarily representing in any
way the views of these generous critics.

A few years ago, a brilliant Canadian educator,
F. Mauger-Clement, E.C., published an excellently
written autobiographical novel entitled, *Les Elus que
vous êtes,* and dedicated it to his fellow teachers, who
"aux frontières des générations, affrontent avec allé-
gresse le terrible quotidien." In a sense any work on
Catholic education is implicitly dedicated to the
working teachers, to the men and women who in
the classrooms of all our schools confidently face the
day-in and day-out burden of attempting to shape re-
fractory and seemingly intractable young minds. But
beyond this tacit and inferred dedication, I have
chosen to offer this work to a distinguished educator
and historian whose kindness to me and my wife both
here and abroad, whose encouragement of my studies,
and whose wise counsel have made me his intellectual
debtor: to John U. Nef, Chairman of the Committee
on Social Thought in the University of Chicago. In
many ways the ideal for educators which I have
sketched in this book has found expression in the
integral humanism of Professor Nef's life, and in all
of his works, ranging from the monumental *War and
Human Progress* to the recent *Cultural Foundations
of Industrial Civilization.*

Since an author's Foreword provides the oppor-

tunity for a last word, I would like to discuss here a
few observations in the text which I myself or some of
my critics have thought required clarification.

First, when censuring, in Chapter One, "many attempts to apply Aristotelian-Scholastic values to modern poetic practice," I was expressing an historical,
not a speculative judgment: that is, I was criticizing
not Aristotelian-Scholastic principles as such, but
rather a tendency which is evident in the writings
of critics who have publicly declared their reliance
on those principles. I think this is the only type of
judgment that anyone can fairly formulate on this
issue since it seems impossible to reconcile the "Aristotelianism" of the Chicago school or the more moderate, though equally moralistic, "Aristotelianism" of
Harold Gardiner, S.J., and Victor Hamm, with the
"Aristotelianism" of J. C. LaDrière and Father William Rooney. It is not for me, the non-Aristotelian, to
adjudicate among these various camps; but writing as
an educator, it is for me to point out, as I have in
the text, that it has not been the Aristotelianism of the
Catholic University critics which has influenced the
teaching of literature in our schools, but rather that
brand which is to be found in *Critics and Criticism,
Norms for the Novel*, and *The Pattern of Criticism*.
It is the critical tendency exemplified in these books,
among others, that I refer to in Chapter One.

Second, in my strictures on the abuse of analytic
methods, in Chapter Four, I have suggested, in brief,
that analysis is not a technique for comprehending an
art work, but rather an instrument for communicating what has already been comprehended; my point is

that a more nearly adequate approach to such communication is the creation of a climate of metaphor
around the object by means of which it is revealed.
No doubt in grasping the art object there is implicitly
and synoptically some analysis, but the actual paths
which the mind and sensibility pursue in this act of
comprehension are so multiform and devious, so
uniquely personal, so subtle and, as Newman would
say, so "omnigenous," that they cannot be reduced to
a single pattern or process. Those aspects of comprehension which do admit of such reduction are a few
general rules, a few general principles (e.g., those of
scansion), the value of which in grasping this or that
concrete artifact is, by reason of their very generality,
at best merely propaedeutic: that is, when these principles are not, as in fact they often are, irrelevant and
distracting, they are merely of incidental worth. Analysis has the relation to an art work that a description
of a kiss over the telephone has to the real thing.

Third, I must emphasize, as I have done in the text,
that in criticizing the *Companion to the Summa*, I
certainly intend no criticism of its author. Walter
Farrell was a great teacher and a great spiritual director, and I was honored that his last published essay
appeared in the *Journal of Arts and Letters*. But I
cannot escape the conclusion that his influence
through the *Companion* books, and even more, the
influence of some of his vocal supporters, was a reactionary force at a time when a more kerygmatic, one
could say, a more humanistic temper was developing
in the field of religious education. This is not to say
that Msgr. Cooper's four volumes are superior to

Father Farrell's; quite the contrary. But Msgr. Cooper's catechetical works, as well as those of Msgr.
Russell, failed, if at all, only by reason of faulty execution: their direction was toward the loftiest and
most praiseworthy intellectual goals. Whereas the impact on religious instruction of the work of many
advocates of "theology" has been to intensify that rationalism from which Catholic education has too long
suffered.

I realize that it has for the past decade or so been
academically "chic" in some circles to disparage any
attempt at emphasizing the place of sensibility, of the
imagination, of the affections in the teaching of Christian doctrine, and even in the teaching of the humanities. The assumption seemed to be that the more
abstractly sterile presentations of dogma were, and the
more aridly clinical the considerations of an artifact
were, then necessarily the more scientific such teaching would be. What might be called the "prophetic"
element in education, whereby the teacher in enthusiastic response to the object he was disclosing
would be moved by it to "speak forth," to engender
by his declamation a climate of metaphor—all of this
has often been scorned as emotional ranting. Yet the
great teachers, from Agassiz and Kittredge to a Msgr.
Julius Haun or a Msgr. Martin Hellriegel or a God-
frey Diekmann, have not been esteemed for their
aridity, *or* for their dilution of content. Certainly, too
great a stress on the teacher as "poet," on the class as
an esthetic experience, *can* lead to abuse: vapid senti-
mental blustering *can* be substituted for a genuine
response to the object. But this is merely an abuse,

and here as elsewhere, abuse does not take away use. As Archbishop Ullathorne said, there are prophets and there are prophets. Some are truly augurs: they speak with vision and insight. Others are merely augers: they only bore.

Finally, it has been suggested that, in Chapter Two, I should have taken into account more fully the social conditions of the times, the state of learning, and other historical factors that may have influenced the various founders of religious institutes. If I have failed to present an entirely balanced picture, I think a fuller perspective might be gained if this chapter were read in conjunction with two earlier essays: "The Religious Life: Fundamentals and Accidentals" (*Worship,* September, 1953), and "The French School" (*Journal of Arts and Letters,* Summer, 1949). I would regret any disproportion that may appear in my treatment of this topic, not simply because of the claims of comity or justice, but because it is precisely this sense of history and of the evolution of social structures that seems to me most lacking in much discussion of traditional religious institutes and of the great founders.

Indeed, the rediscovery of the genuine spirit of these founders is one of the most urgent tasks facing religious educators in America today. As a layman, I would like to suggest in this context that while we may always benefit by the elevation to the altars and by the public exaltation of the heroic sanctity of founders of the religious institutes, it might be more edifying, in the radical sense, as Dom Lambert Beauduin has pointed out (*La Maison-Dieu,* No. 21), if

there were less competitive eagerness and more dis-
cretion displayed in the efforts of some communities
to secure the canonization of their members. (One
does occasionally have the feeling that certain religious are too much taken up, for unconsciously temporal motives, with pairing off the numbers of saints
or doctors of the Church in their Order with those of
another.) Now, given such new mechanical processes
for cataloging, sorting, and duplicating original documents, and given the relative wealth of American religious houses in contrast to those in Europe; given,
too, the siphoning off of some funds from the necessarily large amounts now expended on promoting
the cult of this or that holy person—since we must
be taught by precept as well as by example—given
all these conducive factors, it is to be hoped that the
various communities, ranging from the smallest and
most recently founded Sisterhoods to the ancient and
established Orders, would create research centers in
America devoted, not, certainly, to perpetuating the
obscurities of nineteenth-century hagiography, but,
first, to the production of closely documented essays
on limited topics related to the origins of their institutes and, second, to the publication of broadly inter-
pretive studies which would distill from these historical data a sense of the real spirit of the great founders
and foundresses.

Excluding Katherine Burton's biography, what do
we know about either the life or the religious temper
of Mother Butler of Marymount? Excluding Sister
Bertrand Degnan's *Mercy Unto Thousands*, what do
we know about Mother Mc Auley? What do we know

about Basil Moreau, about the Venerable Libermann, about the elder de Lamennais? What do we know of the manner in which they would face the issues of our time? We do not even have in English a series of introductory books, on the founders of the smaller religious institutes, comparable to those Gaétan Bernoville has written in French. Here is an exceptionally arable field lying fallow.

Before uttering my, "Go, litel book," I must thank my wife who not only bore with me while I was writing this work, but who helped me considerably in the revision of the manuscript.

J. G. L.

ACKNOWLEDGMENTS

The author and publisher wish to thank the following for permission to quote copyrighted material:

The Bruce Publishing Company, Milwaukee, for *The Whole Christ* by Emile Mersch, S.J., translated by J. R. Kelly, S.J.; and for *The Jesuit Code of Liberal Education* by Allan P. Farrell, S.J.

Cambridge University Press, New York, for *Desiderius Erasmus Concerning the Aim and Method of Education* by W. H. Woodward.

Harcourt, Brace and Company, Inc., New York, for "O sweet spontaneous earth," by e. e. Cummings, copyright 1923, 1950, by e. e. Cummings, reprinted from *Poems 1923–1954* by e. e. Cummings; and for *Essays Ancient and Modern* by T. S. Eliot, copyright 1932, 1936 by Harcourt, Brace and Company, Inc.

B. Herder Book Company, St. Louis, for *Christian Perfection and Contemplation* by Reginald Garrigou-Lagrange, O.P., translated by Sister M. Timothea Doyle, O.P.

P. J. Kenedy & Sons, New York, for *The New Tower of Babel* by Dietrich von Hildebrand; and for *Meditations on Various Subjects* by St. John Eudes.

Alfred A. Knopf, Inc., for "The Sense of the Sleight-of-

Hand Man" by Wallace Stevens, copyright 1942,
1954 by Wallace Stevens; and for "Homunculus et
la Belle Etoile" by Wallace Stevens, copyright 1937,
1954 by Wallace Stevens. Reprinted from *The Collected Poems of Wallace Stevens.*

The Marquette University Press, Milwaukee, for *Humanism and Theology* by Werner Jaeger.

Montfort Publications, Bay Shore, New York, for *True
Devotion to the Blessed Virgin Mary* by St. Louis
Mary de Montfort, translated by Frederick William
Faber, D.D.

National Society for the Study of Education, Chicago, for
Forty-first Yearbook (1942).

The New Scholasticism, Washington, for "English and
Philosophy," by Margaret Townsend O'Brien.

Our Sunday Visitor, Huntington, Indiana, for the Rev.
Richard Ginder's column appearing in the April 13,
1958, issue of this newspaper.

Pantheon Books, Inc., New York, for *Religious Art* by
Emile Mâle.

Random House, Inc., New York, for "Under Which Lyre"
by W. H. Auden. Reprinted from *The Collected
Poetry of W. H. Auden,* copyrighted by Random
House, Inc.

St. Martin's Press, Inc., New York, for *Memoirs* by Mark
Pattison.

Mrs. Maisie Ward Sheed for *Life of John Henry Cardinal
Newman,* by Wilfrid P. Ward.

Sheed and Ward, Inc., New York, for *France Pagan?* by
Maisie Ward, copyright 1949, by Sheed and Ward,
Inc.; for *A Humane Psychology of Education* by
Jaime Castiello, S.J., copyright 1936 by Sheed and
Ward, Inc.; and for *The Satin Slipper* by Paul
Claudel, translated by John O'Connor.

The Tablet, London, for the letter from this review's

Rome correspondent which appeared in the December 16, 1950, issue.

Vanguard Press, Inc., for *The Mechanical Bride* by Marshall McLuhan.

Joseph F. Wagner, Inc., for the quotation from Brendan McGrath's view of Mr. Lawler's *The Christian Imagination,* which appeared in the May, 1956, issue of *The Homiletic and Pastoral Review.*

CONTENTS

CONTENTS

INTRODUCTION

THE BEST THING GOING ON TODAY IN AMERICAN EDUCA-
tion is criticism and self-criticism. Until Sputnik,
criticism was taboo. We were supposed to have the
best of all educational systems. Now we are far from
sure. The chauvinists are hushing up. Dr. Conant and
his associates have spent hundreds of thousands of dollars in a study of what is wrong with the public high
school. Under the leadership of J. Lloyd Trump, the
Commission on Experimental Study has spent time
and money on how to improve the staff in the high
school.

All this is a good sign. Self-criticism is the life of
schools as well as the life of man and of human institutions. A school system needs to keep checking itself,
as does a nation-state or a church or a family. Scruti-
nizing itself, reassessing itself—according to Socrates,
this is the human life. This law of self-criticism holds
also for persons, as we all know in the case of the

artist, scientist, saint, businessman, or the cook. Examining oneself is a law for the person as it is for the community.

Sometimes it is said that the church-related school lags. Yet the Catholic schools in America have led in self-criticism; even before Sputnik they were engaged in it. Msgr. Ellis' work of 1955 was the first, and up to now it has been perhaps the most notable. Since that initial challenge, which was mainly from the point of view of history, we have had others speak on the subject: Father Weigel as a theologian, Father Ward as a moral philosopher, and Professor O'Dea as a sociologist. Along with some popular statements these add up to a continuing dialectic, and of course can only be good for the future of Catholic education in the United States. Few if any will agree with everything in any of the works of these authors. But the best of all features in this body of sincere and critical work is the way in which it has been received. It has been viewed with intelligent concern and not with alarm. By and large, it has been welcomed.

While these studies were appearing, the Sister Formation Movement came into being. A major aim of this is to see to excellence in the spiritual and intellectual formation of Sisters who are to teach. Leadership in the movement has been strong and well advised. Three volumes on plans and developments have been published, and the Report of the Everett Curriculum Workshop is the best thing that has been done for some time by any American educational group.

The present book by Professor Lawler happily

carries on this self-examination and constructive criticism. It too will be welcomed as significant. It is well
balanced, and it is mainly looking in a positive, creative direction. It is especially good on several points.
For one thing, it has a realistic grasp of the place of
the layman, and rightly emphasizes that in society generally, and in the work of the world, he has his own
task to do. The layman has a sense for temporal realities and a responsibility for them. As the author says,
in fields such as economics and politics and labor the
layman may be expected to acquire an "empathic
awareness" of the human condition. As a layman he
is to testify to this condition; he is prudently and intelligently to witness. It seems to me that St. Paul
would at once agree.

Then too the intellectual life is a life and like any
other good thing is to be sanctified. As Professor
Lawler has so well said in an essay on Teilhard de
Chardin, we must discover and affirm the "ontological
radication of the Christian intellectual life . . . in
the essential nature of God's universe." Confusion
and misfortune inevitably come from taking only one
thing as holy, namely the direct service of God in
convent or monastery. We have suffered in America
from this assumption of an exclusive holiness; for the
life of the mind and the work of the world must also
be developed and loved as holy things. Otherwise we
should be approaching the early Protestant error that
only one thing, namely the word of God, is holy: all
the rest is the work of the devil and cannot be sanctified.

A "pious pragmatism," says Professor Lawler, will

not do as a philosophy of Christian education. On the higher levels the mission of the Catholic scholar and therefore of the Catholic college and university derives from making one world of a vast world of natural truths and a vast world of supernatural truths. The ideal, as this book affirms, is not one set over against the other, not one sealed up here and one sealed up there, but a single, over-all, integrated cosmos of learning. Obviously, any such resultant supposes a perpetual, conscious working and reworking, at least on the part of some scholars, above all those with a sense for unity. Therefore it would be fatal—perhaps we should say that it is fatal—to approach all subjects with a once-for-all, preconceived set of values and standards. It would be equally fatal to attempt to limit Catholic higher learning to one intellectual tradition or to the heritage of any single historical period. Though of course we must have experts and specialists and emphases, the Catholic intellectual life must be free and must be as wide as the universe. And it is toward the attainment of this breadth and this freedom that *The Catholic Dimension in Higher Education* is a challenging contribution.

LEO R. WARD

University of Notre Dame
Notre Dame, Indiana

THE CATHOLIC DIMENSION
IN HIGHER EDUCATION

PERSPECTIVES

FOREIGN VISITORS, WHO HAVE SPENT A FEW WEEKS traveling through America, often remark, on their return to their homelands, that we are a people not given to introspection or self-examination; it has been said that we are a nation so addicted to looking only to the future that we do not pause to glance at the present or to consider the past. Simone de Beauvoir has suggested it; D. W. Brogan has assumed it; and even sympathetic critics like Siegfried, Maurois, and von Kuehnelt-Leddihn have given it countenance. In the game of international one-upmanship, this is the sort of stereotyped judgment to which Americans are accustomed; and with the advent of sociologists and psychologists into this same arena, it is the kind of assessment which, we are told, is now

capable of being backed up by those various batteries
of scientific apparatus that the social sciences have at
their disposal.

Yet notwithstanding the repetition, in various ways
and media, of this affirmation of our lack of interiority, one often feels that it, like those other trite and
overworked proclamations of our materialism or our
anti-intellectualism which worried continental tour-
ists or anxious pollsters often make, represents, as far
as profound insight into our national character goes,
little more than so much hackneyed verbiage, stimulating or pedestrian only to the degree in which its
enunciation is or is not clothed in some semblance
of literary style. Simone de Beauvoir's strictures are
interesting because, when all is said, it cannot be denied that she can write; it is less easy to take the
authors of *The Lonely Crowd* seriously. But if we
are a people not given to self-examination, this need
not be regarded as an entirely unhealthy situation:
certainly if one looks to the rage for auto-critique and
self-revelation which swept the continent after the last
war, and to the published extravagances which followed in the train of that storm of introspection, it is
rather difficult to bemoan our presumed indifference
to self-scrutiny.

Yet, in mere point of fact, self-examination and
self-study have long been numbered among the favorite pastimes of the American scholar—but with results that have sometimes been far from satisfying.
Every industrial and business group, every social stra-
tum, every religious body, seems to have had its
public conscience, and to have been possessed, at one

time or other, by a kind of competitive eagerness to publicize to the community at large its findings, its flaws, its defects. The spontaneous and unconscious response to this kind of intellectual exercise is one largely of revulsion; and this I think is a healthy reaction. There is something verging on the pathological in an excessive preoccupation with probing into one's motives and forever reopening healed wounds.

But here a caveat is necessary: for just as in the spiritual life one distinguishes between the serene examination of conscience and that scrupulous and harassed introspection which borders on moral hypochondria, so too, with regard to institutions or social agencies, one must not confuse a morbid, obsessive self-consciousness with a calm diagnosis. And it is in the latter category that I would place the three recent general studies which, along revisionist lines, have had the beneficial effect of awakening the Catholic educational community to a long overdue examination of its ideal objectives and its actual achievement.

The three general studies to which I refer are: *The Younger American Scholar: His Collegiate Origins* by R. H. Knapp and J. J. Greenbaum; *The Chicago Sunday Tribune's* appraisal of the major American institutions of higher education; and Msgr. John Tracy Ellis' examination of American Catholics and the intellectual life. *The Chicago Tribune* series of articles, though marred by occasional political overtones, merely reiterated the results of a number of earlier findings and included no Catholic college or university among the nation's forty outstanding schools;

the Knapp-Greenbaum study listed Catholic schools, with one exception, in the lowest groups of all colleges surveyed; [1] and while Msgr. Ellis' criticisms have been widely publicized and have been subjected to some strictures, no one as yet has effectively disputed his general thesis.

All three of these objective and impartial appraisals, which directly or implicitly place the Catholic scholastic tradition on the same low plane as that of the disciples of Judge Rutherford and similar fringe cults, have been explained away by a number of widely accepted clichés that it is necessary, by way of preface, now to examine. The first of these clichés is that good teachers are not always good writers. As a consequence of this alleged fact, it is said to be impossible to assess the caliber of a school by the quality and quantity of its faculty's publications. This explanation certainly represents a partial truth; yet one cannot help wondering why Catholic schools should have such a monopoly on talented but inarticulate scholars.

Nor can one avoid wondering about the validity of another self-justifying explanation which has been proffered: that the intensive counseling and extra-curricular programs, as well as the time-consuming spiritual exercises of the religious faculties of Catholic colleges, allow little opportunity for creative scholarship. Both of these latter explanations are of dubious merit, for it is quite obvious that the counseling programs in Catholic colleges are not notably superior to those of other schools; and while the extra-curricular activities do in some schools influence the curricu-

lum, even to the point where courses have been introduced—generally speech and journalism—in order to
provide training for these extra-curriculars, it is
nevertheless apparent that, athletics excepted, such
activities are not particularly outstanding. With regard to the claim that the demands of the spiritual life
distract one from creative intellectual work, it can
only be pointed out that such a spiritual life is either
not in accord with an organic apostolate of *tradere
contemplata,* or else the form of the apostolate itself
is warped, since it admits of no influence from the
supernatural order.[2] A prayer life which does not contribute to the work of Christian education implies
either defective prayer or defective education. Moreover, this scholarly inertia, to which these various
surveys and appraisals bear witness, seems to have
afflicted lay faculty members almost as severely as the
religious.

It is, of course, self-evident that the absence of creative scholarship does not reflect *perfectly* the state of
Catholic higher education; but then there is no perfect reflection, no truly comprehensive measurement
of any spiritual undertaking, and it is equally evident
that this lack does indicate *some* inferiority. A scholar
writes because he has something to say. The fact that
what he writes is published indicates that what he
says is of some concern or of some value to the intellectual community at large—it is, after all, not very
difficult to impress a class of undergraduates, or a
busy administrator, or the editor of the local diocesan
newspaper with one's learning: but a jury of one's
peers is quite another thing. If action follows being,

then this lack of scholarly activity would certainly point up the poverty of our insights into the transcendental aspects of being: into truth, goodness, and beauty, the contemplation and comprehension of which are the proper work of the school.

Nor does it seem that one can explain away the failure of Catholic schools to appear on the periodically published lists of outstanding colleges and universities by asserting that Catholic schools, being poorly endowed, cannot afford to attract eminent teachers and scholars. For there are Catholic schools which have operating budgets and student populations approximating those of many secular colleges that have consistently been listed among the nation's best schools. Moreover, one can point to Catholic colleges which have expended large sums of money for building projects not directly related to increasing student facilities or faculty competence (e.g., stadia and fieldhouses), and which have continued to pay salaries both inconsistent with the splendor of their physical plants and with any elevation of academic standards.

If one recognizes some measure of inferiority and some degree of deficiency in Catholic higher learning, then these must, I believe, be attributed to something other than merely technical factors. It should not be necessary, of course, to point out that many of the defects of judgment and of planning in Catholic educational work are evident to some degree among non-Catholic schools as well; yet for the reasons developed below, it would seem that these defects are sometimes more deeply rooted and more widespread within Catholic circles.

I

One of the first causes to be examined of the present failure of our higher learning is the inordinate preoccupation, apparent among some Catholic educators and administrators, with methods of organization and programs of study. Underlying this academic obsession is a theological heritage tinged with the voluntarism of the sixteenth and seventeenth centuries: a voluntarism which assumed that merely by planning, by arranging, by employing the right techniques one might attain natural as well as supernatural wisdom— far from dispensing with technique, these educators relied upon it exclusively. This heritage has been so strengthened by the educational yoga of the teachers colleges that rarely does one encounter among Catholic administrators the realization that wisdom is, as Maritain has said, "a grace of the natural order," and that it is not embodied in any scholastic recipes or plans. There was no "Oxford Plan" which Jackson, Copleston, or Jowett adhered to in their various reforms of that university; and at Harvard today, *General Education in a Free Society* is a dying tract. Yet both of these universities are living schools because they have intensified their curricula, while demanding a high level of competence and ability from faculty and students.

In this context, there was something a little disturbing in the interest aroused by much of the recent discussion on various "Christian culture" programs for college instruction; such excitement over an academic question seemed in a few cases to reflect not so much serious intellectual concern, but rather a longing for some panacea to cure the educational malaise blighting Catholic schools. That the proponents of "Christian culture" could ignore Aristotle's dictum, "History is less universal than poetry," or that they could ignore Cardinal Newman's axiom, "Homer and Aristotle were to be the schoolmasters of all generations,"[3] is much less significant than their ignoring the fact that the present crisis in Catholic education stems more from inadequate, incompetent, indifferent teaching than from defective curriculum. The issues facing our higher learning are spiritual rather than technical, personal rather than administrative. Such programs as those for which the advocates of "Christian culture" have been so zealously lobbying, when promoted with excessive urgency, conviction, and passion, inevitably suggest that the system is more important than the teacher; and while Mr. Dawson himself would certainly not assert this, yet some of his American defenders and disciples, in the various forms which their historicism and neo-medievalism have taken, do leave the uncommitted observer with this impression.

Two important illustrations of this primacy of the man over the system, of the teacher over the program, come readily to mind and may well be considered here. First, Thomism may undeniably be said to offer a magnificent framework for philosophical reflection; but that Thomism—as so many continental scholars have remarked—has frequently remained in America only a kind of metaphysical taxonomy is to be attributed not to the philosophy, but to the philosophers. Second, Mr. Hutchins, when Chancellor of the University of Chicago, declared, "A university without theology or metaphysics cannot exist"; and his successor, Mr. Kimpton, has declared, with equal vigor, that "metaphysics is impossible"—yet notwithstanding these irreconcilable differences, the particular university in question has gone on existing.[4] Now all of this is not intended as any belittling of educational theory, but simply as a clarification of Mark Hopkins' "law": if you put a good teacher in the company of good students, you will have a good school whether the program be based on the *De Magistro,* the *Ratio Studiorum,* or *The Essay Concerning Human Understanding.*

Far, then, from belittling educational theory, the observations which follow tend rather to underline its pre-eminent importance when its role is rightly understood. First, however, it is necessary to introduce these observations on the value and function of theory with some additional remarks which will serve to point up the unfortunate abuses flowing from the epidemic of theorizing that ravaged American schools after the establishing of professional training institutions for teachers, and after the emergence of the accrediting agencies as a dominant factor in higher education.

One cannot overlook the fact that, since the onslaught of instrumentalism and pragmatism, the professional educationists have theorized on everything from cloakroom comportment to classroom seating;[5] while their well-annotated dissertations have dissected, in all due seriousness for the importance of their research, such allied subjects as punctuality charts and the positioning of blackboards—now tinted a therapeutic green. Moreover, all of these pedagogical exercises have been undertaken so earnestly and with such religious fervor that those who were teaching without benefit of these professional rites could only wonder by what strange combination of fortitude and luck they had managed to communicate with their students at all; and this wonderment was compounded by the growing realization that almost invariably the poorest teachers on a faculty were these same professional educators, while the mere "amateurs" consistently taught more interesting and stimulating classes.

Nor can one overlook the fact that the field of educational theory has allowed every teachers college graduate to play the role of a generator of great profundities and a marshal of great ideas,[6] and that as a result of all this there has been a frightening unconcern with such an elementary principle as that of Norman Foerster in *The Future of the Liberal College:* "The *sine qua non* of a liberal school is simply the liberal spirit." Though one cannot ignore all such facts which attest to the abuse of educational theory, neither can one ignore the plain truism that abuse does not take away use. And although it may rightly be said that the best working theory for a Christian school is often that which, while inchoate and inarticulate, yet informs the teaching and research of its best faculty members, it nevertheless must be replied that generally it is necessary to enunciate such working theories, if only to refurbish and refresh them.

But it in no way minimizes the importance of the role of educational theory to point out that that college will be an excellent school which, though without any specific, lengthy, theoretical program, is staffed by teachers of a liberal and humanistic spirit who are both devoted to their students and competent in their individual disciplines. The history of education bears out this statement, for it has not been those schools with the most comprehensive and the most clearly articulated theoretical schemata which have achieved the highest academic distinction, but simply those with the best faculties.

As an illustration of this, there might be examined, on the one hand, the fate of what was to have been the Catholic University of Ireland, which had as its theoretical scholastic program Newman's great *Idea;* and, on the other hand, the University of London, which has flourished and attained a position of some eminence even though its theoretical basis has been only a few vague egalitarian and scientific notions. It is an even more remarkable fact that although this British institution may have been founded on grounds that were generally opposed to those later set forth in *The Idea of a University,* yet by a kind of homing instinct in all serious educators, by a kind of natural gravitation toward ultimate values, the University of London may be recognized today as a school where the liberal and humanistic tradition has become deeply rooted.[7]

Thus while one cannot in justice disparage the importance of educational theory, for it goes without saying that no human work can be without its theoretical orientation, yet one can point out that the precise and rigidly scientific explication of such theory is frequently a mixed good. For such detailed programs often tend to idealize a single point of view, and to concretize what, given the fluidity and breadth of the field of education, should remain flexible and adaptable. Furthermore, in attempting to encompass systematically the mobile expanse of human knowledge, these theoretical programs sometimes alienate the liberal members of a faculty, whose views may not conform to the pattern which has been cut out for them, and often isolate the school from any meaningful intellectual intercourse with other institutions; usually it will be found that faculties dedicated wholeheartedly to some specific and tightly concatenated theoretical program, rather than participating in any genuine dialogue with other schools, are engaged only in what may be described as talking to themselves.

This is not to suggest that there is any particular virtue in incoherence and imprecision; nor is it to succumb to what has been termed the dogmatism of non-dogmatism. It is simply to argue in favor of a prudent flexibility from the preceding observations, as well as from such additional historical illustration as is offered by the educational tradition of Benedictine monasticism. For it is a fact that the Benedictine schools, founded upon a rule of a few thousand words, have preserved their unique character, while adapting themselves to the demands of successive historical periods,[8] with far greater ease and success than have the schools of a number of sixteenth and seventeenth century congregations which, in the present age, now find their educational work hampered by lengthy constitutions that meticulously detail every refinement of pedagogical practice.

However, even after considering these critical evaluations of the role of educational theory, it is still necessary to examine the nature of this role itself; only after such an examination can one hope to dissipate the confusion and disorder—the evidence of which Msgr. Ellis has collected—so widespread and so deeply rooted in Catholic higher education.

It is necessary first, however, to insert here a note of appreciation, in which all serious educators must share, for the work of those critics who have succeeded in creating the present healthy atmosphere of self-criticism. Anyone examining the literature which has developed since the publication of Msgr. Ellis' essay, and anyone considering the intense and sympathetic response this development has elicited, must conclude that in a climate of such courageous reappraisal the future of Catholic education is relatively bright.

While it is more than twenty-five years since Abraham Flexner published his important study, *Universities: American, English, German,* it is evident that such a work had little impact on Catholic educators who either were overburdened as teachers with large classes and heavy teaching schedules, or were, as administrators, immersed in the necessary but rudimentary task of "fund raising." As a result, the few voices that could be heard in criticism of the Catholic higher learning, during the last two decades, were often drowned out by that strident and self-complacent claque which chanted the praises of Catholic schools on the assumption that, as they had theological truth, they had little to look for in the profane world surrounding them.

Now that it has become something approaching a fad, within the past few years, publicly to criticize hitherto unrecognized deficiencies, and now that even eminent administrators, who in their day seemed to be ardent defenders of the *status quo,* have been found competing with one another in exposing flaws and revealing defects, there is a real danger, first, of going to the opposite extreme by masochistically berating real achievements and demeaning notable successes, and second, of ignoring the moderate suggestions of such earlier critics as Francis McMahon, Sister Madeleva, Virgil Michel, and Leo Ward. The last named of these is the most important of all, for even a decade after its publication, Father Ward's *Blueprint for a Catholic University* remains the most valuable and comprehensive study on the distinction between true and false reform in Catholic higher education.[9]

In general, however, one may say that the present collective examination of conscience is a healthy and not a morbid exercise of responsibility on the part of Catholic educators, and that rather than fostering too severely critical an attitude, its assessments have really not gone far enough, being diagnostic rather than remedial, and even in this diagnostic phase being generally confined to the immediate, practical flaws in school structure while ignoring those broader theoretical foundations which are at once the strength and the weakness of the Catholic position. Thus many of the remedies which have been proffered by recent critics are concerned with such improvements in the order of technique as increasing faculty salaries, unifying small local colleges into one united system, introducing more laymen into the schools; and while all such suggestions have some merit, nevertheless they are only temporary palliatives for an affliction which demands not *hic et nunc* improvisations, but an extensive study of theological and historical data from the entire continuum of Christian learning, and the application of these data to contemporary issues. In the present lively concern over healing the educational body, there is serious danger of mistaking this or that nostrum for a true curative.

Before discussing, in Chapter Five, what seems to be a more nearly adequate rationale for the Catholic intellectual life, and consequently for the Catholic school, it is necessary to sketch briefly what has been the cause of failure in so many recent attempts at defining such a theoretical foundation. This failure, I would suggest, is largely the result of two misconceptions: first, the identification of the Catholic intellectual heritage with the culture of the Middle Ages; and, second, the assumption that a comprehensive educational program need concern itself only with metaphysical principles.

II

The first misconception equates the Catholic heritage
with the particular historical period in which Catholic doctrinal positions were most widely accepted. In
this equation one may recognize an error concerning
past and future history. With regard to the past, the
equation ignores the foundations of the medieval
world-view in St. Paul, in the Fathers, in Plato, and
in the Sapiential literature of the Old Testament:
foundations which are undeniably as necessary to the
man of our age as the Aristotelianism of the Scholastics. With regard to the future, the equation
ignores the political and economic aberrations in
medieval society as well as that superstition and that
suppression of conscience of which Acton has written
so eloquently; while canonizing the "thirteenth, greatest of centuries" as achieving the one ideal, various
neo-medievalists have distorted history by exalting
what is optimistically called the renaissance of the
twelfth century to the detriment of the Renaissance
of the sixteenth; and as a consequence of this, in the
educational order, Catholic educators have generally
ignored the impressive pedagogical treatises of Vives
and Vittorino, while exaggerating the merits of such
works as the *De Magistro* of St. Thomas or the
Didascalion of Hugh of St. Victor.

It would be a digression to examine in detail the
motives of this systematic glorification of medieval
culture as an educational ideal, but it is apparent,
even from a brief examination, that they often derive

from a well-disguised or an unrecognized loyalty to
an insular definition of Catholicism, rather than from
any exigency in the educational order itself, and that
they have been nourished by such works as Belloc's
Europe and the Faith, Adam's *Christ and the Western Mind,* Haecker's *Vergil, Father of the West,* and
a number of other books that will enter this discussion as it progresses.

Within the neo-medievalist educational camp one
may discern two distinct groups which, though they
have much in common, are divided from one another
by their separate modes of interpreting reality. The
one group—which I will call the "temporalist"—relies
for its program of studies primarily on the examination of historical sequence; the other group—which I
will call the "structuralist"—relies, for the development of its curriculum, on the study of some essential
pattern of ideas within a given historical period. The
temporalists are generally historians; and the structuralists, philosophers. Now these two modes of interpretation are the only ones available for any
consideration of human culture, and so there can be
no argument with the neo-medievalists on the grounds
of their having employed an inadequate distinction
to analyze the materials within their field: any series
of events or themes can be related only by some historical or metaphysical scheme. The argument with
the neo-medievalists can be drawn only on the
grounds that they have limited themselves to the era
which has been questionably called "the age of Christian culture."

The group which I have labeled "temporalist"

often seems to assume that because the Greco-Latin period is more remote from the present time than the Middle Ages, this mere fact of chronological proximity makes them more relevant to the educational work of this century. Such an assumption, in addition to suffering from those limitations common to the entire neo-medievalist camp, distorts the historical fact —and it is a fact the acceptance of which implies no lack of the Catholic spirit—that it was the periods of the Renaissance, the Enlightenment, and Romanticism which have, in the midst of abuses no less lamentable than those of the thirteenth century, enriched our age as much as any specifically medieval heritage, and which have borne fruit in the democratic and personalistic bearings of modern society.[10] It is a fact of recent history, worthy of consideration here, that the Christian democratic movement of the twentieth century, even when not tainted with Sangnier's popular sovereignty thesis, was condemned only fifty years ago by the neo-medievalists of that day as "political modernism"; and one might consider, too, that Charles Maurras for good and bad reasons looked back to the Middle Ages as his political ideal. I mention all of this only because it seems undeniable that if one is going to develop an educational program for the Catholic school in a democratic and pluralist society, a fidelity to the theory and practice of the medieval era will often raise as many problems as it resolves.

From the educational standpoint, I have already quoted Cardinal Newman's strictures on the type of temporalist pedagogical theory which has in recent

years received its best exposition in John Julian
Ryan's *Idea of a Catholic College* and *Beyond
Humanism,* and its most vigorous defense in Vincent
McCrossen's *New Renaissance of the Spirit.* One
more text from Newman may be cited here because
it argues from universal educational experience, and
because it reflects the attitude of a brilliant theorist
on the place of a tradition which can hardly be called
medieval in the continuum of liberal learning. Cardinal Newman wrote:

The medieval sciences, great as is their dignity and utility, were never intended to supersede that more real and
proper cultivation of the mind which is effected by the
study of the Liberal Arts. . . . The simple question to
be considered is, how best to strengthen, refine, and enrich the intellectual powers; the perusal of the poets, historians, and philosophers of Greece and Rome will
accomplish this purpose, as long experience has shown.[11]

It is possible to carry the argument further and point
out that an even more devastating criticism of the
temporalist, and concomitantly of the structuralist,
positions is that these two points of view are necessarily interdependent, and thus to accent one or the
other of them exclusively, to the detriment of their
inner reciprocity, is to distort one's image of history
as well as of reality.

The widespread acceptance of the temporalist position is partially the result of an attempt to translate
into pedagogical terms that broader understanding
of historical forces which has marked our age, and

which has been embodied in such divergent treatments as those of Spengler, Sorokin, Cassirer, Berdyaev, and Toynbee. But this acceptance is, to a
greater degree, the effect of pressures and demands
within the educational sphere itself. When the educationists who mint the jargon of the profession discovered a few years ago the notion of "integration," and
heard the clear scientific ring in this latest catchword
they were putting into currency, there arose immediately a great concern for this "felt need" in pedagogy;
and when this new term had undergone all the successive avatars and transmutations which the social
sciences alone can impose on simple Latin substan-
tives, the "non-professional" educator who was teaching science or the humanities realized, like a man
discovering his prose speech, that his enduring efforts
to unify the curriculum had been at last professionally canonized. In the resultant urgency and eagerness
to exploit this principle of integration, the educationists, as well as some scientists and humanists, turned
to history as the best instrument for shaping an organized program of studies. There was then born a
number of plans which were based on the study and
analysis of chronological sequence.

Many of these temporalist plans, in addition to exaggerating the historical importance of the medieval
period, commonly embraced one or the other of two
extremes. First, they overlooked that qualitative
value which makes a given age culturally rich, and in
a kind of cinematic leveling of the diverse forces of
history, stripped away those distinctions, subtleties,
and nuances, the understanding of which is so im-

portant for the knowledge of the past as well as for the cultivation of intellectual taste. In an attempt at depicting a universal view, and because there is nothing more chaotic or seemingly fortuitous than the course of civilization, such educational programs oversimplified history by imposing an unreal pattern on it; and the students of these programs were then left the victims of a superficial, journalistic understanding of the interrelation of ideas, men, and events.

The second extreme into which the temporalist program often fell was, conversely, to avoid the pitfalls of an easy journalism by presenting the student with as much history as he could digest in the framework—since it cannot be called a structure—of chronology alone. This approach to general education had the advantage of being faithful to the historic fact; but, on the debit side, it tended to leave the student with little more than a mass of disordered and disconnected data which, by reason of their very universality, subjected him to an empty relativist view of history; his vision of the world approximated the non-teleological conception of Simone de Beauvoir's *All Men Are Mortal.*

Both of these extremities represent actual abuses to which some temporalist programs have succumbed. But even when these extreme positions have not been taken, the basic criticism of the Catholic temporalists —their neo-medievalism—still stands.

Before one examines the structuralist position, it should be noted that this particular group of theorists has generally been more influential than the temporalists in developing the Catholic school curriculum. This is not the result of any superiority either in ideology or in execution, but merely of certain sociological factors in Catholic education. Because the structuralist is usually a philosopher, and because philosophy has been until the recent past largely a clerical precinct, the structuralist has generally been a priest and therefore, in the Catholic college, he was more likely to be an administrator; the temporalist has usually been a historian turned pedagogue (e.g., Ryan, McCrossen), and so was more likely to be a layman and hence usually without administrative authority.

If, as has been suggested above, the temporalists have yielded to the temptation of paying too much attention to the chronological sequence of ideas, and too little attention to the ideas themselves, the structuralists have succumbed to the opposite error; they tend to treat notions that were shaped in the matrix of a given historical period, and that reflect a particular set of circumstances and a particular historical conditioning, as if these notions were abstract and immutable essences. In the actual work of education, the structuralist program attempts to revive in all their medieval splendor the *artes liberales,* and to organize the entire curriculum within the framework of the trivium and the quadrivium. Because the structuralist stand usually precludes any profound examination of the genesis and development of the *artes liberales,* or of the method whereby they were applied in the Middles Ages, the curricula which derive from this stand generally seek to interpret contemporary literature, philosophy, and science through the instrumentality of the seven arts alone.

An artificial *rapprochement* of past and present through the medium of the liberal arts is often what passes in structuralist circles for an application of medieval wisdom to modern times. With their passion for clear ideas, and with their pursuit of pure essences, untouched by temporal trammels, the structuralists have abstracted the liberal arts from the historical conditions which begot them in Greece and which nourished them in Rome, and by this very abstractive process have excised the heart of this traditional scheme of human learning. It is indicative of an even greater indifference to the lessons of history that such excision—like most other Catholic educational programs—has been carried out in the name of Cardinal Newman. For Newman realized what contemporary advocates of the liberal arts generally ignore: the meaning of these arts is to be found not in any definition and enunciation of them in modern terms and in relation to contemporary culture; this meaning and this value are to be discovered in the application of the liberal arts to the classic authors, and to the classic authors *alone*. Thus Newman, speaking specifically of the liberal arts, declares:

Even to this day Shakespeare and Milton are not studied in our course of education; but the poems of Vergil and Horace, as those of Homer and the Greek authors in an earlier age, were in schoolboys' satchels not much more than a hundred years after they were written. I need not go on to show at length that they have preserved their place in the system of education in the *orbis terrarum,* and the Greek writers with them or through them, down to this day.[12]

It is in the classic texts that the naked framework of the seven arts must be clothed. And, perhaps, considering the verbal contortions, the twistings of meanings, and the adroit manipulations which the structuralists are forced to impose on such ancient instruments as dialectic, rhetoric, and astronomy in order to compress them into their procrustean modern curriculum, it might be suggested that the true cause of the liberal arts, as of education, would be best served by a greater fidelity to classic literature than to medieval pedagogy. Because of this emphasis in *The Idea of a University* on the classic authors, rather than on the seven arts themselves, there is good reason for the Oratorian, Louis Bouyer, in his study on Newman, to point out the real sympathy that exists between the educational ideal of Newman and that embodied in Werner Jaeger's *Paideia.*[13] And although Père Bouyer neither documents nor illustrates the existence of this bond, yet I think it will be evident to anyone who is familiar with these two masterful educational treatises. Werner Jaeger himself in a lecture delivered before a group of Catholic educators has stressed—without referring to Newman—the significance of this principle emphasized throughout *The Idea of a University.*

Sometimes modern historians and classicists who were pursuing the humanistic tradition through the Middle

Ages have tried to find it too exclusively in the tradition of the *artes liberales*. Nothing would be more wrong than to underrate the historical importance of that tradition for medieval humanism, but the liberal arts represented the ancient *paideia* in its latest and thinnest form, more the skeleton to which it had been reduced for pedagogical purposes than its true self. The turn from the *artes* to the *auctores* was a return to the *paideia* of the Greeks in the form which it had in its best times when it was still represented by and embodied in the great authors.[14]

It should not be necessary to add that this return to the authors was largely an achievement of the Renaissance, when the first humanists broke with the tropological modes of the medieval era and, as Matthew Arnold said in "Hebraism and Hellenism," learned to see literary works "as they are."

It is, then, apparent that both on theoretical and on historical grounds, structuralists, temporalists, and the whole neo-medievalist camp can find little support for their emphasis in contemporary education on the liberal arts as cultivated in the Middle Ages. And as a corrective to the narrowness of a number of programs in "Christian culture," one may even go as far as to accept the maxim of Erasmus: "I affirm that with slight qualification the whole of attainable knowledge lies enclosed within the literary monuments of ancient Greece." [15]—the "slight qualification" being that the knowledge referred to is conceived primarily as pedagogical; that is, it is not regarded as the sum and perfection of all knowledge, but simply as the kind of knowledge that provides the finest instrument for forming, training, and disciplining the intellect.

At the beginning of Section II, I mentioned two misconceptions which have militated against the development of an adequate Catholic educational program. The first, the identification of the Catholic intellectual heritage with the culture of the Middle Ages, has been briefly discussed above—though it is a discussion to which I shall return in the following chapters. The second misconception is rooted in the assumption that a comprehensive educational schema need concern itself with metaphysical principles only.

Anyone either reading the literature which has been published on the higher learning in America by various Church groups and by different philosophical schools, or examining the forewords to a number of college catalogues, cannot but be impressed by the wide divergence of viewpoint which these various writings represent. There are those which propose, as a goal, training for democratic life; others idealize the education of the "whole man"; others, like Milton, are concerned with "repairing the ruins of our first parents"; and still others envisage an "education for eternity." Some programs are frankly pragmatic; some are philosophically idealistic; some, materialistic; some, based on metaphysical premises; and others yet are so non-dogmatic as to be relativistic. Moreover, while almost every school's prospectus and every academic program employs many of the same terms to describe its objectives, these terms seem to be juggled so skillfully that each particular institution manages to arrive at different conclusions to justify its existence as a separate and unique entity.

It comes then as something of a shock to the layman, who is not initiate in these semantic subtleties, to realize that virtually all of these institutions have nearly identical curricula and—a more striking paradox—appear to be following the same practical paths to completely different theoretical destinations: one is tempted to say that what began as a problem in logic or semantics, ends as a problem in topology. This paradox was recognized by Professor Edward Reisner of Teachers College, Columbia, who introduced a symposium [16] on various educational philosophies with the sardonic comment that "one would have difficulty in establishing a unitary relationship between any given metaphysical position and the educational consequences which are ostensibly drawn out of that metaphysical position." It was recognized, also, by the late William McGucken, S.J., who in his contribution to the same symposium declared:

The confusion and bewilderment of aim so characteristic of American higher education, the utilitarian, anti-intellectual elements that there prevail, which makes Mr. Hutchins despair of hoping for anything but triviality, mediocrity, and chaos from the present American educational system, are unfortunately all too true of most Catholic institutions.[17]

One wonders why, with the splendid theory of education Catholics are alleged to possess in Scholasticism, Catholic schools should also reflect confusion, be-

wilderment, utilitarianism, and anti-intellectualism.
Father McGucken broaches one possible reason:

Naturally enough, Catholic institutions have imitated
the externals of college and university here in America;
perhaps necessarily so. Nor do they cease by that fact *qua*
Catholic institutions to be any the less Catholic, just so
long as they hold fast to their philosophy of supernaturalism, so long as they realize they are training not merely
for time, but for eternity, although possibly inefficient
qua institutions of higher education.[18]

One may suggest, on the contrary, that it is precisely
to the degree in which Catholic institutions are inefficient *qua* institutions of higher education that they
cease to be Catholic; furthermore, it may be suggested
that it is here, in this unwitting defense of mediocrity
in the name of supernaturalism that one encounters
a basic source of our current educational confusion.
"Why?" asked Newman, "why do we educate except
to prepare for the world? Why do we cultivate the
intellect of the many beyond the first elements of
knowledge, except for this world?" [19]

I do not want to draw too much out of Father
McGucken's observations, particularly because he
himself was, in a period of dawning instrumentalism,
a vigorous defender of the humanistic tradition; but
his statements nevertheless must be recognized as
typical of the best Catholic educational thought two
decades ago; and in almost every case this educational
thought relied exclusively on the Scholastic world-
view.

For the Catholic university, there is a principle of integration—not an eclectic metaphysics, but the metaphysics of Aristotle and Aquinas. . . . Nevertheless, for the Catholic university this principle of integration is not merely metaphysics, but metaphysics supplemented by theology.[20]

Again, it is difficult to understand why with this presumably comprehensive principle of integration, Catholic schools were so little integrated, were so often citadels of that utilitarianism and anti-intellectualism which Father McGucken has so justly decried.

One might argue that the existence of this difficulty is a further indication of the unimportance and irrelevance of scientifically formulated educational theories; and while there may be something to be said in favor of such a view, yet it seems more accurate to suggest that far from indicating the irrelevance of educational theory, it indicates merely the incompleteness of the work of a number of educational theorists. As a matter of fact, nothing seems easier for the philosophical mind than to delineate an abstract ideal to be sought after by a school; and nothing seems harder—judging from the rarity of its appearance—than to show the correlation of such an ideal program with the actual work of education.

Among Catholic educators this task of delineation is usually entrusted to theologians, either because of academic reasons, or because of the clerical character of American Catholic schools. The academic reason rightly asserts that students of the "queen of the sciences," from the superior height of their position, can take a broader view of the inferior orders of learning beneath, and so regulate them more prudently. There is no need to proffer any criticism here of this theological assumption or designation of authority, except to note, in passing, that men whose field is necessarily dogmatic and precise are inclined, in their encounter with such fluid disciplines as art and literature, to impose on them an inflexible and unyielding regimen which tends to stultify their natural spontaneity. It was to some degree the theologian's passion for precision which, in its encounter with religious art, begot the static canons of the school of Beuron. In addition to this danger of a contemporary reduction of the arts to theology, it is also to be noted that there is little historical precedent for theological direction in the period which theologians generally invoke to justify their pedagogical hegemony. In the medieval schools, theology did not dominate the arts; as Newman observed, ". . . both the teaching and the government of the University remained in the Faculty of Arts, in spite of the genius which created or illustrated Theology and Law." [21]

However, the important criticism, in the present context, bears not on the *fact* of theological direction, but rather on the relegation to professional educationists of the task of applying this direction to the actual work of the school. Frequently, what results from this division of labor is that the theologians weave their splendid theories while the educationists, though paying prudent homage to theology, follow the bent of their own training, which is generally pragmatic. So, there is created a kind of academic

limbo or no-man's land, which the theologians spurn
as beneath their dignity as devotees of the "queen of
the sciences," and the educationists fear as beyond
their scope: dismal visions are readily conjured up of
the Homeric gods playing on Olympus while the
mortals struggle below. The curriculum—such as it
is—which results from this division of labor is a hy-
brid, two-headed thing, with theologians pulling it
one way, and educationists the other, while scientists and humanists are stranded between these two
poles.

One would hope, then, that those theologians who
regard themselves as "educators," in the noblest sense
of that title, would undertake the work of meshing
these two areas and of organizing a unified program
of studies. And this would be a task no more beneath
their dignity as theologians than it is beneath the dignity of their colleagues concerned with moral theology to attempt the application of their principles to
practical ethics and casuistry.

It is now more than twenty years since Msgr.
O'Connell in *Naturalism in American Education*
analyzed this discrepancy between theory and practice, and expressed well-founded amazement that
schools directed by religious teachers and oriented
toward humanistic ends could embrace doctrines and
ideals which were plainly naturalistic and pragmatic.
And it is a sad illustration of the self-satisfaction and
complacency of Catholic educators in his day that it
has been only within the past decade that any concerted effort has been made to cure this schizophrenia,

and so bridge the chasm between the abstract ideal and the actual work of instruction.

III

It would not be entirely accurate to say that Catholic learning is without definite direction, and that this very real lack of teleological bearing is one of the major causes of the present educational confusion. Such a statement is not completely true because there is a general tendency toward the affirmation and defense of Christian humanism apparent in most Catholic schools; and while this tendency is in the practical order occasionally smothered or ignored, yet its influence continues to be felt by reason of that natural instinct for liberal learning present in all genuine educators—to which I referred in Section I—and also by reason of the rich intellectual patrimony to which the American Catholic school falls heir. That, as a result of this dependence on traditionary wisdom, Catholic schools in this country are often forced to live off the capital of past ages without contributing anything of value to the amassed cultural treasure, certainly gives cause for concern; but it does not negate the fact that this heritage has, up to the present, preserved Catholic educators from much of the confusion of their secular colleagues.

However, it must again be acknowledged that sometimes too great a reliance on this heritage, and particularly on the medieval portion of it, has had the inverse effect of breeding an intellectual smugness which is the antithesis of any genuine humanism.

This prideful attitude has been apparent particularly in many of the works on education by those American Catholic journalists who author popular apologetic pamphlets and who write for the large diocesan newspaper syndicates. Many of these works have overtones of: "We give thee thanks, O Lord, that we are not as these others—materialists, pragmatists, instrumentalists, as that John Dewey there; we read our catechism twice a week. . . ." Nevertheless, in spite of all such abuse, it cannot be denied that this cultural heritage, when not confined to the Middle Ages, along with the instinctive good sense of the "working teacher," has been the most important force in maintaining the intellectual character of the Catholic school.

Yet a tradition which moves forward only under the impetus which has been given to it by an earlier age cannot be called a living tradition. For if this tradition is not truly vital, it will be defined too narrowly, or as something complete, ready-made, and, therefore, static: like Orlando's horse it will have the best qualities and all the virtues, save one—it will be dead. Now in such limited definition lies the real cause of the current bewilderment in American Catholic education; and hence it *is* accurate to say that Catholic higher learning has been without the strong foundations it requires, and that this lack, along with a fidelity to certain fragmentary traditions of recent origin, is the source of the mediocrity and the deficiencies about which so much has been written lately.

After more than a century of Catholic higher education, anyone seemingly brash enough to declare

publicly that, to a considerable degree, Catholic educators do not know exactly what they are doing,
would seem to have, by the extravagance of his statement, given up his right to be heard. But considering
the historical circumstances of the development of
American Catholic schools, the poverty and the peasant background of many Catholic immigrants, the
existence frequently of language barriers, the demand
for clerical training, and the isolation of Catholics, as
a result of all these factors, from the intellectual life
of the nation—considering these circumstances,[22] it is
cause neither for surprise nor for recrimination that
it is only in the past three decades that concerted
attention should be directed toward the less utilitarian bases of Catholic education.

Historically the American Catholic college, sometimes only an outgrowth of the secondary school, or
more often simply an extension of the seminary, had
for objectives merely a refined version of the goals
which these two institutions pursued. And these goals,
as a rule, were concerned more with the training of
the will than with the cultivation of the intellect, and
more with the moral life than with the life of the
mind. This ethical bent the early American Catholic
college had in common with most nineteenth-century
schools; but whereas few of the outstanding sectarian
colleges in the twentieth century, and fewer still of
the secular schools, would now regard their mission
as primarily moralistic, there are some Catholic colleges that continue to defend this nineteenth-century
ideal.

Such a defense is generally made on the grounds of

Pius XI's encyclical on Christian education which emphasized the need for a cultivation and formation of the "whole man." By that strange fate which often meets papal pronouncements, this phrase, sensible and comprehensive as it is, when rightly understood, has become the *mot justificatif* under whose wide shelter a number of goals, hazy, dull, and ranging from athleticism to pragmatism, has taken refuge. What the defenders of the school as an instrument for moral direction overlook, in the interpretation of this blanket phrase which they have appropriated for their own pedestrian ends, is that the encyclical had reference, not to college and university education exclusively, but rather to the whole cycle of scholastic training from primary grades to graduate school. When the phrase "perfection of the complete human person" is examined in this context, it becomes apparent that moral training outside the circle of the family falls mainly within the province of elementary and secondary education, and has a place in a college or university only as an incidental objective.

While relatively few serious educators regard the primary mission of the Catholic college or university to be the preservation of virtue and the inculcation of the precepts of morality, there is a large body of administrators and teachers, who, in their laudable desire to maintain the intellectual character of the Catholic college and to bridge the gap between theory and practice, have sought a workable rationale for their academic programs in the philosophical synthesis of Scholastic philosophy. Moreover, not content with defending the existence of the Catholic university and college on the supposition that they are needed to minister to the wants of the Catholic community, these educators have claimed that Catholic schools are essential to *any* community, are essential to *any* educational order in *any* society, because they can provide a reasonable *Weltanschauung* which is absolutely necessary for the progress of research and the advancement of learning. In a democratic polity such a claim seems exorbitant, since it smacks a little of intellectual totalitarianism, and seems redundant since an adequate justification for Catholic education can be found in the simple obligation imposed on every segment in a pluralistic society of tending to its own private wants. But no matter what the claim may superficially *seem* to be, I think it is defensible and valid, and I will try to show it as such in Chapter Five. But I do not think the basis for such a defense is to be found in any specific body of knowledge, whether philosophical or theological, whether Scholastic or non-Scholastic, which the Catholic possesses.

Scholasticism, it has been asserted, can offer to all inquiring minds of this age a type of unified and coherent wisdom not available elsewhere; in its comprehensiveness it furnishes all students with a worldview of unparalleled perfection. Now, although such a position is usually weakened by its dependence on a constricted notion of Scholasticism itself, this stand does have the merit of safeguarding the properly intellectual mission of a college or university and, from this viewpoint, can be said to afford a *raison d'être* for Catholic education far more tenable than that of most other confessional schools.

Obviously any approach to education will rely, at least in part, and intentionally or unwittingly, on Scholastic principles. But without implying any rejection of this important element of the Western tradition, it must be affirmed, in mere honesty, that there is a number of other intellectual constructions as broad as the Scholastic and equally as capable of yielding a reasonably complete and unified vision of reality to the twentieth-century mind. Thus, on the grounds of Scholasticism alone, I do not think it is possible to defend the Catholic university—as Father George Bull attempted in his now-famous address to the Fordham faculty—as a unique and, therefore, a necessary intellectual agency in American society.

But even assuming the immanent superiority of the Aristotelian-Scholastic synthesis, as Catholic educators would be justified in doing, there is still some basis for rejecting it, as the exclusive rationale, on the assumption that the purpose of the Catholic college or university is not primarily to provide a corpus of answers to the "big questions," but rather to give to its students the experience of wondering afresh on the mysteries of the universe, and to give to its faculties a prudent freedom to search toward the elucidation of those same mysteries. Now, it is certainly no argument against Scholasticism that, when applied to the educational order, it often takes the form of a mechanical apparatus which grinds out the "right" and the "true" solutions to whatever problems are posed: this may be an argument against the abuses to which such reliance on highly systematized world-views readily leads; or it may be an argument against the direct application of any closed body of philosophical theses to education, on the premise that such application sterilizes the formative work in its very sources by reducing the pursuit of truth to a primarily technical process, lacking all the passion of discovery and all the incitements of exploration.

It is on the principles of this second argument that even a Catholic educator would be justified in taking his stand against an exclusively Scholastic rationale for his educational program. From the point of view of such an educator, the great teachers would not be those with the greatest knowledge of the philosophical system—*ces ergoistes,* as Montaigne termed them— but rather the great teachers would be those who were most capable of reflecting anew on the age-old questions, and most capable of communicating such reflection to their students. And from that same viewpoint, the great administrators and educational philosophers would be those who regard the tradition they are to draw from for their synthesis as embracing something more than the medieval period, and something more than merely the philosophical school of that period, and something more yet than a philosophical school which, at least in its educational aspects in America, has not shown itself open to many insights either of the Patristic age, of the Renaissance, or of the nineteenth century.

Furthermore, given the temper of the modern spirit with its profound sense of "subject-ness," and given that gradual development of Christian sensibility which has been evident from the time of de Lamennais' *Essai sur l'Indifférence,* which has received a clear formulation in the *Grammar of Assent,* and which has flourished in this century in the *Metaphysik des Fühlens* of Haecker, and in the work of Blondel and Marcel—given all these various forces shaping the Christian person, one may well wonder whether an academic training based too exclusively on the Aristotelian-Scholastic synthesis will correspond to the longings and the needs of contemporary man, and will assuage his intellectual anxiety in the face of a universe so mystifying and, in many ways, so unlike that of the Schoolmen. In passing, one may also wonder what would be the benefits of a narrowly Scholastic world-view on young students who might feel with Newman: "For myself (without denying the argument from final causes), my reason would not lead me to Him from the phenomena of the external world." [23]

It is not inconceivable that an educational philosophy, while including, certainly, Scholastic principles, might yet reject Scholasticism as the last word in education and turn to such a work, for example, as Haecker's on the *analogia trinitatis* as the basis for developing another form of educational theory which would be derived from the interrelationships within the Trinity, and from that deeper awareness of the person-as-subject which has marked recent philosophical discussion. Again, it is not inconceivable that, in a manner similar to that in which Father William Rooney has applied the insights of Dietrich von Hildebrand's Christian phenomenologist position to a philosophy of literature, someone may also apply such insights, drawn from the entire tradition, to a philosophy of education. And all such possibilities have in favor of their realization the following factors: first, while rooted in the Christian heritage, such world-views do not engender excessive certitude on questions which ought from an educational standpoint to remain open; second, these world-views are much more susceptible, by reason of their poetic, discursive tone, of being translated into an experienced comprehension of reality; third, they are, with their awareness of the distinction—emphasized in Blondel and Marcel—between problem and mystery, much better adapted to aid in an assessment of the imponderable and, perhaps, insoluble issues facing the students of the twentieth century who, far from seeing in the universe the well-ordered cosmos of the Aristotelian-Scholastic system, see instead, in this age of possible annihilation, a world of awesome and frightening terrors: a world, compared with which even the nineteenth-century darkling plain of Arnold and the scientific mélange of Henry Adams are as mere passing clouds on a bright landscape.[24]

Unquestionably the students in our schools need the insights of Scholasticism; but they need in the specifically pedagogical realm the experience of how such insights came into being; and this experience is not often gained by the simple expedient of turning to the conclusion of this or that article in the Scholastic *summae,* nor—as Newman showed—by examining the various links in a sorites. As an immediate illustration of the bad pedagogy against which this paragraph is inveighing, one may cite the notion of "being" which educators of an exclusively Aristo-

telian-Scholastic bent often inculcate: *being,* conceived as little more than the gerund form of the
transitive verb, with a consequent loss of all sense of
mystery and existential urgency that this notion
carries with it in other less tightly codified educational schemata.

Similarly—drawing the illustration from the arts—
it is difficult to avoid seeing a certain clumsiness or
ineptitude in many attempts to apply Aristotelian-
Scholastic values to modern poetic practice. From
Aristotle's emphasis on music and art, as merely pragmatic instruments serving a kind of hygienic function, to the writings of the Chicago school of critics,
there is evident a suspicion of the arts in general, and
of their non-rational, non-logical components in particular. Critics in the Scholastic tradition have too
often viewed poetry as a kind of inchoate philosophy,
a kind of metaphysical angel with clipped wings, and
so they bring to the appreciation of the poetic work
the same epistemological machinery they employ so
effectively in the analysis of nature.[25] It is a Scholastic
who tells us that "whether or not he [the student] remains nominally a student of literature, the time
comes when he wants nothing but philosophy." This
is truly a remarkable assertion, particularly since it
runs counter to the experience of so many teachers
who have found students avid for a type of knowledge
which, in contrast to what they are often given as
"metaphysics," is not fixed in static formulae. This
Scholastic philosopher goes on to assert:

In reading *Troilus and Cressida,* for example, he [the

student] cares less for Shakespeare's version than for the
theory implicit in Ulysses' speech about order (or "degree") in society. If he follows that back to its clear state
in political philosophy, he will not rest until he finds
Aquinas.[26]

And possibly students in other countries, afflicted
with this same rationalism, may not rest until they
find *Materialism and Empiriocriticism*. All such pursuits, all such expressions of unrest, noble or ignoble
as they may be, with their presumption that the poet's
"hard Sophoclean light" is somehow dimmed by the
metaphysician's "immaculate imagery," overlook
what even the philosophers must concede, that esthetic knowledge is its own excuse for being.

So sophisticated a group as the neo-Aristotelians of
the Chicago school is forced out of devotion to its
master to reduce the poem to a dramatic action and
to treat the poem's unique language—which may be
said to constitute the essence and existence of the
work—as if it were merely the frosting that makes the
metaphysical cake digestible. Diction for Aristotle
and his followers is simply superimposed decoration,
and not the principle that both forms and informs
the poetic utterance; hence, the disdain of the neo-
Aristotelians for *Verszwang* and metre, and for the
type of linguistic analysis authored by Empson. And
despite its professed fidelity to structure and to the
poem as an intellectual construct, the Aristotelian-
Scholastic criticism, when it is faithful to its principles as now elaborated, must exalt the type of
versifying Arnold condemned in Tennyson and

Wordsworth: "More and more I feel bent against the modern English habit . . . of using poetry as a channel for thinking aloud, instead of making something." [27]

I cannot say whether similar strictures may be brought to bear on attempts to develop, on a rigid Scholastic basis, a pedagogically valid method for evaluating, comprehending, and teaching the natural sciences; but here, too, it would appear that the phenomenologist school would offer insights not dreamt of by many American Catholic educators. Dietrich von Hildebrand has written rather severely in his essay, "Catholicism and Unprejudiced Knowledge," of the "mistaken idea that an attitude which keeps things at a distance and does not allow itself to be touched by them or their world is the only 'objective' and 'scientific' attitude." It would appear, also, that Goethe's criticism of Newton for not encountering the problems of optics with sufficient reverence is one that might be made of many approaches, even to the world of nature, which are too constricted to admit of personalist and subjective perceptions. Moreover, it may be that the failure of many Scholastics to accept such perceptions is the cause of the attacks to which these philosophers are often subjected by scientists as non-Catholic as Philipp Frank, or as ardently Catholic as Teilhard de Chardin.[28]

What ought to be borne in mind throughout the preceding discussion is that an *educational* theory has as its goal, not the development of a program for forming "professional" philosophers, but for forming contemplative and humane Christians; for forming, in the best sense of the expression, *amateur philoso-phers*—which is quite a different thing from forming dilettante philosophers.

A similar body of arguments can be raised against those who find the *raison d'être* of Catholic higher education in the insurance which Scholastic theology provides for guaranteeing purity of truth and for defending the sacredness of man against the errors of materialism and secularism. In this theological foundation for the school, the influence of Cardinal Newman is strongly felt; and rightly so, for nowhere is the role of theology in the university more brilliantly expounded than in the lectures on "The Scope and Nature of University Education." But unlike Newman when referring to theology, most contemporary Catholic educators mean almost exclusively the theological system developed in the Middle Ages. Whereas Newman, in his letter to Dr. Pusey, wrote:

For myself, hopeless as you consider it, I am not ashamed still to take my stand upon the Fathers, and do not mean to budge. The history of their times is not yet an old almanac to me. Of course, I maintain the value and authority of the "Schola," as one of the *loci-theologici;* nevertheless I sympathize with Petavius in preferring to the "contentious and subtle theology" of the middle age, that "more elegant and fruitful teaching which moulded the image of erudite antiquity." [29]

Thus the concept of theology often suggested as applicable to contemporary Catholic education has as little in common with the theology of Newman's

Idea of a University as the four volumes of *A Companion to the Summa* have with the four volumes of Scheeben's *Dogmatik*. If, then, Catholic educators intend to be faithful to Newman's thought, or to invoke his name in defense of their theological rationale, they ought in justice to develop their academic program along the lines, perhaps, of such a work as Scheeben's *The Mysteries of Christianity,* or of Przywara's synthesis of Newman's own philosophical and theological position.

Many contemporary Catholic educators, however, are in accord with Newman—or at least with an element of Newman's educational theory—in their stress on the mission of theology in a school as primarily that of a guardian of truth and a bulwark against error. It is a principle of Newman's nine Dublin lectures that theology in the university plays a primarily protective and monitorial role, similar to that which the theological faculty at Oxford played during Newman's Anglican period. Such a notion of theology severely limits Newman's own concept of this science as it is envisaged in his other writings; but these writings, it must be said, have generally remained little known by educators, with the result that there has prevailed in educational circles this narrow definition of theology as yielding both a surer knowledge of the Christian fact and a regulative control over the other academic disciplines.

This emphasis on theology as a *gnosis* raises a number of problems akin to those discussed above regarding a narrow conception of Christian philosophy. But these problems, I repeat again, may or may not relate to limitations within the corpus of certain philosophical or theological constructions—that would be an issue for theologians and philosophers to resolve to their own satisfaction; the questions with which I am concerned here derive from the pedagogical advantages or disadvantages of a particular system or organization of ideas. In the preceding discussion of the various educational stands which Catholic theorists have taken on purely Scholastic grounds, no criticism of Scholasticism itself can therefore be drawn out of these remarks. This critique has been sketched along educational lines only; and along those lines it may be summarized in the observation that God and creation which, when rightly presented to the young inquiring mind, ought to be objects of contemplative wonder, generally become, when seen in their crystallized Scholastic setting, mere objects of a preposition.

Most students of literature would be appalled by reading the type of "blurb," frequently appearing on vulgarized classics, which solemnly declares—to take a random, but real example—that James T. Farrell has pronounced *War and Peace,* "probably one of the great novels of the nineteenth century." Yet James T. Farrell on Tolstoy is infinitely less incongruous than the title of many college courses—again, a random, but real example—which define their subject matter under the heading: "St. Thomas on God." And the students of theology do not seem much disturbed by this! The only point of the illustration, which really ought not to need sharpening, is that many Scholastic theologians, by the impassioned conviction with which they have assaulted alien views, even when orthodox, by the surgical precision with which they have dissected certain sacred themes, and by the certitude with which they have set forth their "answers" to divine "problems," have often unconsciously, and from so noble a motive as the clarification of truth, appeared to be unaware of the tremendous mystery they were probing. From the standpoint of education, this attitude has had few beneficial effects.

That in the development of Christian doctrine this incisive analytic temper has borne the good fruit of elucidating dogma is an evidence both of the infallibility which oversees the deposit of Revelation and of the vision of the theological School. One may also say that, in the Scholastic emphasis on *ratio,* the discursive work of the mind, rather than on *intellectus,* the intuitive insight of the mind, there has been achieved providentially a highly refined organization of knowledge which may be verified and certified by the instruments of logic. There has, then, been developed a body of truth that is as pertinent to the man of this age as it was to the man of the medieval period, and it would be sheer illusion and the wildest romanticism to attempt to eclipse this construction by any synthesis which would oppose or contradict it.

On the other hand, it cannot be denied that this body of knowledge, sometimes by reason of its very perfection, more often by reason of its abuse, has bred an indifference to that sense of experienced immediacy which, however irrelevant some may think it to be to scientific philosophy and theology, is indispensable to education. Educators of a Scholastic background recognize the difficulty—not to say, the impossibility—of maintaining this sense of immediacy, for it is not born of analysis of abstractions, but from those flights of the spirit which often transcend verbal coherence, and which are communicated by the stammerings of mystics and artists, and embodied pre-eminently in the Scriptures. But having recognized the fact that, from the viewpoint of logical comprehension, the only good intuition is a dead intuition, these educators ought then to go further and acknowledge that if one is developing a balanced educational schema, he cannot do so on Scholastic formulae alone, but must draw his data *explicitly and directly* from the Scriptures, from what Maritain has called the "holy learning" of the Fathers, and finally from the painters and the poets.

Considering the failure of many theologians to look beyond the confining horizons of the medieval period when preparing an educational program, it comes as no surprise that the most widely used textbook of college theology, *A Companion to the Summa,* is remarkably free of quotations from the Fathers and from the Bible. Too often in theological manuals intended for student reading, the piercing sword of the Word of God has become, in its Scholastic translation, what Bruni d'Arezzo five and a half centuries ago called "that vulgar threadbare jargon which satisfies those who devote themselves to theology." [30] This early humanist educator may not have realized that historically the neat Scholastic formulae were necessary for the purification of doctrine, but he did realize that pedagogically they sterilize the young mind.

No one, then, can question the value of such formulations, so important in guaranteeing theological accuracy, and in the work of the professional theologian; yet again it must be repeated, the task of the school is not to train professional theologians. These formulae, freighted with the anguished prayers of the great Schoolmen, and, with St. Thomas, drawn from meditation on the Cross, are not to be rejected—as the Modernists sought—because they are inadequate theologically; nor are they to be re-interpreted metaphorically—again, as the Modernists attempted—to bring them into conformity with certain contemporary philosophical schools. Rather they are to be recast and amplified in the educational process because they are inadequate pedagogically.

Those seemingly trite phrases of the Scholastics, which summarize a long discursive labor of the mind, may be compared to the prayer of simplicity in the spiritual life; for the prayer of simplicity, like a theological formula, is the culmination of a natural intellectual discipline pursued over a long period of time, and of the inspiring movement of grace—in short, the culmination of "long study and great love." In the spiritual life to seek to attain the prayer of simplicity without an initiating formative period is, in a sense, to sin by presumption. Similarly in the work of education, if this initiative effort is not made, the Scholastic formulae become empty catch phrases which, far from climaxing the activity of the mind, rather deter it from seriously undertaking the pursuit of truth. And the end product of such a constricted training is too often that mockery of instruction which Bloy excoriated in a typical passage as a "pretense of religious education which shadowy likenesses of priests, stuffed with formulas, wring like seminary linen over young and uninterested brows." [31]

IV

This chapter has been centered on a negative critique of Catholic higher education; a number of practical evidences of the failure of the Catholic college and university has been described, and it has been suggested that this failure often results from an attempt on the part of many educators to organize a Christian program of studies on, first, neo-medievalist grounds: structuralist or temporalist; second, on grounds which do not allow any co-ordination of educational theory with educational practice; third, on moralistic grounds; fourth, on the grounds of Scholastic philosophy alone; fifth, on the grounds of Scholastic theology alone. In every case, the critique has set itself against an educational doctrine of exclusivism and neo-medievalism, and it is these two doctrines, in the various forms they have assumed, which the remainder of this essay will continue to analyze; for they represent, I submit, the basic source of weakness in Catholic higher learning. Certainly, no one school reflects all these tendencies that I have criticized, and I would doubt that any one school has carried any of these tendencies to the extreme to which I have pushed them; but I am sketching an abstraction in broad lines which is intended to be true, not of this or that isolated school, but of the entire complex picture of Catholic education.

Such a picture is not defined in terms of curriculum, but in terms of the spirit which animates the curriculum. It is not, then, so much a question of courses—since nearly all schools, Catholic or non-Catholic, teach the same subjects—but of the principles on which a program of general education is founded. Only in those courses in which the Catholic school is free to teach whatever, and however, it deems best, that is, in courses in theology and philosophy, does one meet with limitations in subject matter. For that reason, this chapter has been concerned primarily with deficiencies in method, with deficiencies in the underlying assumptions which inform all the courses; with deficiencies, if you will, in the principle of integration. It would be absurd to say that Catholic schools have introduced medieval standards or medieval theories into such fields as literature or physics; on the other hand, I think it a fact that Catholic schools have often approached all subjects, even physical science and the arts, with a mechanism of sensibility, with a preconceived set of attitudes and values, derived from medieval premises. It is, as I have said, not primarily in the courses offered by a school that this neo-medievalism is apparent; it is in the *manner in which* they are offered, in the *spirit in which* they are taught. And from this point of view, it is no exaggeration to say that the tenor of Catholic education in America has generally been rationalistic.

TWO:

AT THE SOURCES

THERE IS IN THE CONSTITUTION OF ALMOST EVERY congregation founded since the sixteenth century, as well as in the rules of some of the older orders, a distinction made between the primary and the secondary ends of the community. With regard to religious institutes of a "mixed" or "active" character, this primary end is generally summarized in the phrase "pursuit of perfection and the salvation of one's soul," while the secondary end is defined in terms of that particular apostolate in which the community is engaged. Now it is the fate of many such distinctions—as, for example, that between the primary and secondary ends of marriage—that they are generally never brought back to the original unity where they find their true source and significance; instead, like many

54

simplified formulae, these distinctions tend to become concretized as divergent elements, with the unfortunate result that far from being regarded as harmonious aspects of a complete whole, or as reciprocally related causes of an organic unity, they are often conceived to be in opposition to each other.

Furthermore, since religious are bound to a tradition which is largely contained in written rules, and since these rules are seldom viewed—as are, for example, the rules of art—either as enforcements that are accepted only that they may be transcended, or as directives that are to be subsumed in fidelity to a higher principle, it often happens that in those communities devoted to teaching, the apostolate, seen as a secondary end, becomes a "second-class" end. In such a conception, the educational work may then be merely tolerated as a necessary but encumbering trammel, or it may actually be feared as a dangerous source of temptation. The nature of a "secondary end," as the bodily element of the religious institute, is seriously distorted; and consequently the congregation, the members of which suffer this distortion, fails in the application of its spiritual doctrine to the social order. Whereas a religious institute that recognizes a harmony in the synthesis of primary and secondary ends, a religious institute that envisions its "body" as the secondary social end, and its "soul" as the spirit of Christ refracted through its founder, a religious institute possessing this unity will be a vital religious organism; it may, then, be compared to a living person, rather than, as in the case of some communities, to an Aristotelian separated substance—or, as in a few other cases, to an angel driving a machine.

The relation of primary and secondary ends ought to be the relation of efficient to instrumental cause. Just as efficient causality does not destroy the real nature of the instrument, but perfects it, so, too, the primary end ought not to so subordinate the secondary end that its structure as a real end is circumvented, and it becomes a mere *means*. In the order of intention this secondary end may be regarded as a means, but in the order of execution, the secondary end must be pursued for what it is: as *an end in itself,* though not the ultimate end. Paradoxically, only when the secondary end is recognized *as an end* can it fulfill itself as a means.

The failure to understand fully the interrelation of primary and secondary ends leads some religious educators into an anti-intellectualism which they justify in the name of their prior obligation as religious, in the name, that is, of the pursuit of perfection. However, it must be inserted here, this is a tendency which, no matter how deplorable it may be from the viewpoint of education, is not entirely to be condemned. The flight to the mountain and the rejection of the world is a Christian temptation resulting from the tension between the "other-world" and the "this-world" poles in the life of faith; while that anti-intellectualism which derives from sloth, from indifference to the plight of man, from acquiescence in sense impulses, or, finally, from a naturalistic faith in the mechanical manipulation of cultural forces—such an anti-intellectualism, which is as deplorable among pagans or Christians as among laity or religious, is beneath discussion.

I

If, as I have said, many religious persons assume an anti-intellectualist posture under the guise of pursuing the life of perfection, such an assumption is often not without support from spiritual writers of various schools and varying shades of orthodoxy. Generally this anti-intellectualism is rooted in a pessimistic understanding of the relation of nature to grace, an understanding which, though paying lip service to the maxim "grace presupposes nature," undercuts the meaning of such homage by lengthy and detailed descriptions of the evils residing in man's "corrupt nature." One may, for example, read in the writings of Abbé Moreau, a founder of the Congregation of the Holy Cross, an acceptance of St. Jane de Chantal's axiom: "Everything for grace, and nothing for nature"; one may read in the writings of St. de La Salle such a maxim as, "Nature destroys grace"; or again, one may read in St. Grignion de Montfort:

The sin of our first father has spoilt us all, soured us, puffed us up and corrupted us, as the leaven sours, puffs up and corrupts the dough into which it is put. The actual sins which we have committed, whether mortal or venial, pardoned though they may be, have nevertheless increased our concupiscence, our weakness, our inconsistency and our corruption, and have left evil remains in our souls. Our bodies are so corrupted that they are called by the Holy Ghost bodies of sin, conceived in sin, nourished in sin, and capable of all sin—bodies subject to thousands of maladies, which go on corrupting from day to day, and which engender nothing but disease, vermin and corruption.[1]

All such opinions are not so much unorthodox as they are incomplete and narrow. Moreover, one can cite innumerable passages from other saints and spiritual writers, less caught up in the conflicts of their historical period, which run counter to those I have quoted above.

However, I would like to repeat what I have said in *The Christian Imagination* (Chapter II) on the sources of much of this anti-naturalism and anti-intellectualism. Its repetition is necessary here because of its direct bearing on the largest group of religious congregations teaching in America today: the communities stemming from the seventeenth-century Catholic revival in France. For although an institution may not always be the lengthened shadow of one man, it is nevertheless true that a religious congregation, because of its traditionary character and its fervent family loyalties, inevitably reflects to some degree the spirit of its founder.

The French school of spirituality—one aspect of which we are concerned with here—as well as the climate in which it flourished, has been translated into the twentieth century by such communities as the Brotherhoods inspired by the great educational apostolate of St. de La Salle: the Brothers of the Christian Schools, the disciples of the elder de Lamennais, the disciples of Edmund Ignatius Rice, the

Marist Brothers, the Brothers of the Holy Cross, and the Marianist Brothers; by the many communities of Sisters of St. Joseph; by the Sulpicians; by the Vincentians and the Daughters of Charity; by the Eudists; and, to a lesser degree, by the communities of St. Peter Fourier and St. Jane de Chantal. When one realizes that most of these congregations are engaged almost exclusively in the work of secondary, collegiate, or seminary education, then the need for understanding the sources of this anti-intellectualism, so rampant in seventeenth-century France, and often so evident in Catholic education today, is all the more urgent and imperative.

The historical perspective in which this discussion must be placed is the age of the Renaissance and the counter-Reformation in France.

In 1553 Rabelais died. Whatever else the author of *Gargantua* might have been, it may be said that he is a representative symbol of late Renaissance humanism. His death marked the close of an era in which naturalism had been completely exploited; and it marked, too, the beginning of that equally distressed age in which the reaction to sixteenth-century licentiousness was so strong that human nature itself came to be regarded as corrupt. In the arc of the historical pendulum, France pledged complete allegiance to unbridled passion in one century and, in the next, erected a code of morality suppressing virtually all natural tendencies, sometimes even the most innocent. It was the extremist humanism of Rabelais—in its turn a reaction to the integral humanism of such earlier Renaissance figures as Guarino and Vittorino—

which begot, as a contrast to its own excesses, the anti-humanism of Port Royal in the following century. Similary the abbey of La Trappe with its exaggerated austerities is in a very true sense the logical historic successor to the abbey of Thélème whose motto Rabelais inscribed as: do what you please.

In general, this was the picture throughout Western Europe: the riotous living of the Stuart court set in motion the historical forces which culminated in that cheerless protectorate of errant saints who, as the first Samuel Butler said, "proved their doctrine orthodox by apostolic blows and knocks." From Hampton Court to Fontainebleau to the Quirinal, the Renaissance humanism invariably produced an austere—though sometimes beneficial—reaction in the age which followed, whether in the rigorism of a Saint-Cyran and the cruelty of Peters, the Puritan executioner, or in the reforms of a St. Pius. And it was on the crest of this wave of rigorism, reform, and anti-naturalism that the religious institutes of this period entered upon the historical scene.

This explains one of the most disturbing attitudes of the masters of the French school: that contempt for human nature which pierces through the brilliant passages of their writings and their teachings like a stream of darkness.[2] However, there is another explanation for their anti-naturalism. It represents, not only a reaction to the passionate humanism of the preceding period, but also signifies how strong was that Platonic and Augustinian tradition which temporarily replaced the moribund Scholasticism of the commentators. With the decline of a virile Thomism, an oversimplified notion of man was created to conform to the ready-made devotional patterns of the first anthropocentric spiritual writers, and of Thomas a Kempis in particular. This conception emphasized the Platonic dualism, with its stress on the conflict between body and soul, between the real world of ideas and the world of images. As Conrad Pepler, speaking of the condemnation of human learning on the part of the Brothers of the Common Life, has noted, "It was an over-spiritual attitude which is to be found hidden in every oversimplified appeal to divine wisdom against the possibility of human error." [3]

There comes into the sphere of the seventeenth-century spiritual writers both an anti-intellectual and an anti-natural trend. And there is among the most influential theologians of this period, Olier, de Condren, Eudes, de La Salle, de Montfort, what amounts almost to an obsession with man's "corrupt" nature. A third reason for this anti-intellectual and anti-natural bias may be found in the type of apostolate carried on by the greatest spiritual leaders of the French school. The religious degeneracy of the poor classes among whom de La Salle, Vincent de Paul, M. Olier, John Eudes, and their disciples carried on their apostolic work demanded that the purgative way be stressed in the simplest catechetical and pastoral form. Their constant preaching and teaching of the need for repressing aberrant natural tendencies could thus in time also contribute, along with the factors mentioned above, to modifying their entire outlook on human nature.

St. John Eudes, in a letter to the queen explaining the reasons for the destruction of the Louvre by fire, illustrates how priests and religious working in such an environment might easily assume a pessimistic and anti-natural bias. The Saint writes: "This fire meant that Paris was full of atheists who trample God underfoot and do things to shock even the demons." [4] No doubt similar conditions met the priests of the Mission of Vincent de Paul; and one may presume that the misguided gamins of the parish of St. Sulpice, or the delinquent waifs of Rouen, whose depravity is pointed up in many a contemporary chronicle, could readily induce a pessimistic strain among the disciples of M. Olier and of St. John Baptist de La Salle.

Thus, if one considers the historical background of this bias, one is better able to understand why so many great saints of the French school were inclined to succumb to it. Nor can the influence of Jansenism be discounted. For while objectively repudiating the Jansenist doctrine and upholding the Bull *Unigenitus,* it is nevertheless evident that subjectively the French school was affected by this heresy. History is not written all black or all white—there are many areas of gray in which it is difficult to determine the exact stand of a man on a particular issue. But it *can* be determined that the same intellectual climate begot the heresy of Port Royal as the pessimism of the French school, even though the latter was kept within theological bounds by the fidelity of the greatest founders to the Holy See.

Of course, it is not a question of heresy among any of the masters of the French school. It is merely that this deviation from traditional teaching, in response to the ethos of the age, represents a monistic view, an overemphasis on the "other-world" pole of Christian life; and whenever the delicate "balance of orthodoxy" is upset, fearful consequences are unleashed. It is not, then, heresy; but neither is it integral Christianity. As Jean Guitton remarked at the 1950 *Semaine des Intellectuels Catholiques:*

It was difficult for them to realize that what is superior and more profound does not absorb what is inferior and less profound when it impregnates it, but that it elevates and sublimates it.

I have discussed elsewhere, in *The Christian Imagination,* the obligation of historical research—both to the religious community itself and to the souls it tends—imposed on the members of a particular institute. For only after such historical studies, interpreted in the light of the theological tradition, have been undertaken will it be possible to separate the substance of a religious founder's heritage from the accidental accretions which may have obscured it over the centuries. Such research is doubly necessary in the present crisis in American Catholic education, since it is obvious that an atmosphere of anti-humanism and anti-naturalism is not going to conduce to the cultivation of the intellectual virtues. It would be a naïve expectation to hope that the majority of religious teachers, working in such an atmosphere— even though they may have the best of intentions, and may have equipped themselves with the best educational instruments, with fine buildings, with impressively up-to-date methods and curriculum—will be able to develop, in the face of a narrow and unbalanced tradition, a comprehensive educational program.

II

Derivative from this heritage, though common also to much counter-Reformation ascetic practice, is an attitude of disdain for the free and spontaneous exercise of man's intellect, will, and sensibility. Moreover, this is an attitude which, unlike the anti-intellectualism of the French school, being found in many contemporary spiritual writings, often affects the layman as much as the religious. There is little need to be concerned here with such observations as Père Lallemant's that "next to sin and the passions nothing is so injurious to a soul as eagerness in study"; for such remarks may be attributed, as I have suggested in the preceding section, to their authors' historical background rather than to their theological wisdom.[5] Nor is it a question of the general dangers which all human activity entails, and for which the only solution would be a permanent state of what may be called passive retaliation; nor again is it a question of denying the very real temptations which any apostolate will encounter, and which Abbot Chautard has so profoundly analyzed in his classic *The Soul of the Apostolate*. What is of sole interest here is the effect in the educational order of a spiritual doctrine which, in the name of higher virtue, rejects the Christian's work in the world, not, certainly, as an evil, but as a discordant element in the harmony of religious perfection.

This disdain for human effort has been expressed by Père Teilhard de Chardin in terms drawn from the advice that a confessor might well give to his penitent:

Without doubt the material of your acts has no ultimate value. That men should discover a truth or another phenomenon, more or less, that they should create lovely music or beautiful pictures, that their political organizations should be more or less successful—all of this has no direct importance for heaven. Nothing of these discoveries nor of these creations shall go to make up the stones from which the New Jerusalem is constructed. But what is important for the next life, what shall always remain, is that you will have acted in all things conformably to the will of God. Obviously, He has no need of the products of your industrious activity, since He is able to draw all things unto Himself without your help. What interests Him exclusively, rather what He desires intensely, is the faithful exercise of your liberty, and the right choice you make among the various objects surrounding you. Learn well this lesson: on earth you are given things only to exercise yourself upon them as a means of purifying your mind and heart. You are being put to the test, so that God will be able to determine if you are worthy of heaven, of entering His presence. You are on trial. From this viewpoint, it makes little difference what is the value or the result you draw from the fruits of the earth. The only question is that you should know how to make use of them in learning obedience and love. Do not become attached to the gross envelope of human work; it is mere straw, a fragile vessel. Rather learn how to fill these base vessels with the precious elixir of your docile spirit and your union with God. If earthly objects have no value in themselves, yet you are able to love them for the means with which they provide you of proving your fidelity to our Lord.[6]

It is impossible to translate this paragraph and do justice to—what Abbé Michonneau has called in another context—"the clerical unction" of its phrasing. Yet this is no travesty of the type of religious counsel often inculcated by the "manuals of perfection." Far from being Jansenist, or in any way unorthodox, this doctrine represents really an oversimplification of the loftiest reaches of Catholic piety. The attitude of the above paragraph reflects the admirable desire on the part of earnest spiritual guides to guarantee a crystalline purity in all profane action, so that the Christian soul may be assured of traveling the *via unitiva* without stumbling over temporal scruples or being distracted by the evanescent beauties of the passing landscape.

There is no reason for taking issue with those authors who are mapping out every twist, bend, and dip on the spiritual way, on what a Kempis calls the "royal way of the cross"; for, while there may be those who believe the best spiritual prescription to be something approaching the brevity of "Love and do what you will," and who feel consequently that the highly technical ascetic manuals of the post-Reformation era (largely of Latin origin), however psychologically fascinating, nurture only an increased

self-consciousness—notwithstanding all this, it must
be said that both for speculative reasons and for the
practical direction of souls, such manuals, in the
hands of intelligent confessors, are not without their
value. One may, however, take issue with that oversimplification which these manuals often rely on in a
misguided effort to exalt grace at the expense of nature. For, along with the presumably praiseworthy
aim of anatomizing the way of perfection, there seems
generally to arise a temptation to make this way so
straight and narrow that it appears better adapted to
angels than to men. More precisely, one can say that
such manuals treat of the spiritual life of all Christians in terms drawn almost exclusively from the monastic principles of the purely contemplative orders.

In such a conception of the spiritual life, the pursuit by the convinced Christian of scientific research, of
the humanities, or of any "secular" discipline is often
regarded, if not as an evil, then as an imperfection
which can be rectified only by ordaining it with a
pure intention to the supernatural plane. The effect
on the Christian scholar who is told that his work
may suffer imperfection unless formally directed to
some supernatural end, is often to introduce a psychological conflict which usually is resolved by diverting
the work to some ulterior religious objective. What
one would like to see emphasized in the manuals, as
a corrective of this monastic conception, is that the
Christian whose vocation may be to education and
research, whose person is enriched by the gifts and
the virtues, and whose efforts are undertaken in an

atmosphere of grace, is, by these very facts, pursuing his highest perfection.

It may be objected that this corrective to a narrowly monastic and monistic spirituality would lead to naturalism. This I do not think is true. Such a corrective is not sought primarily for the equanimity of Christian scholars or for the advancement of Christian scholarship, but simply for the clarification of spiritual doctrine. And such an objection has, in point of fact, been answered by Dietrich von Hildebrand who, in *Liturgy and Personality,* shows that the central theme of the liturgy is that every good must be sought as an end in itself—but sought always *in conspectu Dei*—if it is to have its proper effect in transforming the person in Christ. In another place this layman, who is certainly one of the great spiritual masters of our age, has written:

It is not from what we undertake with a view to our transformation, but from the things to which we devote ourselves for their own sakes, that will issue the deepest formative effect upon our habitual being.[7]

This is not naturalism: it is, in the best sense of the word, *supernaturalism.*

That such a notion of the intrinsic worth of Christian activity in temporal affairs has not always been recognized is apparent in the life of Gerard Manley Hopkins whose continuing tensions, while culminating in a unique poetic achievement, were not by that fact any the less severe. However, Hopkins' natural sensitivity and his rigid ascetic temper served to increase this religious-esthetic discord, so that perhaps better examples of this excruciating tension are to be found in the lives of Frère Marie-Victorin and Père Teilhard de Chardin: both scientists of the first rank and internationally esteemed as such, both men of physical and intellectual vigor and apparently in no way given to excessive self-probing, and yet both obsessed, at one time or another, during their religious life, with the fear that in taking up scientific studies they were compromising spiritual principles.[8]

That the nature of this obligation of tending toward the highest perfection raises a number of critical issues can be seen in the interest which was evoked a few years ago by the publication of Father John Hugo's *Applied Christianity*. This was a work, written with the best of intentions and allegedly based on the best traditional sources, which made a dogmatic system of rigorism and contempt for the world. What is particularly germane to the present discussion is that this book was accepted by the superiors of at least one religious community of educators as the best contemporary expression of the spiritual doctrine of their founder: the founder being in this case a priest of the French school of spirituality. It is indicative of deficiencies in the theological training of many religious Sisters and Brothers, as well as of a real ignorance of the historic conditions surrounding the origins of their communities, that this work which they so eagerly embraced was almost universally condemned for its extravagances by the theologians.

One of the texts on which Father Hugo relied was the following from Garrigou-Lagrange's *Christian Perfection and Contemplation,* where, under the heading "imperfections for religious," the eminent Dominican wrote of

. . . certain ways of amusing oneself or of taking pleasure in scientific or artistic things; in study, and activity that has been branded as "natural" because it is not sufficiently supernaturalized by the motive prompting it. We may place in this class the omission of something which we think is better for us, and to which at the time, from a lawful but less perfect motive, we prefer something less good: for example, when, although we could make a visit to the Blessed Sacrament, we prefer to spend our time at a useful philosophical study which could be postponed. This act in itself is not evil, nor is it so for us unless by a special vow we are obliged to do what is more perfect. Therefore it is good, since concretely no deliberate act is indifferent; but it is less good than the other. We should not stigmatize as evil what is only less good. But we should keep in mind this imperfection in the order of good, remembering that, as venial sin disposes to mortal sin, imperfection disposes to venial sin.[9]

Garrigou-Lagrange had reference here to acts of imperfection for religious, who are by their state obliged to tend to perfection, and so the direct application of such a doctrine to laymen or even to non-regular clergy would be somewhat arbitrary. But bypassing for the time this whole preliminary question on the counsels to perfection being offered to all Christians in a universal external invitation, which is rendered

effective by a particular internal solicitation—bypassing this question of the nature of the religious vocation, since it is not immediately pertinent to the
present topic, I would suggest that if Father Hugo
stumbled over this declaration, it is not too surprising.

We have here one of those extremely intricate
statements so precisely worded that—as Claudel has
remarked of certain perfectly etched poems—"one
grain of snuff would be enough to upset the fragile
wonder." It is this ability to synthesize such practical
details with the most acute theological principles
that has made Father Garrigou-Lagrange the favorite
spiritual writer of those who, particularly in this age
of tension, are seeking a more definite and exact
method of sanctity. One must then pay tribute to
this theologian who, in the best tradition of Bañez
and Nuño, has been defending the Thomistic position with such vigor and assurance. But after having
paid this just tribute, one may yet feel that there are
in the above passage on imperfections some statements which may be open to serious misinterpretation and—what is more important—which would,
when faithfully accepted by religous educators, erect
a barrier between the intellectual life and the pursuit
of perfection.

Since it is a question of imperfection, not of sin,
and hence concupiscence does not enter in even veni-
ally, one wonders whether the imperfect ways "of taking pleasure in artistic things" would include the de-
lighting in them purely for their own sake without
bothering about whether or not they—as pious authors

say—"raised the mind to God." For is there not a danger in demanding that we sanctify the "profane" by a purer intention, of superimposing upon it an adventitious religious veneer which inhibits us from seeing the object as it is, and so prevents it from witnessing in its own way to God's power and beauty? Furthermore, from the standpoint taken in this text, is one not finally driven to conclude that there is no such thing as a "useful philosophical study," since certainly any philosophical study could be postponed for the greater good of praying? And if the *Summa* seemed to Thomas on his deathbed "as so much straw," might one not conclude it an imperfection in him to have devoted so much time to "useful philosophical studies" when he could have been absorbed in the more efficacious work of prayer? And if it is replied that for Thomas the means of tending to perfection was philosophy, has one not made philosophical and consequently theological understanding depend *exclusively* on obedience, rather than on its dignity as a science; and by defining this dependence, has one not undermined the natural structure of all thought and action? Surely, by such definition, it would have been as perfect an instrument of perfection for St. Thomas to have devoted himself, like Brother Juniper, to gardening, had obedience so ordered. One might suggest that for the Christian whose "vocation" is to philosophy—which it is for many laymen in the world—there will rarely be any such thing as "a useful philosophical study which could be postponed"; assuming that truth resides at the end of an ascending and interminable line of investigation, one would have to be a Tithonus in order to justify the postponement of a "useful philosophical study."

Furthermore, if one defines, with Father Garrigou-Lagrange, imperfection with a small *i* as the pursuit of a lesser good which one is entirely free to pursue—e.g., saying nine *Aves* instead of eleven—and if one also defines, again with Father Garrigou-Lagrange, Imperfection with a large *I* as an act which always disposes to venial sin, then, having formulated such definitions, is one justified in equating these two terms, these two "imperfections"?

The example offered above, of saying nine *Aves* instead of eleven, may seem an absurd one—in fact, I'm sure it is—but I do not see how, in many cases, the spiritual doctrine being discussed here could lead to anything other than this type of mathematical weighing of imponderables. There is much truth in the following observation of Newman, even though he relied on the common Anglican interpretation which identified the theological doctrine that Rome enforces with the devotional observances which it tolerates:

When religion is reduced in all its parts to a system, there is hazard of something earthly being made the chief object of our contemplation instead of our Maker. Now Rome classifies our duties and their reward, the things to believe, the things to do, the modes of pleasing God, the penalties and the remedies of sin, with such exactness that an individual knows (so to speak) just where he is upon his journey heavenward, how far he has got, how much he has to pass; and his duties become a matter of calculation.[10]

An example more relevant to the work of education might be found in the case of a religious with definite and outstanding scientific gifts, and of sincere and mature piety, who is obliged in obedience to teach, let us say, English grammar and "to devote his free time to this subject." Such a command, unless perhaps dictated by ignorance, by the demands of penance, or by the unique situation in a particular school, would probably be imprudent—but not for that reason any the less binding. Would it not be an imperfection, as defined by Father Garrigou-Lagrange, for this religious, after an adequate preparation of his grammar, to devote some time to satisfying the natural inclination of his mind, presuming that he was motivated in no way by pride or concupiscence? That such a case, though certainly only a parody of actual situations, is not entirely unrealistic may be seen in the last days of Hopkins, when his poetic sensibility was blunted both by his Irish exile and by an exaggerated fidelity to his duties as an instructor in Greek. (As an evidence of this gradual dulling of sensibility, I would point to the "terrible" sonnets which, in contrast to the earlier poems, are intense and austere, though undeniably moving poetry—I am a little afraid the "evidence" will be lost to those who are inclined to exalt *Paradise Regained* over "Lycidas," or the Last Quartets over the *Missa solemnis*). This is not so much a criticism of Hopkins' religious superiors who, after all, could not

under any circumstances have been expected to recognize the genius of the poet, as it is a criticism of a type
of religious formation which augments rather than
moderates the tension between the "other-world" and
the "this-world" poles of Christian life.

All of these examples are intended to suggest the
impossibility of defining a doctrine of imperfection,
whether for the spiritual life of religious educators or
for the Christian living in the world, without weighing, along with abstract principles, the abilities and
gifts of the natural order with which God may have
adorned for His own glory the Christian person.

Finally, the last question which one may ask, when
faced with the above paragraph from Garrigou-Lagrange, is whether the enunciation of such a doctrine
on imperfection, in works directed to the Christian
community at large, and to the members of religious
congregations, constitutes a present service to religion, or whether it is not true that even robust
temperaments seriously guiding their lives by such
manuals may not find themselves so excruciatingly
harrowed and psychologically encumbered that their
last state of perfection will be worse than their first?
And one may pose this question for much the same
reasons that one may doubt the wisdom of introducing such textbooks in casuistry as Father Healy's
Guidance series into college classes in religion: such
materials have perhaps great value for confessors and
directors of conscience—their value to the faithful as
a whole, or to individual religious, seems debatable.

All these questions and suggestions are presented
by the untrained lay mind with the hope that the

theologians may unravel this knotted and twisted issue. In the meantime, I imagine that in the practical order the layman or the religious will often take refuge in the urbane assertion of the great St. Teresa: "In small things I went according to my natural inclination—and I still do—instead of considering which was the more perfect course." [11]

This lengthy and somewhat detailed discussion has been necessary because it is generally under the guise of perfection and to the detriment of what is disdainfully called "secular learning"—as if the development of the intellect, will, and sensibility of an immortal being could ever be entirely of "this world"!—that many religious people and, among these, many religious educators have justified their scorn for human culture and their refusal to make a firm commitment to the humanistic and scientific disciplines.

It is not hard to imagine the effect on a group of young religious teachers who have heard the gift of knowledge defined—as it is in *Christian Perfection and Contemplation*—as "making us judge created things supernaturally, either by showing us their nothingness, or by disclosing to us the divine symbolism hidden in them." [12] Quite probably these young people will be inclined to interpret this highly orthodox, though perhaps excessively negative, definition to mean that one must never seek created things as ends in themselves, but must instead seek in them some manifest vestige of divinity; and the probable result of such an interpretation, in the educational order, will be to augment in future years the number of those ingenious exercises aimed at proving such things as Dryden's Catholic spirit, Father Tabb's poetic eminence, or the indebtedness of modern science to Friar Bacon: exercises, it may be said in passing, which will generally be written in the style of John of St. Thomas while combining the intellectual insights of *Pilgrim's Progress* with the piety of the *Imitation.*

One can justify a certain asperity toward the proponents of the spiritual doctrine I have been discussing, only because it constrains and even cripples potentially splendid young minds by exaggerating the polarity of nature and supernature. There is an unremitting tension within the Christian life, but it is a tension nevertheless which can be partially resolved by such a principle as that which I have already cited from Dietrich von Hildebrand's masterful work, *Transformation in Christ;* and it is a tension which can be tempered by recognizing the profound truth in the following observation of Father Conrad Pepler who, at the time of the publication of an anthology commemorating the tenth anniversary of *The Life of the Spirit,* declared:

Here the vices of the world have to be considered, but not in the negative manner so characteristic of spiritual reading and sermons of recent centuries. Many a Christian has come to regard the life of holiness as a series of dark nights in which he had to struggle with devils and avoid a whole host of sins. The compiler of the anthology has called this part the "Sacrament of the World," a well-chosen phrase which reveals the more positive approach; for all created things which may perhaps be snares and temptations are also "sacraments," the signs of God's presence and will, to be accepted in one way or another if the Christian is to be made whole and holy.[13]

III

All of the above remarks center on a comprehensive understanding of the interrelation of the "this-world" and the "other-world" poles of Christian life, and on the need for avoiding the twin pitfalls of excessive naturalism and excessive supernaturalism. Now it is possible that the development of a balanced assessment of this polarity has been made more difficult in our country by that peculiar historical event in Church history which is called "Americanism." It seems to me that this is only a possibility; for, while it would be rash to assert, as some have, that "Americanism" was a tendency to be found only in the imaginations of certain continental theologians, and that it was entirely a "phantom heresy," yet it would be equally rash to attribute too much influence to a movement which represented simply the growing pains of a young and vigorous church, and which had as much about it to be praised as to be condemned.

In any event, it is not with the "heresy," but with its aftermath, that the historian of education must be concerned; and, viewing this period following the promulgation of *Testem benevolentiae* as objectively as one can for such recent history, I think it not improbable that a reaction set in similar to that declenched by the condemnation of de Lamennais or of Modernism. I would take, as an illustration of this reaction, the bitter and mordant article on "Americanism" published in 1903 in Vacant's *Dictionnaire de Théologie Catholique* in contrast to the restrained treatment of the same topic in the *Enciclopedia Cattolica* of 1948.[14] The little essay in theological one-upmanship published in Vacant, with its reference to Father Hecker as a "dreamer" and to the *"hardiesses dogmatiques du P. Hecker,"* reflects the temper of the time. In a religious climate where opinion was moving to the other extreme from an alleged naturalism such statements as those following from Archbishop Ireland would have seemed dangerously suspect:

The supernatural rests on the natural, which it purifies and ennobles, adding to it supernatural gifts of grace and glory. Where the natural is most carefully cultivated, there will be found the best results from the union of nature and grace. It is a time of novelties, and the religious action, to accord with the age, must take new forms and new directions.

Lay action is today particularly needed in the Church. Laymen have in this age a special vocation.

The common! We are surfeited with it: it has made our souls torpid and our limbs rigid. Under the guise of goodness it is a curse. The want in the world, the want in the Church, today as at other times, but today as of never before, is of men among men, of men who see farther than others, rise higher than others, act more boldly than others.[15]

Ireland was also—as Josephine Ward suggested of de Lamennais—"born out of due time."

It is difficult to say with certainty whether the reaction which took place after the condemnation of Americanism had any effects in the educational order; but recognizing, first, that Catholic education takes its *form* from the spiritual ideals of the Sisters, Brothers, and priests who carry out the actual work of teaching, and recognizing, second, that no spiritual writer of any celebrity within the English-speaking world from Archbishop Ireland to Father Leen (for there is a definite relationship between Leen's two books, *Why the Cross?* and *What Is Education?*) and Abbot Marmion (a period roughly from 1900 to 1930) seemed possessed either of the theological equipment, or the ability, or the influence to outline for American Catholics a balanced doctrine on nature and grace—recognizing these two facts, it seems quite justifiable to attribute the mistrust of the humanities and of the intellectual life in general, so prevalent among religious educators, at least in part, to this sentiment against Americanism.

It is somewhat ironic that Leo XIII's letter to Cardinal Gibbons closed with the remark that "Americanism, in the bad sense of the word, leads one to conclude that there are some who seek a Church in America which will be different from the Church in the rest of the world." For what is needed in American Catholic education today is a basis for the religious life, as for the intellectual life, which will be more in accord with that in other Catholic countries. And, as a matter of fact, this basis can be found sem-

inally in the works of Archbishop Ireland which
were never intended to be criticized by *Testem be-*
nevolentiae.

IV

In the preceding sections, I have touched upon the
issues raised by various misconceptions of the spiritual life which are derived, first, from the seventeenth-
century French school, second, from certain monastic
and monistic principles in the manuals of perfection
of the counter-Reformation era, and third, from the reaction to Americanism. It is now necessary to examine
the educational consequences of the predominance of
Latin devotional forms among American Catholics.
This issue merits consideration here because of the
non-intellectual structure of many of these devotions
and because, in the emphasis on Latinized forms of
piety, any communication with the other cultural
forces in a civilization which is fundamentally Anglo-
Saxon is seriously inhibited. Only when piety seeks a
mature spiritual experience will it generate a mature
intellectual order, a mature educational work; and,
reciprocally, only when piety is not in needless disconformity with the cultural life of the nation will it
be able to influence and be influenced by that life.

When John Henry Newman wrote in the conclusion to the *Apologia* that he felt the loss of the Ger-
manic and English element in the Church to be a
"most serious evil," he did not realize that his own
works, particularly in the realm of Christian spirituality, would do a great deal to redeem that loss. This

English-German element, whose absence Newman so lamented, can now be recognized as the same force which brought forth the Christian social renovation in von Ketteler; which, beginning with Abbot Herwegen, treated liturgy as an instrument for shaping the Church's inward spirit, and not as the exclusive concern of rubricians and archeologists; which formed from the polemic theology of the Schools a theology of prayer and of mystery in Scheeben and Möhler; which took the spontaneous religious instincts of man, so feared by post-Reformation asceticism, and in Odo Casel showed them to be channels of organic holiness.

This spirituality, then, which Newman, in his great contribution to modern religious life, fostered and cultivated is nothing other than the spirit of personal and corporate worship, the spirit of that piety which the great Cardinal wrote of in his Anglican sermons and studies on the breviary, and in his Catholic essays on Benedictine monachism. It is the piety, he shows, which has received, not the stamp of Latin culture alone, but also of that Anglo-German temper symbolized by Boniface of England, bishop of the Germans, who may well have described his people in the words of Claudel:

It is no small thing to be apostle of the Saxons and bishop of the introvert, shut-up flock of a people corked fermenting. . . . I will have a people more akin to matter and more bent thereon and more mingled therewith and more fit than any other to soak into it and be imbued therewith, a people outside of all dry categories,

outside all the unbending nations, to be at the stage of
longing, in face of everything, a mighty storehouse in the
centre of Europe, semi-fluid, a conforming negation, an
impulse thrusting and filling and maintaining all together, an inward and shrouded man in whom the word
of God does not turn at once into action but to simmer-
ing deep-down fermentation.[16]

One does not long for the reaffirmation of this English-German element out of any patriotic loyalties or
because of that religious xenophobia which is, by
definition, the antithesis of catholicism. Far from being spiritual chauvinism that leads one to hope for a
renewal of this English-German element, it is rather,
on the contrary, a deep sense of the universality of
the Church and of the contribution which every nation is intended under Providence to make to the
temporal expression of the Body of Christ.

The salvation of the nations, as Père Daniélou so
beautifully attested, implies that once a people has
received the Faith, it is intended that, in turn, these
newly converted should offer their own highly personalized gift to the Mystical Body. Yet it remains a
sad truth that, with the exception of Newman himself, most spiritual writing in English during the past
two centuries has been stamped with the seal of continental piety. And, as I have already mentioned, this
piety has not infrequently, in its popular expressions,
been characterized by a severity and an emotionalism
which are at once the cause and the unconscious
panacea for a narrow and semi-Jansenistic conception
of man. The great contribution of the English spirit,

both in devotional forms and in theological insights, has been shrouded by the imposition, as the one ideal and the only standard of prayer-life, of a religious vision that remains largely alien to the needs and longings of the Anglo-Saxon world. That rich period stemming from Caedmon and Bede, from Cuthbert and Alcuin, moving through the days of More, Colet, and Lynacre, and terminating in Campion, Allen, and Martin—that rich period, which has been illuminated so well and so reverently in our time by Margaret Williams' translations, remains a dead historical epoch to modern American Catholics.

There is no doubt that the Tudor persecutions, with their attendant demand that priests be formed and educated in continental seminaries, as well as the unfortunate excommunication of Elizabeth, have been the major cause of this spiritual uprooting; but it is equally true that, more recently, with the gradual decline of this spirit of the counter-Reform, little more than lethargy has been responsible for such continued indifference to the older tradition.

One further cause of the predominance of continental forms of piety may be found in the quite understandable equation, by many Catholics, of Latin devotions with Roman doctrines. Notwithstanding the great ardor with which successive popes have fostered the non-Latin liturgies and, within the framework of orthodoxy, devotions with a distinctively national character, many Catholics still persist in asserting the superiority of this or that practice imported from the continent over forms of piety native to the English-speaking world. This derives partially

from the fact that most of our religious communities
are of Latin extraction; but even more is it the result
of the religious conflicts within the Church in the
nineteenth century. Most of the ultramontanists in
England, passionate believers, like their colleagues on
the continent, in an extreme notion of infallibility
and of the temporal power—men such as Faber, Ward,
Vaughan, and Manning—were also strong advocates
of Latin devotional practices, and with the consequent acceptance of the Vatican decree, their position
on prayer-life and piety seemed also to have been
vindicated. This is *lex credendi, lex orandi* with a
vengeance.

That even in the twentieth century, Father Faber's
books are more widely known than Newman's sermons—which were also intended for popular reading
—is a good indication of the extent to which ultramontanism has prevailed in the realm of piety. And
furthermore, it is not so much that Catholic critics
have made the great mistake of overstressing Newman's intellectual work to the detriment of his
equally impressive spiritual achievement, as it is that
the tenor of modern American religious thought,
wherever the liturgical revival has not been felt, is
more attuned to emotion and sentiment, and hence
cannot harmonize with Newman's serene and objective piety.

Not, of course, that Newman is lacking in feeling
and sensibility. But this sensibility, as evident in the
sermons, in the *Apologia,* and even in *The Dream of
Gerontius,* is controlled and guided by the restraints
of reason and theological wisdom. It was precisely the

absence of these controls that Newman deplored in Wesley and criticized in a number of Catholic writers:

How is it fair to throw together Suárez, St. Bernardine, Eadmer, and Faber? As to Faber, I never read his books. I never heard of the names of de Montfort and Oswald. Thus a person like myself may be in authority and place, and know nothing at all of such extravagances as these writers put out.[17]

Newman would certainly have criticized the competitive spirit occasionally displayed by the various advocates of different devotions; he undoubtedly would have felt great distaste at the overemphasis on those measurable forms of piety that reflect a kind of "counting complex" and give a thaumaturgic value to numerical repetition; and he would certainly have deplored the efforts on the part of devotees of this or that private devotion to make it appear as if their particular practice had a monopoly on grace. But, as is evident from his own pastoral apostolate in Birmingham, he would not have condoned wholesale attacks on these devotions, for he realized that many of these practices are often necessary for certain persons, in certain spiritual conditions, and at certain stages of religious growth. Concerning these practices, he wrote:

I venture to say the majority of Catholics in England know nothing of them. They do not colour our body. They are the opinions of a *set* of people, and not of them even permanently. A young man or woman takes them up, and abandons them in a few years.[18]

The relevance of Newman's teachings to American Catholics—and, in the present context, its relevance to educators—is in the fact that America's religious development is no more polyglot than America's language, and that underlying all assimilated European traditions is a strong Anglo-Saxon strain which must be strengthened if our religious life is to be the supernatural complement and fulfillment of our social, political, economic, and intellectual life.[19] This reason, of course, is of far less significance than the all-important truth that what Newman himself called "the English and German element in the Church" fosters a piety which is in perfect accord with the liturgical spirit and which is, as he shows in his essays on Benedictinism, intimately connected with the life of worship. But it is this less significant, pragmatic reason, drawn from the requirements of the educational order, that I would stress here.

No one would dream of displacing devotion to the holy house of Loretto, or our Lady of Częstochowa, or the Infant of Prague, or our Lady of Sorrows with devotions to our Lady of Walsingham. This would be unparalleled religious snobbery. But to suggest, as Newman did, that the loss of the English-German element in the Church has been a most serious evil, and further to suggest, with him, that this loss must be redeemed, not merely for cultural reasons, but because it deprives the Christian community of a great spiritual force, and the Church—which is clothed in variety—of a gracious adornment, is to make an observation at once so compelling and so self-evident as immediately to enlist the services of all sincere Christians in its fulfillment.

V

All of the tendencies which I have discussed in these five sections are strengthened by two complementary attitudes that militate against the intellectual life and against a truly liberal educational program: pious pragmatism and the spirit of activism.

The victims of the first of these attitudes do not examine the universe, do not pursue scientific or humanistic research, in order to achieve a deeper insight or a more profound vision of the Creator and creation; rather, in the name of virtue they squint at all reality as something tainted, unless it can be directly employed in some evident, tangible, or measurable religious work. The notion that knowledge is its own end—a notion to which the pious pragmatist may pay lip service on occasion—is dismissed in the practical conduct of life as being pertinent only to the natural order, or rather to an order which is conceived as "naturalistic." And since the pious pragmatist regards himself as a religious being, as a person of some virtue, he justifies his incompetence in the intellectual realm by invoking his eminent piety. His only reason for entering upon any "natural" undertaking is that it may be used in the apostolate; only a *"useful* philosophical study," for example, would be of importance to him.

An implicit Pelagianism, which apparently presumes that God's activity in the world is dependent on men, produces among the pious pragmatists a type of "immediatism": what is not immediately germane to the apostolate, what is not immediately aimed at "saving souls"—as if *man* saved souls—is of little value, justifiable only as diversion or recreation. It was this pious pragmatism which Newman so trenchantly condemned:

The only thing of course which it is worth producing, is *fruit*—but with the Cardinal [Wiseman], immediate show is fruit, and conversions the sole fruit. At Propaganda, conversions, and nothing else, are the proof of doing anything. Every where with Catholics, to make converts, is doing something; and not to make them is "doing nothing." And further still, in the estimate of Propaganda, of the Cardinal, and of Catholics generally, they must be splendid conversions of great men, noble men, learned men, not simply of the poor.[20]

Certainly there is some truth in the assertion, "God has need of men"; but this element of truth presumes that God has need of men *as* men. There is in the attitude of most pious pragmatists a hidden and unrecognized temptation to arrogate to themselves the very work of God. God has need of men, not that they may attempt to encroach upon that transcendent activity whereby He speaks His Word to the world, but that they may act as instruments *according to their human nature* in the work of the world. The Christian intellectual—to confine the discussion to education—must by his office determine the true, the good, the beautiful; he must bring souls to the threshold of God's realm, and by this fidelity to his own obligations as an intellectual and to the natural structure of things, he will be of inestimable value to any form of apostolate—though the apostolate may not be his immediate goal.

It is somewhat presumptuous to criticize genius, but it is difficult to avoid in this context all reference to Claudel and his "convert classes"; and, at least in his relations with Gide, it is difficult to avoid the impression, from the whole botched business, that with Claudel, zeal for God's house so consumed him that in his haste to "make" a convert, he sought to bring Gide not to its threshold, but into its very sanctuary. Without ignoring Gide's native sophistic bent, one may yet wonder about the remarks of Claudel on "a mediocre chap without virtue, talent, or intellect such as Rousseau, de Gourmont, or, for that matter, Kant or Renan." And while recognizing the passion of genius in Claudel, one may wonder whether less eagerness might not in the long run have been more effective. Like many Catholics, Claudel seemed to approach his "convert-making" with about as much suavity as Charlemagne approached the Saxons: from fishers of men, they become hunters of souls. They stalk their prey too earnestly; and they betray often an indifference to the object itself, being concerned with it only in view of the transformation they may work upon it. Claudel wrote to Gide: "I am praying for you. I am sorry for you. But I am growing a little tired of all this delay."

It is this unconcern for the object, this unresponsiveness to the value in itself, and this obsession with reshaping it according to one's own pious image rather than helping it gradually evolve toward its proper perfection, which inflates the ego of the pragmatist, and which generally nullifies his work in the eyes of men. The pragmatist in his preoccupation with whether the artist's creation be "spiritual"— whatever that may mean—with whether the scientist's experiment be apologetically useful, with whether the humanist's scholarship be "uplifting," has fallen victim to the first of Satan's temptations: you shall be as gods. By attempting to impose his own private pattern, his own personal vision of the world on objects and activities which have already received their form and structure from the Creator who engenders and sanctifies them, the pious pragmatist unconsciously assumes the role and prerogative of deity.

In the educational order one sees an index of the attitude of the pious pragmatist in the following observations from a work which is still widely used in Catholic colleges and universities. In *A Humane Psychology of Education,* Jaime Castiello wrote:

Goethe was supremely curious of all human things, yet he was unwilling to sacrifice much for any man. He was too wrapt [sic] up in himself; ultimately he was the end of all his aspirations. What a contrast to the tragic figure of Beethoven, whom he disliked precisely because Beethoven was not cooped up in himself nor too interested in self-advancement or in the trivialities of a court life. Of the two, Beethoven was surely the Christian humanist.[21]

A statement such as this in a book which has had a strong influence in the formation of young Catholic teachers indicates to what historical errors—of fact and of interpretation—the attitude of pious pragmatism can unknowingly lead one. In treating the obvious limitations in such a statement, I will pass over with slight emphasis such incidents as Goethe's intense practical activity in the government of Weimar, or the implications of Beethoven's supremely self-centered—though understandably such—Heiligenstadt Testament; for the present purpose, too, one can pass over an observation such as that of Peter Wust on the native sacredness of Goethe's vision, or a valid interpretation of Goethe's reserve, such as that offered by Karl Vietor, that Goethe refrained from too much immersion in the world in order "to guard against paralyzing shocks . . . [this] seemed to him permissible and even necessary if he was to keep emotion and imagination, all the powers of poetic creativity in a pure and vigorous state" [22]—all of these sympathetic judgments may be passed over here, because this is not the place to defend Goethe against the flaws of bad scholarship or clichéd history. All that is relevant to the present topic is how typical this attitude, in the quoted paragraph above, is of that which I have characterized as "pious pragmatism."

Almost automatically the pious pragmatist seems to assume that the life of the mind must, under pain of being worthless, involve some external, visible dedication to the cause of religion and humanity. Yet, as I have already suggested, that intellectual life which is cloistered, isolated, and remote from the affairs of men, that life which may be pursued even in the ivory tower, is often more likely to be fruitful for future ages, and this precisely because it has been sheltered from incidental trivia and transitory problems. Does not the Christian acknowledge in the liturgy that the Seat of Wisdom is also the Ivory Tower? And must he not also acknowledge, with Baudelaire in "Les Phares," that the ivory tower of one generation may be the beacon light of the next?

Two additional factors, the one deeply Christian and the other non-Christian, have often confirmed the pious pragmatist in the righteousness of his ways. The first of these factors is the pragmatic source and motivation of the educational work of many religious communities. It took an honest commitment to historic fact for Father Allan P. Farrell to write at the height of the Hutchins' criticism of American higher education:

. . . Ignatius used education as a means to an end, and the end was religious, to wit, the quickening of the Catholic spirit, the "levying of immediate posterity under the Catholic banner." He did not pretend to view education as an end in itself. "For ourselves," he wrote in 1555, "theology would do well enough with less of Cicero and Demosthenes." [23]

Although this judgment can hardly be said to apply to contemporary Jesuit schools, many of which modified their traditionally strong liberal arts programs only under pressure from accrediting agencies, and from commercially inspired Catholics, such a text of Ignatius does have present significance in that it pro-

vides a convenient shelter for various religious ob-
scurantists, anti-intellectuals, and reactionaries, all of
whom, rather than viewing such declarations as em-
bodying the attitude of one age in the Church, regard
them instead as sempiternal verities.[24] When one
notes, too, that one can read similar statements in the
writings of many other founders of educational communities, it is obvious how much ammunition the
pious pragmatist has at his disposal. The fact that
such declarations have as little bearing on twentieth-
century education as Loyola's other injunctions that
his Society ought everywhere to maintain gratuitous
schools, generally goes unnoticed by those who embrace the accidentals of a tradition while ignoring its
substance.

The second factor which fosters pious pragmatism is
to be found in the dominant educational philosophy
in America today. For whether one call it progressiv-
ism, pragmatism, or instrumentalism, it remains undeniable that the type of scholastic ideal which has
been spawned by professional educationists and which
has come to be identified with Teachers College,
Columbia, has received widespread support from
Catholic schools. While generally denouncing vigorously the theories of Dewey, Kilpatrick, and Thorn-
dike—not always for the best reasons—Catholics have,
as readily as their non-Catholic colleagues, subscribed
to the practical application of these theories in such
important fields as the organization of curricula and
the training of teachers. It is not, then, too surprising
that a distinguished biographer of St. Jean-Baptiste
de La Salle, Gaétan Bernoville, can praise the founder

of the largest men's educational congregation on those very grounds where he most resembles the educational pragmatists of our time:

His distinctive mark, by which he separates himself from his age and stands as a forerunner of modern times is his having eliminated the humanities, and his taking for the foundation of his educational work those notions which equip the child for the material and moral struggles of life.[25]

That Catholic educators have frequently joined the dubious crusades of the educationists is to be attributed in part to the affinities which exist between the pious pragmatism of many religious persons and the impious pragmatism of many graduates of the teachers colleges.

Turning now to an examination of the second of the two attitudes, which militates against the intellectual life of the Christian educator, a spirit of activism, one encounters the same voluntaristic and Pelagian roots mentioned above. Here, too, as in the case of the pragmatist, the motive is "to do good for souls." Unlike the pious pragmatist, however, the activist may theoretically favor the intellectual life; but because of his conviction that the Christian must *do* good for souls, in the practical order, he sacrifices the intellectual life.

This conviction has been supported by a few Catholic actionists who have, in the face of a long ascetic tradition, beginning with the trial catechumenate of the early Church, asserted the novel doctrine of "formation through action." Now, it must be said in favor of this assertion that certainly there is a reciprocity between the action and the agent; and it is certain, also, that the active life does strengthen an already matured spirituality. But to take these certainties as a guarantee of apostolic achievement on the part of untrained and immature religious persons would be to presume exorbitantly on actual grace, and to ignore the fundamental law of all life that action follows being.

In all cases, too great an emphasis on the *agere* at the expense of the *esse* sterilizes one's spiritual capacities and dries up the fountains of thought. Activity becomes, then, an aimless wandering on the periphery of things, a skittish manipulation of techniques, according to some vague principles, once cogent, but since grown feeble. Inevitably as one withdraws further and further from that contemplative unity which should ordain activity to its proper end, one tends more and more to fill up the resultant vacuum with a deeper immersion in matter, in multiplicity.

As a consequence of this movement toward multiplicity, in the educational sphere, the activists, rather than opposing the incessant fractionizing and increasing of courses and programs of study in the American school, have fostered this very complexity. And while these apostolic activists may remember enough traditional thought to deny Herbert Spencer's assertion that Science—with a nineteenth-century capital S—is "the most valuable knowledge," they would have to agree with him, if they are to be consistent with their activist tenets, when he declares: ". . . organic progress consists in a change from the homogeneous to the heterogeneous . . . and this law of organic progress is the law of all progress." [26] Spencer regarded this as a pedagogical thesis; and it would be so regarded by those present-day educators who, having lost sight of the original unity of spirit, have become absorbed in the multiplicity of matter. Activism engenders this materialization of the educational work, and this particular brand of activism is fostered both by the doctrine of "formation through action," and by the type of devotional practices, already discussed, which scatter one's prayer life over so wide a field that simplicity of view is obscured.

VI

The complexus of spiritual attitudes analyzed in this chapter is, in its broad lines, often as prevalent among the laity as among the members of the various religious congregations. However, because almost the entire American Catholic school system is directed and staffed by religious or by non-regular clergy, this complexus as it affects the academic world can generally be recognized more readily in the work of religious educators.

It is necessary, then, to examine in detail those salient traits of the religious life which, when abused, are a further cause of undermining any serious educational achievement.

The Hidden Life

In addition to the three vows of poverty, chastity, and obedience, one of the foundations of the religious life is withdrawal from the world. This turning away from temporal affairs and conversion to the things of eternity is for all religious communities one of the basic sources of their mission both to their own members and to the souls among whom the apostolate is exercised. When occasionally this pursuit of the hidden life puts the members of a community out of touch with the social or cultural activity about them, invariably there are those who immediately declare that religious engaged in teaching should break off their cloistered isolation, should become conversant with secular affairs, and should by these questionable means adapt themselves to contemporary life.

Of course, there must be adaptation, as this is a law of all life, but the complete destruction of one of the bases of the religious state can never be defined as adaptation. Rather it is a kind of revolution. And no matter how valuable a work may result from it, and no matter how beneficial to individuals such a revolution may appear to be, nor how successful an apostolate may seemingly derive from it, the adherents of such a novel movement cannot be regarded as members of any of the traditional religious congregations. I am not, then, concerned here with any of the various reforms or revisions of traditional rules which have been suggested for a number of apostolic lay organizations or for secular communities, since these groups are not active in American Catholic education. There is no question being raised as to the advantages or disadvantages of traditional forms of religious life; nor, it should hardly be necessary to add, is there any criticism implicit here of the structure of the religious life itself. The topics of interest now are: first, the *abuses* of the legitimate religious principle of the "hidden life"; and second, the consequences in the educational order which flow from these abuses.

With regard to the religious women who maintain the majority of American Catholic colleges, it seems likely that an erroneous concept of the hidden life has brought about an extension even to the academic world of St. Paul's injunction, "Let women be silent in the church" (I Corinthians 14:35). It is a remarkable phenomenon that American Catholic education, though preponderantly a woman's field, has never shown itself open to any distinctively feminine element save in such non-academic areas as "home management," "library science," and business training. With the impressive figures from the past before the mind's eye of Mary Ward, of Louise de Marillac, of Catherine McAuley, one must be content in our time and in our country with a small handful of outstanding educators, such as Mother Butler, Georgia Stevens, Sister Ritamary, and the Franciscan authors of the *Christian Impact* series; while a vast host of other religious women appears content either to follow the lead of clergy or laity on all important academic issues, or—yet more unfortunate—to take refuge from the intellectual disciplines among courses that could as well be taught by cooks, librarians, and stenographers.

This deplorable state results partially from the inadequate theological and spiritual formation in many religious communities of Sisters; and although this inadequacy is being gradually corrected by the foundation of theological schools for women, the influence of such schools on the large body of religious congregations has not yet been widely felt. As a consequence there is a tendency among some teaching nuns, even among those of a broad humanistic or scientific culture, to place an excessive reliance on the judgments of the clergy, and often to accept the opinions of the community confessor on many non-religious questions, as if these opinions had the guarantees of theological wisdom to confirm them. It sometimes happens, then, that the ultimate court of appeals, even on strictly academic issues, in some Catholic women's colleges is the chaplain.

It is worth noting that the reason alleged by two different authorities of two different nations for the decline of vocations to the religious communities of women is the failure of these communities to provide a comprehensive theological and spiritual training. As a result of this failure, wrote Dom Ernest Graf in 1951, "in practically all the Orders and Institutes of women, vocations have fallen off and are still falling." A year earlier in France, a committee of priests offered the following reasons for this decline in vocations: emphasis on the married state to the detriment of virginity; complex spiritual life not sufficiently oriented to the liturgy; customs which are often incompatible with the work of nuns.[27]

All such observations, as well as those I have quoted in the notes, are directly relevant to the educational problems with which we are concerned here, and this relevance is underlined by such practical regulations as prevail in some dioceses that priests must administer high schools staffed by religious women. Now there is nothing about holy orders that infuses administrative gifts, so that regulations of this type, when not dictated by prudential requirements of overwhelming importance, tend to perpetuate a myth of inferiority and inefficiency. Moreover, on historical grounds one can point to such medieval monasteries as Whitby where an abbess ruled over both monks and nuns. And since it was at St. Hilda's Whitby that English Catholic literature was born, one might suggest that this is an aspect of that "feminine" element, of that element of *anima,* I alluded to above, which contemporary religious women ought to further in education: in the face of the omnivorous physical sciences, the religious woman would be doing a real service if, rather than taking refuge among the kitchenware, the glue-pots, the card catalogues, and the IBM machines, she would devote herself to asserting the claims of the arts and of *belles-lettres.*[28]

There are regulations in other dioceses—as Sister Janet showed in her N.C.W.C. survey of secondary education—that restrain nuns from teaching religion even in their own schools: by a strange paradox, the religious woman is assigned to teach those subjects labeled secular, while the clergy who are called secular are assigned to teach those subjects labeled religious. Yet there seems good reason, presuming adequate training and intellectual competence, why religion classes should be taught by nuns in their own schools. Such teaching to be effective would, of course, require, in additional to theological knowledge, a sympathetic understanding of the lay mind and of the role of woman in modern society: an understanding which can be obtained only through prudent contact with life outside the convent, and through the elimination of a number of minor hampering regulations, e.g., those which forbid the attendance of nuns at evening lectures.

Ignoring the anti-feminist spirit of some of the Fathers, and ignoring also a number of traditional anecdotes about the sin of Eve in seeking knowledge, there is no ground either in the theological tradition or in modern socio-religious psychology for assuming that woman succumbs to temptation more readily than man. It comes as a bewildering discovery, then, to learn that the members of lay religious institutes for men enjoy a freedom—in almost all ways, but particularly with regard to such activities as studying at non-Catholic universities or attending public lectures—which does not prevail within communities of women. An educational consequence of this is that Catholic men's colleges have generally outgrown their nineteenth-century seminary origins, while, on the contrary, a number of women's colleges have continued to uphold a mid-Victorian convent-school ideal, if not in the curriculum, then in the prevalent social and religious atmosphere.

There can be little doubt that this lack of freedom to pursue legitimate intellectual goals within women's religious communities is the result of prejudices which have no doctrinal foundation whatever, and which are largely of non-Catholic, Puritan origin. Yet

so deeply rooted are these prejudices—as well as those
others which so apotheosize the "good Sisters" that
the effectiveness of their goodness is often impaired—
that to impute them to anything but the purest
Gospel spirit leaves one open to being accused of
scoring a point for militant Protestantism. One is
tempted to suggest that a suffragette movement would
not be without its benefits. More seriously, one might
hope that contemporary neo-medievalists would take
up the cause of the religious sisterhoods and strive for
a kind of prudent liberty of action, *mutatis mutandis,*
in contemporary secular society, similar to that which
prevailed in the "sacral" society of the Middle Ages.
Is not this perhaps one lesson to be drawn from the
fact that the outstanding Catholic woman educator
in America, Sister Madeleva, is also the outstanding
authority on Chaucer's nuns?

One other consequence of an abuse of the notion of
the hidden life must be discussed here. This is the
problem raised by the athleticism so rampant in many
American Catholic men's colleges. The introduction
of this subject under the heading of abuses of the
hidden life may appear somewhat arbitrary; but it
has seemed to me, as well as to a number of other
Catholic teachers with whom I have discussed this
problem, that the extraordinary success of Catholic
schools in athletics has patently not been due to the
exceptional physical prowess of Catholic youth. Nor
does this success seem to stem from the greater need
which Catholic schools have for attracting public
notice; nor, again, from the greater pressures which

Catholic students may be able to exert on faculty and administration. As to the first possible cause of such success, there is little reason why Catholic schools should seek the type of publicity athletics brings with any more eagerness than do other non-Catholic schools of similar size and character; as to the second possible cause, I think it is generally and rightly realized that the students in Catholic colleges are usually more docile to administrative decrees than are the students in most non-Catholic institutions.

This athletic success derives, I would suggest, in great part—and making due allowance for the normal incentives of competitive sport—from the type of escape valve that it provides and the common social focus it offers to men who are necessarily cut off from many of the diversions and distractions of a more active life. I have reference particularly to those Catholic schools (it would not be difficult to name several) that would enjoy no national eminence, and that would, in some cases, probably be unknown outside their locales, were it not for their athletic teams. It would be impossible to document the existence of this nexus between rampant athleticism and the abuse of the hidden life, but I think the general accuracy of the observation will be supported by many educators, lay and religious, who have taught in Catholic secondary schools and colleges. However, should one believe this judgment to be faulty, he can still examine the isolated fact of athleticism, and its exorbitant demands on faculty and students, while reserving judgment as to source and provenance.

Because a number of educators have already la-

mented the strangle hold which an athletic department often gets on a college, I do not want to repeat
what these others have so well said. It is not necessary
to do more than allude, in passing, to the shameful-
ness of such situations, accepted by many Catholic
administrators, where the highest paid members of
the faculty are on the coaching staff. Nor do I want to
treat of the strong probability that any Catholic college which has fielded successful teams over a period
of a decade or so, would be found almost always to
have devoted a larger budget to athletics than to any
department within its school of arts. Neither do I
want to discuss at length the implications of so extraordinary a situation as that in which, in a mass
circulation news magazine, a public statement can appear proclaiming a particular school's athletic purity:
a statement signed not by a gym instructor, not by a
coach, not by an athletic director, not by a dean, not
by one of three or four vice-presidents, but by the
president of the university! One is then expected to
sympathize with further protestations from these
same quarters affirming that athletics does not play a
dominant role in the life of such a school. One is a
little reminded, when listening to such protestations,
of E. M. Forster's Mr. Pembroke; Mr. Pembroke
with his school "is the world in miniature": Mr. Pembroke, with his "exhortations to be patriotic, athletic,
learned and religious that flowed like a four-part
fugue" from his mouth.

Nor do I want to emphasize the scale of values reflected by such news items, released to the press, which
underlined not academic, but financial, reasons as the

cause for two large Catholic universities discontinu-
ing intercollegiate football. And in like manner, it
does not seem necessary to devote much space here to
a discussion of that remarkable evolution which has
taken place between the period twenty years ago—
when the fortunes of such teams as the "Galloping
Gaels" or the "Fordham Rams" were as enthusi-
astically followed as those of the "Fighting Irish"—
and the present "athletic moment" (to give it its due
importance) : during which two decades, the student
ideal of many Catholic men's colleges changed from a
stocky, squat anthropoid type to a gangling, lanky,
long-armed youth. There may be mercenary cynics
who will suggest that this evolution of ideal types—
this truly biological "sport"—arose in that marked
transition from football to basketball which occurred
when it was discovered that it is less costly to finance
five young men than eleven. A more charitable interpretation, and one to which most Catholic educators
would incline, is that the great faith of the administrators of those colleges where this evolution took
place has succeeded in what hitherto—to men of lesser
faith—had been deemed impossible: merely by taking
thought these administrators have added a cubit to
the stature of their athletes.

All of the various expressions of administrative
weakness, pusillanimity, and abdication before the
mob spirit which I have touched upon in the preceding exercise in apophasis are only indirectly related
to the fundamental issue raised by athleticism. What
has been discussed above is the abuse, not the necessary consequence, of athletics; and so it would not be

very pertinent for me to suggest eliminating athletics entirely from the school. Certainly there must be some programs of athletics in Catholic colleges, and it seems probable that these programs should be organized under some kind of academic supervision. Indeed, this is one aspect of our Renaissance Christian heritage; for no group of educators, since the classical era, so stressed the importance of athletics in the life of the school as did the Humanists. Yet it was a Renaissance educator, Erasmus, who could declare: "We are not concerned with developing athletes, but scholars and men competent to affairs, for whom we desire adequate constitutions indeed, but not the physique of a Milo." [29]

It is not, then, the presence of athletics in a school that is deplorable. It is its omnipresence, its insertion into all elements of collegiate life, its attritionary effect on the academic disciplines and on the academic faculty, and its diversion of student energy and interest from scholastic channels—these are what one must oppose. But what is even more to be deplored, from the viewpoint of the college's obligation to bear witness to Christian wisdom, is that athleticism identifies the life of the school, not with any humanistic or scientific achievement of its various faculties, but with the physical exploits of a semi-professional band, the members of which (coaches, public relations people) are often opposed, on principle, to the intellectual life. The murky climate in which athleticism flourishes enervates the teaching staff of a school both by militating against its rightful dominant influence over the students, and by diminishing the funds at its disposal for salaries, laboratory equipment, and research materials.

Community Spirit

Closely related to the above abuses, which may flow from a faulty understanding of the hidden life, are the following consequences of an exaggerated fidelity to one's own religious institute. Not infrequently among certain religious persons a legitimate family loyalty to their congregation degenerates into an idealization of every aspect of its work, so that any criticism of this work is interpreted as unfaithfulness. Often, then, it happens that schools staffed by such religious are not regarded as instruments to be corrected, improved, and so perfected: they are seen as ultimate ends in themselves. I have discussed in *The Christian Imagination* the results of this attitude which interdicts all self-criticism, so that it will be necessary here only to point out some educational effects of such an exaggeration of community spirit.

In the realm of ideas this exaggeration may demand a complete submission to the intellectual and spiritual tradition of a particular institute, so that any criticism of the established point of view is regarded as a kind of deviationist heresy. It is alleged by most critics that some of the tension in Hopkins' religious life arose from the Scotist principle to which he subscribed in opposition to what they regard as the "accepted" philosophical line of the Jesuits. Inasmuch as this allegation is valid, it will serve to illustrate the type of abuse being discussed here; that such a judgment is not entirely valid seems to me evident from the closer bonds which, on the subject of individuation, unite Scotus to Suárez than Scotus to St. Thomas —had Hopkins been a Dominican, these critics might be justified in speculating that his Scotism would have been a cause of real conflict. Moreover, one can only be edified by the type of spiritual freedom upheld by the Jesuits, which allows, for exmple, Henri Renard publicly to defend the Thomist doctrine of the real distinction, and which allows other scholars, such as Fathers Daley and Doyle, to censure rather severely the achievement of Hopkins. These are illustrations of academic freedom in its best sense. Yet, so rare is this type of intellectual liberty among other communities that one often finds their schools obliged to use inadequate and inferior textbooks simply because these have been written by members of the congregation.

When reading vociferous defenses of a particular community's theological tradition, one is inclined to wonder whether, had their authors as young men entered an institute embracing quite a different body of theological doctrine, they might not have been equally as enthusiastic in the promulgation of those different or opposing teachings; one wonders, for example, what might have resulted in the De Auxiliis controversy if Diego Nuño would have entered the Society of Jesus as a young man. Never, of course, can one question the sincerity of certain vigorous apologetic writers whose ferocity in expounding their order's position is obviously so religiously motivated; yet such vehemence sometimes appears reminiscent of the attitude of a Tertullian or a Swift, rather than of the spirit of the Gospel. Moreover, by reason of its passion, this attitude generally clouds the objective bases for argumentation. Unquestionably such ardent apologists are convinced men, but this conviction often seems to result as much from psychological factors in their formative years as from any deeply personal commitment to truth.[30]

In the educational effort of the Church in America, this excess of community spirit has occasionally interfered with the strengthening of important faculties in the larger Catholic schools. There has been a number of regrettable situations in which a competent specialist, whose work was confined to teaching rudimentary courses in the one undergraduate college of his congregation, has been obliged by his superiors to reject invitations to teach more advanced classes in the graduate schools of Catholic universities. Occasionally one encounters such examples of intellectual frustration as that of an outstanding student of comparative literature obliged to teach elementary grammar, or that of an eminent bacteriologist forced to teach freshmen courses in what is called "hygiene." These examples, it must be said, stand in marked contrast to the truly catholic practice of such communities as the Marianists, the Augustinians, the Dominicans, and the Redemptorists in this country, and of the Brothers of the Christian Schools in Canada. The example of this Canadian institute is particularly relevant to the many congregations of Sisters and Brothers which do not maintain a university or a graduate faculty, and which, on the one hand, must demand that their more talented members sacrifice progress in their intellectual apostolate on the altar of religious duty—and in some cases the sacrifice may not be undesirable—or must, on the other hand, provide the necessary outlet for these outstanding scholars by allowing them to teach or do research in the larger Catholic or non-Catholic universities. The latter policy, which would benefit all American higher learning, might also aid in developing the great centers of graduate instruction which critics have declared Catholic education lacks.

Another result of an exaggeration of community spirit that serves to cripple Catholic higher education —and that partially explains the amazing proliferation of women's colleges—is to be found in the fact that some of the smaller colleges in America are really little more than disguised seminaries and convents which are maintained primarily so that the student-religious, the juniors and the scholastics of the community, can satisfy the requirements imposed by the accrediting agencies for teaching in elementary and secondary schools. The attendance of lay students at such "colleges" is often required merely to defray the expense of supporting the institution. Furthermore, since such communities of religious are devoted mainly to teaching in primary and secondary schools, the faculty of this one college must be drawn almost entirely from the lower educational levels. And because the purpose in founding such a school was largely economic, and because the object was to train young religious rather than to achieve any far-reach-ing educational work, such a faculty will often find no inconsistency in pursuing non-intellectual ends.

Also derived from the exaggeration of legitimate family loyalties is the assumption maintained in the practical order—though often denied in the theoretical—by some administrators that the student may be sacrificed, ostensibly in the name of "school spirit," for the good reputation of the institution. Thus gifted students may be induced to take up non-academic extracurricular activities, even though participation in such publicity-winning activities interferes with the students' scholastic progress. The private justification for this inducement is generally that, if the school is to survive, if the religious institute is to continue its teaching work, if it is to attract the attention of the lay public, then such non-academic activities have to be fostered, and—it should be said—if necessary to secure these objectives, must even be overemphasized.

In another segment of the academic sphere, the attitude of exaggerated family loyalty may concretize as the scholastic ideal a tradition which, because its very sources are tainted with anti-intellectualism or voluntarism, is totally unadapted to the culivation of the mind. When speaking of "tradition," there is, of course, no reference here to the tradition of the Church which is guided by the ecclesiastical magisterium and a sacramental liturgy; I have in mind only that petrifaction of outmoded custom which sometimes passes for a vital tradition; and some of these customs are incorporated in the practices and observances of a few present-day educational communities which were originally founded for missionary, hospital, or grade-school apostolates. With regard only to its effect on higher education, the following illustration speaks for itself: if a religious community is large, and consequently cumbersome and unwieldy in its organizational structure, it will be next to impossible to modify obsolete customs in this country since, perhaps, they are still vigorous and flourishing in other parts of the world. As a result, the lowest common denominator may become the intellectual standard for religious communities of an international composition. Thus, if a congregation staffs, in the majority of other countries of the world, primary schools, orphanages, or parochial missions, and in this country maintains colleges and universities, the religious who are teaching in the American schools will receive the same spiritual formation and will be indoctrinated with the same "traditions" as their colleagues elsewhere. From the viewpoint of higher education, the results of such a primitive formation will often be disastrous.

The "Latin Question" which disrupted the colleges of the Brothers of the Christian Schools, and by that fact disorganized all American Catholic higher education in the nineteenth century, offers an historical illustration of the conflict which may arise when traditions adapted to one age and to one apostolate are compulsorily imposed on members of a religious family who are engaged in a different work in a different historical period. As a result of an unyielding loyalty on the part of the European superiors to a proscription on teaching Latin, which had been written into the constitutions of the institute in the seventeenth century, a number of eminent Brothers of the Christian Schools who were teaching classics in American colleges in the nineteenth century were exiled, and many of these colleges were closed. Led by Archbishop Ireland, a large part of the American hierarchy appealed this decision; but the appeal was rejected by the religious superiors who apparently identified uniformity with unity, and submission to obsolete custom with religious fidelity. It is an ironic footnote to this tragic chapter of Catholic educational history that in the twentieth century all of the hundred or so schools maintained by the Brothers of the Christian Schools in America have permission to include Latin in their curricula.

However, even if the traditions of some communities were open to the light of contemporary needs and insights, the modification of these traditions might destroy what those ignorant of history regard as the very *raison d'être* of the congregation. Thus—to take an example similar to that above—a community established originally to conduct rural missions and seminaries finds itself in the twentieth century controlling the destinies of American colleges and universities. The members of such a community can try to take a middle-of-the-road position between their spiritual tradition and their present educational work; but this obviously is not going to produce any forthright academic policy—as a matter of fact, there can be no policy as such: everything must be improvised for each new occasion as it arises. On the one hand, if the congregation insists on adhering to customs stem-

ming from some of the historic circumstances of its
foundation, it should, perhaps, in the present period
give up its colleges and universities and take up a
work more consonant with its religious tradition; on
the other hand, if the American members of the
congregation, conscious of the requirements of the
educational order, decide to develop a broad intellectual and spiritual program, they may, perhaps, no
longer be regarded as legitimate offspring of the parent body, and this may lead to friction with the
authorized religious superiors. Because not many religious are gifted with the vision, the heroism—or
the *vocation*—of an Isaac Hecker who, in his struggle
against ossified custom and in his defense of sensible
adaptation and assimilation, withstood this friction,
one may expect that the present policy of muddling
through will continue for some years to come.

Such a policy will continue at least until that time
when the American religious communities themselves
will see the need for the gradual assimilation of insular customs by the comprehensive tradition of the
Church. Already this absorptive process is evident in
Europe in the continuing interest of the large orders
and institutes in such extensions of their work as
Frères convers (Dominican) and *monachisme laïc*
(Benedictine); the papal decree *Provida Mater Ecclesia,* which gave a juridical form to lay religious institutes, has received one of its finest commentaries in
an encyclical letter of the Superior General of the
Brothers of the Christian Schools. All of these are indications of a readiness to adapt old traditions to the
needs of modern man; and they are indications which,

although only faintly recognized in the United States, augur a bright future.

More directly related to the traditional religious communities are the results of the International Congress of the Religious Orders which took place in Rome during the Holy Year. Considerable interest in this Congress had been aroused by fantastic news releases in American diocesan and secular papers to the effect that all orders and congregations were to be permanently united under three or four general rules, and that the religious would cease to govern themselves autonomously. In fact, the Congress was convened simply to discuss new techniques and approaches to the apostolate. Father Lombardi, who addressed the Congress at its opening session, pointed out that there need be no change in the spirit of a religious community, but that methods which have not proved effective in the twentieth century should be set aside. He condemned an excessive loyalty to habits and traditions which are merely peripheral. Other speakers emphasized the need for a more profound spiritual formation among religious. Father Omez stressed the importance of a greater respect for the individual personality in the life of a religious community, while Msgr. de Luca suggested that those institutes which have houses throughout the world should take advantage of their international character by exchanging scholars and establishing research centers for higher studies. The Rome correspondent of *The London Tablet* concluded his report by enumerating other agenda of the Congress:

Proposals were submitted for less strict rules regarding
the relations between members of religious houses—especially nuns—and their families; for the abolition of certain forms of mortification; for better sex instruction; for
more dogmatic meditations; and in houses of studies for
a more practical knowledge in spiritual direction and
greater ability to explain theological terms; for the exclusion of unsuitable forms of prayer.[31]

Douglas Woodruff in his column in the same issue of
The London Tablet suggested that it would have
been profitable to invite papers from laymen on the
reforms they would like to see in the various communities—a sound suggestion, since the Church is a
communion which moves and acts as a whole, and a
suggestion which is not without historical precedent,
as the attendance of delegations from the universities
at Church Councils, or the activity of laymen in the
early Church, would testify. And Mr. Woodruff
added: "There should have been more discussion on
the way each age needs new orders to cope with new
situations, and on whether we are not living too much
in the past, and in the nineteenth century."

All of these suggestions, prudently acted upon,
would benefit American Catholic higher education.
And that such admonitions and exhortations are
slowly being heeded in this country gives cause to
expect that much of the present confusion will in
time be dissipated.

Poverty

One of the more frequently reiterated explanations
of the mediocrity of Catholic higher education is

that Catholic institutions do not have the rich endowments of many secular schools, and therefore cannot afford either expensive equipment or "expensive" professors. However, this is an explanation which the activity on many Catholic campuses during the past ten years does not support; for there has been more building, with more money spent on physical improvements, by Catholic colleges during this time than in any previous decade. This expenditure could be justified for elementary and secondary education, in view of the population increases of the post-war years, on the assumption that such education is the right of every Catholic child; but this expenditure cannot be justified on the level of higher education— where the egalitarian principle does not prevail— when it is carried out in the face of such glaring deficiencies as inadequate libraries and laboratories and inadequately endowed professorial chairs.

What, then, might be the explanation of these splendid buildings, of these beautifully constructed libraries, of these publicity offices, of these fieldhouses and stadia? In addition to the noble desire to express in architecture an intellectual ideal, it is to be feared that this accent on the external may represent an unconscious compensation for the voluntary deprivations of the religious state, even—I have suggested this above in the discussion on "community spirit"— as an unwarranted pride in one's religious congregation may be a secret and unconscious compensation for the obligations of personal humility. Group splendor may well compensate for individual poverty; worldly applause, for the cloistered life. And such compensations may be the rapine in the holocaust that destroys the Catholic educational achievement and vitiates the integrity of the spiritual work. Moreover, this attempt to serve two masters may also account in part for the schizoid character of so many Catholic institutions which often seem to stand as proclaimers of Aristotle and kitsch, of Thomism and the split T.

It was Teresa of Avila, the foundress of more than twenty convents, who declared to her followers concerning opulent religious houses: "I hope that, should such a day come, the walls would fall in and crush you all." [32] Yet by the apparent eagerness which some religious administrators have shown to be inscribed in the annals of their communities as "great builders," one would think either that they had forgotten that of these huge structures not a stone shall remain upon a stone, or, perhaps, that they had overlooked that, even from a temporal vantage point, as John Chrysostom says in the office of Confessor-teachers, there is no more lasting nor more beautiful architecture than the shaping of a young mind. It is impossible to say how many academic skeletons are rattling in the closets of many splendid marble buildings, within whose corridors and classrooms dull administrators and uninspired teachers communicate lifeless facts to bored young people. Preferable would it be in place of these stately domes and arcades—even if classes had to be held in Quonset huts—to have more institutions where the budget was as devoted to faculty salaries, and library and laboratory needs, as to dissolving the "building debt."

One is inclined to wonder, too, whether the observation of Abbé Godin may not illustrate a similar compensation for the vow of poverty:

How many teaching orders that are today instructing well-to-do girls were founded to teach the children of the poor? How many societies founded to work in public hospitals end up by opening nursing homes or boarding houses? A founder picks up little street-boys, and his spiritual sons conduct professional schools in which the pupils do not come from the level of the populace.[33]

There is no criticism here of the principles which led the Jesuits to revoke the obligation of gratuitous instruction, or which led the Brothers of the Christian Schools to dispense themselves more and more from their fifth vow of maintaining always and everywhere gratuitous schools: it is apparent that these regulations could be satisfied only in countries in which Catholicism was the state religion or in which Catholic schools were tax-supported. It is rather a question —which disturbs sincere religious as well as laity— raised by practices more and more widespread, such as that of opening new schools only in wealthy suburban areas, or that of evaluating an educational work by counting the number of wealthy and successful graduates it produces.

I will pass over with little comment such remarkable statements as have emanated from those administrators who, until the publication of John Tracy Ellis' criticisms, appeared blandly content with the state of Catholic higher education, and who have now made the astonishing discovery that it is not any failure in humanistic training which points up our defects, but rather the failure of Catholics to be listed in various collections of "notable" Americans. These administrators have not been doing their homework: a suggested reading list might include Tawney's *Religion and the Rise of Capitalism,* Fanfani's *Catholicism, Protestantism, and Capitalism,* and Max Weber's *The Protestant Ethic and the Spirit of Capitalism.* I will pass over the type of reflection such statements sow in the lay mind, to quote instead a startling extract from the "fund raising" propaganda of an important school maintained by a large religious community (both of which shall go unnamed):

NARRATOR: . . . yes, boys, it *does* look like a dream; but the alumni will not let you down. They'll build that GREATER _____ so you, too, can become *big* men, SUCCESSFUL men, like they are. For *our* city and for our Nation _____ has produced thousands of God-fearing, solid citizens. Most of its graduates are outstanding in professional as well as in business pursuits. Hundreds and hundreds are prominent leaders in the so-called three learned professions: theology, law and medicine. These include many priests and religious; numerous jurists and distinguished judges and gentlemen of the robe; and scores of eminent doctors and dentists and other practitioners of the Healing Arts. Besides, in the so-called less-learned professions there are many more brilliant _____ leaders, including world-famous architects and engineers; athletes and journalists; scientists and scholars. But chiefly, _____ has contributed myriads of its graduates to the business and commercial life of our city. It secured positions for most of its alumni and helped them advance to executive and administrative office where many are now tycoons of extraordinary wealth, power and influence. It has given our city two mayors, six bank presidents, four railroad presidents and many other civic and industrial leaders; and it has given the Nation Congressmen and Statesmen and even Admirals and Generals. Perhaps no single college or university in the Nation can boast of as many really outstanding alumni as can _____.

What makes this illiterate twaddle all the more noteworthy is that it was composed, not by any professional "fund raiser" (but by a professed religious), and that it was published and circulated among hundreds of friends and alumni (not all "big and solid," however) of this particular school. Such strident materialism certainly represents an exception, but it is an exception not without some parallel in other aspects of contemporary Catholic education.

Ten years ago I wrote, in effect, concerning certain practices in women's colleges:

It seems unfortunate that a spirit of middle-class snobbishness has made the dominant criterion for entrance into many Catholic women's colleges the "social status"—which is a euphemism for economic condition—of the student. Such a criterion is not found in the entrance requirements of the colleges, but it is evident in the activity programs of these schools. It is perhaps justifiable to say that provision must be made for the influential classes—though they who say this often measure influence in dollars; but when Catholic women's colleges seek to ape in their activities the schools for the wealthy, when many through excessive expenses and luxurious standards of dress, living quarters, publications, and entertainments make it impossible for the young Catholic woman of modest means to secure an education, then a collective examination of conscience is in order.[34]

I cite these remarks now in order to obviate any reflection on schools with which I have been directly associated during the past decade, and also I cite them because I do not think matters have much improved. As I write, I have before me an advertisement for a "select school for girls." The school is so select that the foundress of the community which now staffs it would have been excluded from studying or teaching in it.

Obedience

Just as there are for the other constituents of the religious life a number of practices which, when abused, militate against a truly Christian education, so, too, with regard to that virtue which has often been defined by pious writers as the keystone of the spiritual edifice, there are consequences in the scholastic order that may prove unfortunate. I am speaking of obedience, and of the dangers its unwarranted extension into the intellectual realm may entail.

A hundred years ago Newman wrote of the subsumption of the role of faith by obedience as a characteristically Protestant error:

When Catholics speak of faith they are contemplating the existence of a gift which Protestantism does not even imagine. Faith is a spiritual sight of the unseen; and since in matter of fact Protestantism does not impart this sight, does not see the unseen, has no experience of this habit, this act of the mind—therefore since it retains the word "faith," it is obliged to find some other meaning for it; and its common, perhaps its commonest, idea is, that faith is substantially the same as obedience; at least that it is the impulse, the motive of obedience, or the fervour and heartiness which attend good works. Faith is illuminative, not operative; it does not force obedience, though it increases responsibility; it heightens guilt, it does not prevent sin.[35]

Not until recent years did other Catholic scholars recognize in this reduction of faith to obedience one of the fundamental causes of the eclipse of Catholic thought in the modern world. Père Régamey has written eloquently of the abuse of obedience and its effect on Catholic piety and more particularly on the fine arts; M. Maritain has discussed it in relation to theology and philosophy; [36] and Père Congar has related it to the general life of the Church in terms that deserve to be quoted here:

In a still more general way—one is almost able to say, more radically—Catholics, and especially the men of the Church, are formed and trained to an obedience *ad literam.* This is a very great force, serving marvelously in bringing about submission to what is established (*donné*) in the Church, by which are translated the imperative demands of her constitutive principles. But it sometimes gives place to an excess: that of considering in practice that there is only one virtue, obedience—even as there is only one sin, that of the flesh. This habituates both clergy and faithful to a certain lack of initiative, even where life would demand that it be taken. One might even go to the extreme of conceiving religion as something ready-made, completely determined from on high, extrinsic to the personal decisions of conscience.[37]

Within the school this abuse of obedience may take the form of a suffocating uniformity and conformity which, while occasionally tolerating free discussion, quite frequently interdicts free action, even where prudence would require it. One widely publicized example of this abuse concerned a very outspoken, but undeniably competent, professor of philosophy at a Catholic university, who was indirectly forbidden to determine for himself the content of a series of radio addresses. The professor in question had frequently espoused causes at variance with certain accepted ideas of many "typical" Catholic laymen, but he had nevertheless consistently maintained a most faithful stand on religious principles. Following his refusal to submit to the arrogant demands of a cleric who was overstepping the bounds of authority and justice, the professor resigned his teaching position. There is probably some moral to be drawn from the fact that he was immediately offered a place on the faculty of one of the country's outstanding universities.

In this context, it may be advisable for administrators who are tempted to regard the teaching faculty as so many hired hands, to reflect on the medieval notion of knowledge as a *donum Dei* which a teacher may offer to his students freely, though it cannot be bought or sold.[38] Because he has at his disposition a spiritual gift, the teacher cannot be regarded as a functionary who receives a salary for his work; like the priest, he can be given only an honorarium for his services. And because the teacher—again like the priest—is a minister of spiritual things, he has an obligation not primarily to such abstractions as "school" and "administration," but to his own intellectual integrity and to that of his students.

One wonders to how many administrations of Catholic colleges can be applied Newman's words regarding the attitude of the Irish bishops toward the laymen who supported him in his Irish university venture: "They were treated like good little boys; were told to shut their eyes and open their mouths and take what we gave them—and this they did not relish." [39] The tone of this remark of Newman explains a further declaration, which he made some years later, when he asserted that, if he were to open another school, he would insist that the masters be laymen. [40]

With regard to the religious state itself, Père André Rabut has described the feelings of many young religious who, being subjected to an exaggerated notion of obedience, feel themselves destined to a life in which the personal gifts and the talents they would like to devote to the apostolate are going to atrophy from lack of exercise:

Almost all the virtues that are taught to a young novice seem to fall into the category of docility. Now, while admitting an absolute docility to God and a relative docility to those charged with guiding him, he would center more spontaneously his virtues on the idea of responsibility. Man, he believes, is primarily a being who must choose a mission, and be responsible for this choice before God; if necessary, before God alone. . . . He would like to be one of the long line which began with Jesus, with St. Paul, with the founders of the religious orders, and of which fearlessness is one of the most striking traits. . . . In St. Catherine of Siena and St. Joan of Arc, for examples, one finds convinced spirits who have not been docile in every sense of the word. A certain conception of docility is the equivalent of an abandonment before God of the vocation of man.[41]

In any educational undertaking an obsession with docility tends to exalt mediocrity and passivity, so that often the religious teacher who seeks to advance himself within the scope of his own field fears to propose any method or thesis which is not entirely conformed to the views of his superiors. In an environment where no prudent criticism of authority is possible, and where every novel or critical suggestion may brand its author as lacking in the spirit of obedience, it is certain no genuine research and no creative teaching can exist.

Within a faculty where such an attitude prevails the abuse of obedience tends to eliminate from positions of trust and responsibility capable independent thinkers, and to replace them by lackeys who, however dull and pedestrian they may be, are retained in office because they are, in administrative argot, "safe men." Toadyism may ensnare any organization based on a hierarchy of delegated authority, but it is a peculiarly imminent danger for organizations in which authority is sanctioned by religious vows. One sometimes has the impression that provincial superiors are not disturbed by the fact that their appointees to administrative office often have the intellectual vision of Goethe's Wagner, and that they are therefore forces for reaction rather than for progress within a school. And in turn, these administrators seem little disturbed, in their pursuit of uniformity, that a truly great teacher, a teacher, for example, such as George Lyman Kittredge, might be excluded from their faculty on the grounds that his teaching methods were novel or that his appearance and actions were eccentric. "It must be said," wrote one of Newman's Oxford disciples, "that the wayward and eccentric must and will take their own course, and a university is sure to have a good many such men." [42] It must also be said that the presence of such men, if their teaching is effective, generally indicates a liberal administration and an intellectually healthy faculty.

Finally, the abuse of obedience creates an atmosphere, within the student body of a school, in which the word "docile" loses its root meaning of "teachable," and takes on overtones of subservience and submission. The notion of student government in such a school becomes akin to the polity of the "guided democracies" in the Soviet empire; and the faculty, itself rendered impotent by this same abuse of obedience, rather than forming the students into independent thinkers and free agents, tends to make of them instead, dispirited, malleable, acquiescent dullards who can neither act nor think without some positive injunction from authority. This is one of the reasons, as the student magazine *Today* has often noted, why some employers prefer to hire Catholic graduates; it is not that they are more industrious, but simply that their inbred sense of submission will possibly keep them from agitating for better wages or better working conditions. This again suggests the schizoid character of some of our schools, in which the social encyclicals of Leo or Pius are taught in the classroom, while their effective realization and application in the marketplace are rendered impossible by the authoritarian and, one fears, reactionary formation imparted over four years of disciplined but uninspired training. There rises before one's imagination the haunting specter of many of our students going forth from their high schools and colleges to hew out their own brave new world, reciting collectively: "We are alphas; we are proud to be alphas. . . ."

Pre-eminence of Piety

Because the religious state is by definition a way of life tending toward the highest spiritual perfection, it is understandable that motives of piety should dominate all facets of the apostolate of a religious community. This is both understandable and desirable. However, what is neither understandable nor desirable is that from narrowly pietistic motives important decisions should be made in the educational sphere.

Two situations, in no way inconceivable, serve to illustrate the consequences to which the pre-eminence of piety may give rise in a religious community. First: the delegates from a congregation which maintains a number of elementary schools, perhaps a college, and one or two hospitals, assemble to elect a provincial superior. The choice for such an office will probably not fall on a college educator since then the other two segments of the community may be offended and possibly left without leadership; similar circumstances would prevent the election of a religious from the hospital or the grade-school group. The unhappy compromise in such a situation is likely to take the form of selecting as superior someone whose talents lie in none of these three areas, but who is by virtue of other personal qualities acceptable to all segments of the community. Such a "political" problem may seem somewhat farfetched, but the general truth it serves to exemplify remains: the best that may be hoped for is an application of the monastic axiom, "If a man be pious, let him pray for us; if a man be learned, let him teach us; but if a man be prudent, let him govern us." The worst that may result is that someone with no academic ability or intellectual competence will have the dominant voice and the deciding vote in important educational enterprises.

The second illustration concerns the appointment of religious to the higher offices in a college or university. It is evident that frequently in the past the highest positions, including that of president, have often been filled exclusively on the grounds of the spiritual accomplishments of this or that religious. The obvious reasons for such an appointment will be the same as those mentioned in the preceding paragraph. A less obvious reason is to be found in the fact that the boards of trustees in Catholic colleges are merely advisory groups of a predominantly financial character. Unlike the trustees of secular colleges, the Catholic lay boards have little to say about administrative appointments. And, after considering some of the appointments that have been made, it is difficult to say whether this condition has more disadvantages than advantages. Examining the history of trusteeship in early American Catholic parish life, one is inclined to feel that as little lay interference as possible in administrative affairs makes for harmonious government; but, on the other hand, when one takes cognizance of such facts as that the actual authority in a school is vested absolutely in the local provincial and his council, and that in congregations dedicated to a variety of social works this group will often be composed of religious with no academic background—or at least with no more academic background than the average lay trustee—it does not seem an encroachment to suggest some lay voice in appointments to high academic office. If the current trustee system does not provide this voice, then, perhaps, the revival of such an institution as the faculty senate might prove beneficial.

Furthermore, should a capable administrator be appointed by a provincial council to head a school, his term in office is canonically fixed, in most communities, for a period of six years; and this period can generally be extended only by special permission from the Sacred Congregation for Religious. Thus no matter how important an educational reform may be under way, no matter how capable a particular administration may have shown itself to be in developing and improving the organization or the curriculum of a school, the effectiveness of such improvement over a long period of time will be seriously impaired by the necessarily short tenure of its initiators.

Many attempts have been made to solve this problem: in some cases three or four vice-presidents and deans have been appointed with no restriction on the duration of their terms in office; in other cases, the spiritual direction in a community has been separated from the academic administrative authority, so that while the canonically installed religious superior is changed every six years, his academic counterpart may continue in office for an unlimited period. Unfortunately, in that event the direction of the school may be split because the actual and effective superior remains the canonically appointed one. In yet other cases the rather dubious expedient resorted to has been to rotate a number of superiors every six years among different schools; thus a religious may continue as superior for a period of two or three decades provided he exercises his office in a different school every six years: here the letter of the law is followed, while much of its spirit and practical value is ignored.[43]

This question of tenure is an important one, first, in view of the continuity which any educational work must possess, and second, because of the length of time it requires to complete any lasting academic reform: a fact attested to by the long tenure of most of the outstanding American university presidents.

Another crippling condition which may be said to

result from a narrowly pietistic attitude is the absence of competition on the educational level—though quite a good deal, on the athletic—between Catholic and non-Catholic colleges. The Catholic school enjoys a virtual monopoly in securing students, and this monopoly it often defends, not on intellectual grounds, but on the grounds of sectarian loyalty and confessional fidelity. Being guaranteed a sufficient number of students, the Catholic college need not concern itself as earnestly with the elevation of standards as it would were it in competition for survival with non-Catholic schools. Moreover, the opportunity for such necessary and praiseworthy competition, even among various Catholic colleges, is often rendered impossible by the organization of many diocesan school systems. A new college cannot be established in a given diocese merely because the already existing schools are deemed inadequate: population increase, and not the desire to raise the academic and intellectual levels, is the only accepted justification for opening a new school. Motives of piety supplant scholastic needs.

This exaltation of piety at the expense of technique—to use M. Gilson's terms—is traditionally opposed to the genius of Catholic education, as this genius was once historically manifested in the medieval universities, and as it is exemplified, on the theoretical plane, in the development of Newman's *Idea of a University*.

The criticisms which have been brought to bear throughout this section, on certain religious abuses within American Catholic schools, are criticisms similar to those directed at Newman and his followers during the period of the Tractarian ascendency at Oxford. During the 1830's Newman's interest, as that of his disciples, in university reform was along narrow clerical lines which were drawn in definite opposition to the liberal stand taken by the followers of Dr. Arnold and later successfully defended by Jowett. As Goldwin Smith rightly observed, the Tractarians wanted to impose on the university a celibate, monastic pattern which was almost exclusively religious in orientation, and which was, among the more ardent Newmanites, almost anti-humanistic in character.[44] It would be a mistake to attribute such an anti-intellectualism to Newman himself, but it would be an equally grave error to view the healthy and vigorous humanism of the two parts of *The Idea of a University* as merely a refined or "Catholicized" version of Newman's own Oxford teaching. Mark Pattison, whatever defects his critics may impute to him, accurately stated the scope of Newman's earlier educational tenets when he wrote:

Religion was evidently to Newman in 1830, not only the first but the sole object of all teaching; there was no thought then of a cycle of learning, a genealogical chart of all the sciences; there was not even the lesser conception of education by the classics as containing the essential elements of humanism.[45]

Pattison could not recognize the causes of that development in Newman's thought which, rejecting all narrow pietism and repudiating all exclusivism, culminated in the intensely liberal program of the Dub-

lin discourses delivered to the first members of the
Catholic University of Ireland.[46]

I would suggest that this gradual but definite
change in Newman's educational position stemmed
primarily from his encounter with the authentic
Catholic tradition of higher learning, particularly as
this tradition was crystallized in the medieval universities. And it is to these universities that contemporary Catholic educators—so strongly tempted, as
was the young Newman, to exaggerate the role of
piety to the detriment of the intellectual disciplines
and of academic freedom—must look. With Newman,
they will marvel at what they see:

When was there ever a more curious, more meddling,
bolder, keener, more penetrating, more rationalistic exercise of the reason than at that time? What class of questions did that subtle, metaphysical spirit not scrutinize?
What premise was allowed without examination? What
principle was not traced to its first origin, and exhibited
in its most naked shape? What whole was not analyzed?
What complex idea was not elaborately traced out, and,
as it were, finely painted for the contemplation of the
mind . . . ? [47]

It is necessary to touch briefly upon one other result of the pre-eminence of piety before closing this
discussion: it is the abdication of human reason in
the name of an omnicompetent religiosity. For, if a
Pelagianism has often polluted Catholic educational
theory so that wisdom is sometimes seen as the end
product of the right techniques and recipes, then, on
the contrary, an anti-Pelagianism, which demeans the

role of the natural faculties, has frequently plagued
Catholic educational practice. There are some religious communities of educators whose superiors, as
Newman said of the Irish bishops, "regard any intellectual man as being on the road to perdition." [48]
This attitude derives, as I have already pointed out,
from a misunderstanding of the mission of the founders of the religious congregations, and from a refusal
to face afresh in each generation the mystery implicit
in the human vocation. But that this attitude finds
expression in those who are dedicated to the cultivation of the intellectual virtues is another of the many
paradoxes resulting from the spiritual tendencies discussed in this chapter.

VII

If at the conclusion of this detailed catalogue of
problems, disorders, and abuses, resulting from a
misunderstanding of valid religious principles, one
may be inclined to wonder why the Catholic schools
of other nations have not suffered from similar aberrant tendencies, I can reply only by indicating a
number of historical facts. First, the aftereffects of
such social conditions as the poverty of the Catholic
immigrants and the anti-Catholicism of the various
Nativist movements have impeded the progress of our
higher learning; second, in those countries where
Catholic education has been as widely organized and
as exclusively a clerico-religious precinct as it is in
America today, the scholastic training has often been
equally as mediocre; third, where excellent Catholic

universities or graduate faculties now exist, they do so in an atmosphere of competition and co-operation with the secular schools; and fourth, the layman in education, on the collegiate and universtiy levels, has played a much more important role in Europe than he has in the United States.

It is to the nature of this role that I now turn.

THREE

THE LAYMAN'S ROLE

ONE OF THE MINOR WORKS OF ST. THOMAS IS ENTITLED *Contra Impugnantes*—the "impugnantes" being in this case the critics of the mendicant orders. In this short treatise, St. Thomas defended, among other things, the fitness of the "new orders" to teach in the medieval universities. The Angelic Doctor never wrote a more effective book, nor one with more enduring consequences for posterity, and it is perhaps now time to defend, or rather, to reassert the correlative ancient right of the layman in the Catholic university: a right in the full sense, and not merely a tolerated privilege.

Unfortunately, when the lay educator claims the exercise of this right, not as a concession from religious authorities, not as a decorative gesture by academic administrators to "balance off" the composition of a faculty, but as a moral exigency flowing from his character as a witness to truth, occasionally his claims, his demands, are viewed as temerarious: he is criticized as being out of line. Yet, in mere matter of historic fact, he is much nearer to the line of traditional theology than are his critics. For the tradition affirms that the layman also testifies in his own way to truth; and because this is an area of truth which is generally closed off from full comprehension by clergy or religious, he must have a *place* in the Church and, consequently, a place in any educational work. This place must be reserved to him because only with these two components, religious and laity, can a well-proportioned, balanced, and organically operative institutional structure be assured. The layman acts as an equilibrant in the school, as in the Church.

This is why Newman, in a number of texts I have already cited, insisted that any schools with which he was to be associated should be staffed largely by laymen. Newman recognized in his educational work in Ireland an attitude among the hierarchy which, when it did accord any recognition to the role or mission of the laity, did so as a grudging concession:

The truth is that these bishops are so accustomed to be absolute that they usurp the rights of others and rough-ride over their wishes and their plans quite innocently without meaning it, and are astonished, not at finding out the fact, but at its being impossible to these others.[1]

Again, when he resigned his rectorship of the ill-fated Catholic University of Ireland, he wrote: "That collisions are ahead perhaps between clergy and laity, I do not deny. The breach between them in Ireland is fearful." Partially to offset such imminent collisions, Newman recognized the need for a vigorously articulate and a liberally educated laity, and he recognized further that, if this need could not be satisfied by Catholic universities, it would be necessary to train Catholics in secular schools, or, indeed, with regard to the conditions of his own time, in Protestant schools.

These are truths disclosed by Ward's *Life,* and by the recent publication of Newman's own memoranda on the Irish university, and they are now among those facts of history which have been overlooked in the current campaign being waged by that small group of vocal journalists and pamphleteers which has nosed out some sapping of the foundations of dogma in the following rather questionable computation:

More than 50 Catholic intellectuals are in language and literature, some 27 in physics, chemistry, and biology, 38 in history, 20 in philosophy (including political philosophy and philosophy of science), 23 in political science, sociology, and economics, and three in theology. . . . In other words, if numbers mean anything, one could say that the commission [The Catholic Commission on Intellectual and Cultural Affairs] considers history 13 times as important as theology, and the physical sciences have nine times more significance. . . . If we exclude the 50 priests, the overwhelming majority of the other 235 "Catholic intellectuals" have had no formal Catholic education. More than 80 per cent of their degrees, under-graduate and graduate, were taken at secular universities. They have more degrees from Harvard, Columbia, and Princeton, than from all the Catholic colleges in the United States taken together.[2]

I am not concerned about the statistical judgment in the beginning of this quotation—though it makes one muse that perhaps the clergyman who arrived at it might profit from a little more of that mathematics and sociology which he deduces others to think so many times more important than theology; what is significant here is the assumption that there is some-thing necessarily non-Catholic or anti-Catholic about taking degrees from secular universities. Such an as-sumption might have some basis if Catholic universi-ties were in every way the equal of the non-Catholic; regrettably they are not. To ignore this inferiority is not to strike a blow against militant secularism; it is to overlook, not prejudiced judgment, not mere opin-ion, but fact: a fact which has never been contested by any group of eminent Catholic educators, and which is further attested to by the many members of various religious communities who have taken gradu-ate degrees at non-Catholic schools. Unquestionably the Catholic university has theological truth, but the possession of this truth cannot be said to redound to the honor of Catholic scholarship and to the credit of Catholic education—Faith is a gift.

If one is to have an articulate, intelligent Catholic laity, then some provision must be made for acquir-ing the instruments of intelligently articulating the

Catholic vision; and such instruments, as every course of university training from the Middle Ages to the present day will testify, are not furnished primarily by theology, but by the humanistic and scientific disciplines. Wherever these disciplines are best cultivated, there the Catholic must go. Newman, as I have said, recognized this fact, and attempted to establish his Oratory at Oxford for the benefit of Catholic students there. For this, and for other attempts at forming an educated laity, Newman was criticized by Ward and Vaughan as being an influence for disloyalty and "worldliness." [3] There is here a rather remarkable parallel with the type of accusation that has recently been publicly hurled at the reputation, at the good name, and even at the Catholic spirit of scholars whose lives and works radiate a religiousness and an acumen which are irreproachable.

Newman failed in his attempt to establish the Oratory at Oxford, and after the final decision wrote:

It is on account of things of this kind that I view with equanimity the prospect of a thorough routing out of things at Rome; not till some great convulsions take place (which may go on for years and years, and when I can do neither good nor harm) and religion is felt to be in the midst of trials, red-tapism will go out of Rome, and a better spirit come in, and Cardinals and Archbishops will have some of the reality they had, amid many abuses, in the Middle Ages. At present, things are in appearance as effete, though in a different way, thank God, as they were in the tenth century. We are sinking into a sort of Novationism—the heresy which the early Popes so strenuously resisted. Instead of aiming at being a world-wide

power, we are shrinking into ourselves, narrowing the
lines of communion, trembling at freedom of thought,
and using the language of dismay and despair at the
prospects before us, instead of, with the high spirit of the
warrior, going out conquering and to conquer.[4]

Providentially, we are living in a happier age: an
age in which the hierarchy itself has fostered a vigorous and intelligent laity as well as a balanced educational order, an age in which freedom of thought does
exist (as the present debate on Catholics and the intellectual life may serve to indicate), an age in which
independent Catholic journals like *Cross Currents*
and *The Commonweal,* and important periodicals
edited by the Benedictines, the Jesuits, and the Paul-
ists, and by the Catholic universities, do flourish; we
are living in a more temperate season than that of
which Newman wrote: ". . . nothing would be better than a historical Review, but who would bear it:
Unless one doctored all one's facts one would be
thought a bad Catholic." We, then, need not use the
language of dismay and despair, because following in
the steps of Newman himself, far-seeing clergy, religious, and laymen have dissipated that climate of
fear, of retreat, of inferiority which enervated our
nineteenth-century forebears.

It would be impossible to attempt, and an ungrate-
ful disservice to want, to ignore, or minimize the
heavy burden which has been borne willingly and
often at the cost of great sacrifice by the religious communities in the staffing and maintaining of Catholic
schools. These congregations and orders have, par-

ticularly by their vows of poverty, succeeded in creating an educational system in which almost all students, no matter what may be their economic background, can find the opportunity of coming into some contact with their rightful intellectual heritage. So varied, so extensive, and so self-supporting a system of private schools as exists within the American Catholic community would be inconceivable, in the present and in the future, without the dominant presence of the religious congregations.

Furthermore, by their vows of obedience and by their promises of fidelity to their particular spiritual tradition, the members of the religious orders have provided a structure of continuity, both of methods to be employed and of ends to be pursued, which secular schools generally cannot command. So true is this that, while one can think of a few isolated examples of secular universities where a sense of tradition has been realized, it is more common to identify them with some specific field of study animated by a small group of talented scholars: or, more frequently, one identifies these universities with the prowess of their athletic teams, the attractiveness of their locations, the social selectivity of their student bodies, or the advantages of their physical plants.

It is understandable that secular schools in America, lacking the traditionary moorings of their European antecedents, should be forced to construct a synthetic tradition in order to bring some unity into their programs. Not infrequently, however, the creation of this tradition is the work of one educational leader, and so, with his passage from the academic scene, his achievement in building an awareness of tradition also passes away. Thus one may observe, in the recent past, the work of a convinced Aristotelian undone within a few years by his successor, an administrator of avowedly Kantian inclination. That these fluctuations and reversals have not often disrupted Catholic schools is due in large part to the spirit of continuity embodied in the religious orders.

In the older universities of Europe, even in the midst of outward changes, and even when new variations on an institutional *leitmotiv* may have been introduced with the passage of time, one can still recognize a very definite line of ideas and practices which determined the character of the school, and which fixed the dimensions of its curriculum. Thus with all its repercussions, the transition from the Oxford of Newman and Pusey to that of Jowett and Pater left untouched that body of humanistic principles which had marked the school long before the advent of Tractarians or Liberals. One may recognize the traditional loyalty of Cambridge to science and mathematics in the facetious observation of an eminent Oxonian, Matthew Arnold. "In the very Senate House and heart of our English Cambridge I once ventured, though not without an apology for my profaneness, to hazard the opinion that for the majority of mankind a little mathematics, even, goes a long way." This desire to preserve old traditions is evident today at the Sorbonne in the earnest efforts on the part of humanists to preserve their field against the encroachments of positive science: efforts reflected by such seemingly trivial incidents as the opposition that has arisen against changing the title, Faculty of Letters, to Faculty of Humane Sciences.

With regard to the religious communities, this sense of tradition has been discussed by Newman in his essays on Benedictinism. Newman has pointed out that the Jesuits, taken as a society, seem to personify the spirit of organization and order in an educational ideal accenting the discipline of the mind and the training of the will—though, of course, this accent is not exclusive. The Dominican tradition seems to exalt the role of logic and reason—though, again, not exclusively. The Benedictine tradition, with its agricultural origins, with its sense of mystery in the liturgy and concomitantly in nature, tends to foster a spirit of poetry, of imagination.

Such distinctions as these which Newman has sketched, and which seem at first glance to be merely the product of another of those facile constructions that ingenious historians delight in, are not to be conceived of, even in our time, as empty gestures to the golden age of the past. These distinctions remain as valid now as when Newman discerned them a century ago, and as they were when first defined in the constitutions and practices of the three orders. Today, however, this sense of tradition has sometimes bred a fidelity to any and all crystallization of custom handed down within a religious community, so that—as has been pointed out in the preceding chapter—not infrequently a particular congregation or order has had its authentic heritage obscured by the temporal accretions which have gradually grown around it.

It is at this point that I return to the original topic,

from which I may have seemed to be straying: for, paradoxically, it is the layman who is in a position to aid the religious communities in reaffirming their genuine traditions. Before discussing *how* the layman finds himself in this position, it is necessary to indicate a few examples of the existence of such a reaffirming role.

First, concerning the progress which has been made in America during the past three decades in the resurgence of Scholastic thought, it is beyond question, I believe, that this progress has resulted largely from the work of lay scholars rather than from any extraordinary achievement on the part of the members of that religious order which is by profession dedicated to the defense of Thomism, or on the part of that other order which by its constitutions is obliged to support the doctrines of St. Bonaventure and Duns Scotus. Second, though the Benedictine schools have been brilliantly faithful to their own living and creative tradition, nevertheless, with the exception of Dom Rembert Sorg, it has generally been laymen like Willis Nutting (with his reiterated pleas for collegiate communities as labor-study centers) and Peter Maurin (with his ideal of the "agronomic university") who have reaffirmed the importance of this rural and agricultural element in Benedictinism. Finally, if it be true, as Father Allan P. Farrell has said, that the Jesuit schools were slowly forced to abandon a number of traditional positions under pressure from accrediting agencies and popular opinion, it is also true that the direction back to such positions had been pointed out a decade ago by such laymen as George N. Shuster and Francis McMahon.

The layman is capable of this reforming and revitalizing role because he possesses that liberty of action which frequently religious give up for a higher good. He is often able to range more widely in his ideas, as in his activities, and to speak out more unequivocally against that traditionalism which sooner or later plagues all large institutions. By reason of his relative isolation from the strong pressures of different groups, and by reason of his independence from that *parti pris* which often possesses religious persons who are bound together in a tightly knit community, the layman can divest himself of particularizing loyalties and confining prejudices, and so judge variant and conflicting views more objectively.

I should not have to add here that it would be a serious error to conceive the task of the layman, because he may fulfill this corrective office, under any such image as that of thesis/antithesis; the layman's work in education, though as important as that of the religious, is not one of opposition, nor even of "creative friction," but simply of spiritual and intellectual complement. And indeed, this complemental role points up the basic reason (from what may be called the sociological order, in contradistinction to the theological) why the Catholic university can achieve a broader and a more balanced humanism than any other type of school, whether sectarian, secular, or neutral. Excluding from any consideration here the truths of theology, excluding that deeper comprehension of reality engendered by what I will in Chapter

Five discuss as "the Catholic intellectual comportment," and taking into consideration only the intense
spirituality of the religious communities, their ardent
devotion to the principles of the monastic and communal life, and considering, too, the devout humanism of such non-regular clergy as Bremond and
Dimnet (I intentionally confine myself to European
examples)—considering all these influences and factors, who can doubt that when the layman in America comes of age, that when he is equipped with the
instruments and allowed the freedom to witness to
those truths which properly lie within his own domain; who can doubt that, when these multiple forces
converge on the one task of perfecting a Christian
educational order, there will then be realized a truly
Catholic and a truly universal higher learning and,
with this, a truly Catholic university?

I

Because the educated layman is immersed in the life
of the world, he is better able to understand the hidden roots of that spiritual and religious anxiety which
may beset his fellow Christians and which may often
go unnoticed because unexpressed. Since he sees the
faithful in all conditions of life, and sees them as they
are when engaged in the whole cycle of their pursuits, the layman may come to an awareness of latent
and submerged qualities which might never be observed by others whose knowledge and judgment are
based on more constricted experiences. For example,
one sometimes has the feeling that certain pessimistic

clerical judgments on the state of the faithful have been arrived at by making an abstraction of the condition of the lay body under its aspect of subject to the sacrament of penance. Inasmuch as such an impression is well-founded, it may serve to illustrate the type of constricted experience to which I refer. Certainly, the judgments of the clergy on the ideals and practices of the Catholic community are necessary, but equally necessary, as a complement, is the expressed judgment of the trained lay mind on his fellow Christians. Confession is a sacrament of the dead: a confessional is not always the best place to study the living.

The religious life and the clerical state, because of their detachment from the affairs and the concerns of the world, and because of their rightful and necessary emphasis on regulations and on legal conceptions, tend not infrequently to breed an indifference to the actual realities of day-to-day existence. Is not this one of the sources of those recurrent anecdotes about religious taking the vow of poverty, while the layman keeps it? In general, men who are preoccupied with spiritual and theoretical values, whose commitment to the evangelic counsels divorces them from personal, economic, and social problems, and whose work is largely cerebral, tend to lose sight of the less blatant element of physical and material life. As a result their apostolate, when it enters the realm of pragma, the realm of here-and-now concrete issues, is often ineffectual because unrealistic. For this reason, Cardinal Feltin wrote in the preface to *Catéchisme et mission ouvrière*:

The catechism which is customarily taught to the children in de-Christianized urban areas is twice removed from actual life . . . *because the theory which is taught to these young people is lacking in any bond with their conception of existence,* and above all because the faith and morality which are sought from them are not capable of being lived normally in the pitiable conditions surrounding their families and their homes.[5]

Both causes of the failure of certain catechetical ventures are important and relevant, but it is the one that I have italicized which I would stress here. Chesterton wrote of the "miracle" of the balance of orthodoxy: is it not indicative of a disequilibrium, which inevitably results in practical affairs when traditional theological data are ignored, that one of the solutions proffered for the problems Cardinal Feltin treats of was not to let the layman fulfill his rightful catalytic role of translating social factors into terms comprehensible to the theologians, but instead to immerse the clergy more deeply—and with what disastrous consequences—in the daily working lives of the people?

In like manner, it is the laity's task to aid in interpreting the sometimes remote and abstract formulae of dogma and morality into a language understandable and meaningful to the large body of the faithful and thus, in a sense, to mediate between the cloister and the marketplace. But even more important in the life of the Church is it that the layman fulfill his obligation as witness by reflecting the views and beliefs, the sufferings and aspirations of his fellow

Christians. The layman has an *ex officio* right to testify to the unconscious or unrecognized legitimate longings of the faithful. These are important aspects of Newman's teaching on the duty of the episcopate to "consult" the Church-taught; and this *ex officio* right, flowing from the sacrament of confirmation, ought not to be abdicated by the laity or abrogated by the clergy.[6] Newman wrote:

The Church moves as a whole; it is not a mere philosophy, it is a communion; it not only discovers, but it teaches; it is bound to consult for charity as well as for faith. You must prepare men's minds for the doctrine, and you must not flout and insult the existing tradition of countries.[7]

And Newman's great contemporary, Scheeben, clarified the nature of this "consultation" when he wrote:

It follows that the public profession of doctrine by the body of the faithful, being a witnessing of the Holy Ghost relatively independent, ought logically and briefly to precede the precise declaration of the teaching body, and in such circumstances influence, as a means of orientation, its future judgment.[8]

From this text of Scheeben, it is evident how important is this testimonial of the laity, or, more precisely, the testimonial of the entire Church-taught. For while I am concerned only with the role of that portion of the laity which is called to the lay state, that is, to the state of Christian in the world, and hence I am not treating of the obligation imposed equally on cleric or religious of testifying, each in his own way, yet it should be pointed out that, in matter of fact, all those who go to make up what the liturgy calls the *plebs sancta* are obliged to bear witness to their state of life. This is the meaning of the religious profession: by his vows the religious becomes a "professor" of the evangelical counsels, and, as such, he is obliged to manifest to the world, by his life and by his activity, the poverty, chastity, and obedience to which his person is committed. For that reason, the religious profession has traditionally been compared to martyrdom, to the public witnessing by blood to Christian truth.

It is, then, not only the layman, properly so-called, who is obliged to testify, but rather every member of the Church-taught: it is the whole body of the faithful which, in union with ecclesiastical authority, asserts the glad tidings. As a consequence of this, one of the powers conferred by office upon the bishop is to reflect and to make express the witnessing of the faithful. This is not, of course, to restrict in any way the primary role of the episcopate of teaching in its own right: the bishop is something more than merely the spokesman of his people. To deny this would be to approach that "Catholic presbyterianism" which, as Cardinal Manning said in his later years, makes of the episcopate "only the Pope's vicariate," [9] and which reduces the bishop to an administrative functionary, to a kind of chairman of the board or ecclesiastical manager.

That the "receptive" and the "preceptive" duties of the bishop are complementary can be illustrated by the following declaration of the great Archbishop Kenrick of St. Louis, explaining his opposition to the definition of infallibility: "I feared that such a definition might lead to danger of schism . . . [receptive] and on examining more closely the question itself, in its intrinsic evidence, I was not convinced of the conclusiveness of the arguments by which it was sustained [preceptive]." And it is apparent in Bishop McQuaid's statement before the definition of the doctrine: "I am afraid that there is a determination to pass abstract questions as decrees that may be true enough in themselves [preceptive] but which will be highly injurious to us in America from the handle they will give our enemies [receptive]." [10]

More relevant to the educational order is Bishop Moriarty's observation to Newman, at the time of the Vatican Council, that some of the ultramontanist bishops had not come "into contact with the intellectual mind of the times." [11] They had not come into contact with it because their own subjects, their own lay people, had not been formed intellectually to bear witness to what they believed, as well as to the culture in which these beliefs were held. There is no question here, in the emphasis on being "formed intellectually," of a snobbish religious intellectualism; no one suggests that scholar-laymen like W. G. Ward or Acton should have exercised a more preponderant influence than other less well-trained laymen such as Veuillot. It is a question not primarily of intelligence, but of declaration and declamation; that is, it is a question of education. For unless the laity is articulate, which implies some intellectual formation; unless the laity is capable of enunciating its vision before constituted authority, which implies generally some schooling; unless the laity can make what it sees and experiences intelligently explicit—unless all these factors are present, then the bishops themselves will be impeded in the exercise of their own "receptive" rights. Now it was because this receptive role is so important that there were those theologians at the Vatican Council who argued that the bishops of larger dioceses should have a greater voice in the deliberations than the bishops of mission territories, or than titular bishops without a resident diocese. The bishop may dispense with the testimony of his subjects on the grounds of his primary duty and of his higher wisdom as a teacher,[12] but this does not lessen the layman's obligation to enunciate what he sees, nor does it minimize the obligation of the school to provide the intellectual disciplines, the humanistic and scientific apparatus, which conduce to such enunciation.

But the layman has an obligation not only to testify in union with his pastors to the religious tradition; he has a further obligation to bear witness to all the legitimate longings and aspirations of the faithful. In the formation of an articulate laity capable of bearing witness to the values and dangers in its various professions and vocations, the school must play a major part. But it is obvious that a school which restricts or cramps the layman's role in its own life will inevitably fail in forming Christians competent to engage in any meaningful dialogue with authority;

and this failure will be as detrimental to legitimate authority, which may find its decrees contemned and scorned as unrealistic, as to the body of the laity, which will find its religious needs frustrated by lack either of the ability or of the instruments to testify.

An example of this urgent need for prudent and intelligent lay witnessing may be found in the arts. In this area, it is not uncommon to find clerical critics condemning certain realistic works of fiction—as Léon Bloy was condemned in his day—or certain motion pictures, on premises that are so completely detached from the actual conditions of a Christian who is living in the twentieth century that these condemnations often have little effect other than to lead to a disregard for authority itself. Concerning what have been called the "public arts," a moralist can rarely justify defining occasions of sin simply on the basis of abstract principles and his own personal response to this or that artifact. What is required is a profound knowledge, certainly of theology, but also of esthetics, of the social structure of various groups, of the psychology of attention, and of a host of other factors which generally come within the scope of specialized lay research.

Should an occasional theologian be found conversant and capable in all these areas, there will probably yet be lacking to him that empathic awareness of conditions in the large body of the faithful which the layman possesses, as it were, connaturally. Moral teachings, as the human though not fallible expression of the immutable ethical code, are not precisioned in a vacuum, nor even in a confessional, a pulpit, or a lecture-hall. They are generated at that point where meditative reason, enlightened by theological wisdom, comes to grips with concrete realities; they are not the products of the isolated mind, nor of the community "mind," but they are defined by the entire community acting as a complete *person*. Their "body" is given in all its physical and pragmatic richness by the layman; their "mind" is that ordinance of reason which moralists discern; their "soul" is the sanction of the bishop which purifies and enforces them. And since it is the *Christian* community that defines this teaching, then supernatural grace acts both to enlighten and to inform it. Such a notion of the complexus which engenders the teachings of Christian morality in no way interferes with the prudential judgment of the individual. By asserting with traditional theology and philosophy that casuistry and practical ethics are no less theological and philosophical *because* they are practical, this notion avoids, on the one hand, the pitfalls of a subjectivist situation-ethic and, on the other hand, the false conception that Christian morality is something simply imposed from "on high."

One may think of other areas from which the "body" of morality is drawn, as, for example, certain issues raised by research and discoveries in medicine and biological science: issues ranging from the eugenic effects of radiation, from certain modes of contraception, from various drugs that reduce responsibility and self-determination to such remote questions as those, for instance, concerned with the proscriptions relative to consanguinity in marriage.

In most cases, given the theological precepts, the clear determination as to whether this or that practice—regarded abstractly—contravenes natural or positive law is to be made by specialized students working in concert with moralists under the supervision, more or less direct, of the religious authorities.

With regard to the task of the school and the role of the layman, what is desired is certainly not that the specialized sciences should encroach on the domain of theology, but, first, that lay specialists should have enough theological competence to engage in a dialogue with the theologians; second, that the theologians should, in turn, recognize the value of this lay guidance; and third, that there will be created, by both parties, a climate of intellectual interchange in which this dialogue will be cordial and fruitful. All of this would be another step toward the fulfillment of Newman's educational ideal. Newman, toward the end of his life, in what may almost be regarded as his spiritual legacy, told Wilfrid Ward that two things seemed immediately desirable: ". . . a great development of specialized research among Catholic students; and, secondly, fair and candid discussion between the representatives of the specialized sciences and the theologians."

II

In concluding this discussion, three additional observations are in order. First, the educational stand being taken here is, I believe, in some opposition to certain sociological *credenda* outlined by Mr. T. S.

Eliot in an essay which affirmed that an intellectual revival would be dependent on a revival of the (Anglican) monastic orders:

The first educational task of the communities should be the preservation of education within the cloister uncontaminated by the deluge of barbarism outside; their second, the provision of education for the laity, which should be something more than education for a place in the Civil Service, or for technical efficiency, or for social or public success.[13]

Such romantic appeals exercise a powerful fascination over all traditionalists, but it is a fascination, one feels, that is born of poetic illusion and wishful thinking rather than of historical experience. Historically—or for that matter, etymologically—the tonsure has not always been a preservative against barbarism; and, on the other hand, quite often when the walls of the cloister excluded the barbarian, they also excluded that very intellectualism and humanism which are necessary if education is to be something more than training for the civil service. The near-myth of the monastic devotion to classical culture can be fostered in the present age only if one ignores (as neo-medievalists usually do) the meaning of the Renaissance, and if one imagines some homage to the ancients to be evident in such practices as allegorizing the *Aeneid,* or in such economies as preserving a manuscript of Horace in order to inscribe upon it the Little Hours. It is not in a new flight to the cloister that educational salvation lies, but in the

opening of those cloisters *which are also schools* to
the man in the world, even to the man contaminated
by the deluge of barbarism. A healthy humanism requires a blending of the monastic with the lay, a
blending, in Mr. Eliot's terms, of the "education
within the cloister" with the unrecognized or contemned education of the agora. The importance of
this unofficial education of the marketplace has been
underlined in Herbert Marshall McLuhan's stimulating work on the folklore of industrial man; and he
has well said:

. . . the failure to come to grips with the particulars of
contemporary existence also becomes a failure to con-
verse with the great minds *via* great books. That is why it
can be said that the medievalism of Dr. Hutchins and
Professor Adler turns out to be no more than a pic-
turesque version of the academicism that flourishes in
every collegiate institution.[14]

Second, the role of the layman in the Catholic secondary school, as I see it, ought generally to be subordinate to that of the religious or priest. In the light
of the objectives of high school training—discussed in
Chapter Five—as embracing mainly moral direction,
and emotional and affective discipline, I would think
experience shows that the religious or the priest, by
his public profession of a dedicated life, by his commitment to the observance of the evangelical counsels and, indeed, by the very cloth of his habit, is
better able than the layman to attract the youthful mind, to captivate its nascent idealism, and so
prepare it for the properly intellectual formation of

higher education. For that reason, and with regard to high school training alone, I would reject the drift of the following observation of Erasmus which, at first glance, one might be inclined to think applicable to contemporary American Catholic education:

Nor can I personally, though few agree with me, advise parents to send their sons to school in the Monasteries or in the Houses of the Brethren. For, whilst allowing the teaching Brothers to be often good, kindly men, they are usually too narrow and ignorant to be fit to educate children.[15]

Third, in all that has been said in this chapter, there is certainly no suggestion whatever that the bishops are not the only teachers of the Church; neither is there any observation that might serve to weaken the dominant role of the religious in Catholic education; nor, again, ought these remarks to be interpreted so that the best which could be hoped for would be merely a belligerent truce between laity and religious in the schools. (Though, in passing, one might propose that, since many Catholic colleges now reach a scholastic level comparable to the journalistic attainment of large segments of the diocesan press, there might be a real need for a school which would achieve in its sphere something comparable to what such lay organs as *The London Tablet* and *The Commonweal* have achieved in theirs.) The fundamental point which I would like to make is that there should be a *real* communication between clergy, religious, and laymen, and that there should be within the college or university a fusion of the complementary spiritual, intellectual, and scholastic attitudes of these groups.

III

I have suggested above that the layman acts as a mediator and as a catalyst in the school as well as in the Church: he must have a place in the educational work because there is just as great a danger that the religious teacher will grow out of touch with the concrete life of his students as that ecclesiastical authority may lose contact with the less cerebral, pragmatic issues facing the large body of the faithful. Thus, for example, in some schools there is often present a fierce opposition to teaching courses in contemporary literature, on the grounds that it presents a perverse and distorted vision of man, and that its basic ingredients are little more than license and lust. Even assuming that this is a valid estimate, and that a steady diet of modern works would be both morally and intellectually debilitating, I think, nevertheless, that it has been a serious mistake on the part of some religious or clergy to advocate the exclusion or the bowdlerizing of this literature. The vision of human life it presents may be distorted; it may even be vicious and dangerous; but whatever it *may be,* this is certain: it *is* the picture of life, the picture of man, which is accepted and embraced by great numbers of our contemporaries. And so, if we regard the university or college, not as a seminary, not as a cloistered island of righteousness in the midst of the raging torrents of sensuality and pride, but rather as a training place where young people, living in a conditioned environment, can meet and cope with the issues that will later face them—if, I say, we regard the school, not as a convent, but as a direct preparation for the world, then the only conceivable policy to adopt must be to examine prudently and carefully that written testimony which constitutes the voice and the record of our time. Now, the layman who lives in the midst of the world, who is cognizant of its works and pomps, of its seductions and insinuations, of its dangers as of its merits, is best prepared to undertake such an examination.

In like manner, in the social sciences, I believe only the layman can fully recognize the deep urgency, indeed, the absolute necessity, for those economic and political reforms that have been advocated at various times by recent popes. Certainly, there are those rare religious and clergy who, filled with a burning desire for justice, have not only expounded theoretically—which is common enough—Christian social teaching, but who have also applied it to specific problems: one thinks of Msgr. Higgins, of Fathers Dunne and Cantwell, of Brother Justin, F.S.C. These, and others like them, are significant figures; but they hardly constitute a majority among their brethren. In fact, it will be found, and I think, ever found, that it has been laymen, such as Peter Maurin, Dorothy Day, Catherine de Hueck, John Cort, who have done most to arouse the Catholic social conscience. And in the school it will be equally true that the religious teacher, no matter how sin-

cerely he may be taken up with the cause of economic justice, will not usually be able to understand
or inculcate such desiderata as a living wage, social
security, hospitalization insurance, with the comprehension and conviction of the layman who may himself at one time have been without these very benefits.
The patent proof of this is to be found in the large
number of Catholic colleges and parochial schools
where, although the principles of *Quadragesimo Anno*
and *Rerum Novarum* resound from lectern and pulpit, there is either no provision made for the layman's
economic problems, or, if they have been provided
for, the initiative has been taken by the laity, and
brought to fulfillment, not in the name of justice, but
out of fear that otherwise the layman would take his
services and talents elsewhere.

The above two examples illustrate the layman's
place in the school, from the viewpoint of the educational work itself. But his presence is also required,
particularly in our time, because the school provides
almost the only position of authority for the layman
from which he may expound his own views and express his own judgments on the broader issues facing
the Christian community. The time was when the
Catholic universities had a recognized place in deliberations affecting the whole Church; that time is past.
In the English-speaking Catholic world, as compensation for this loss of place, various attempts have been
made to publish journals reflecting the lay position.
But when one examines the fate of such periodicals
as Simpson's *Rambler* or Acton's *Home and Foreign
Review,* or when one considers in our time the sus-

pension of *The Sun-Herald*, of *Integrity*, and the dis-
proportionately small circulation, relative to the size
of the Catholic population, of such publications as
The Commonweal or *Cross Currents*, then one is
filled with dismay, certainly, at this unhappy state,
but also with renewed conviction that only by taking
his stand within the school will the layman gradually
strengthen his position, and so emerge once again as
an influence for theological and humanistic progress
in Catholic thought.

Frequently during the course of the last few years
it has been remarked in various quarters that the
layman in American Catholic education is "here to
stay." This proclamation of determined presence
seems justified on the basis of probability alone, when
one considers the large numbers of lay teachers and
lay administrators currently in Catholic schools. But
when, in matter of fact, one examines the actual
grounds which have been taken by some laymen in
defense of their position, it is easy to become a little
doubtful about this vaunted permanence. For example, it has been said that the place of lay teachers
is assured because there simply are not enough religious vocations to provide for the needs of Catholic
schools; it has further been said that, as a vocation to
the religious state does not imply a calling to the intellectual life, talented laymen will always be necessary to supply existing deficiencies. Now all such
assertions are unquestionably true, but it seems apparent that if they furnish the only grounds for the
layman in Catholic education, then his place, far

from being certain, is really rather tenuously held, and is conceivably, though not probably, of brief duration. Moreover, even if continuing circumstances and contingencies, such as those arising from a shortage of religious vocations, did guarantee the layman an accidental permanence, one would still be justified in seeking to define his position, not only negatively, as vis-à-vis the religious state, but also in terms of his own intellectual mission. This I have attempted to do in the present chapter.

FOUR:

DOING THE TRUTH

I HAVE ALREADY SUGGESTED, THOUGH NOT WITHOUT repeated apology at my seeming temerity, that many of the problems in American Catholic higher education may be traced both to its reliance on principles drawn almost exclusively from the medieval world-view, and to its having grown up in the shadow of that rationalist and crypto-Cartesian scholasticism which dominated nineteenth-century American Catholic religious instruction. In an understandable desire to affirm the unique nature of Catholic schools, and with the realization that other historical periods and other philosophical outlooks—even when neither non-Catholic nor anti-Catholic—have frequently been claimed as the heritage of Protestants and non-believers, Catholic educators have generally depended di-

167

rectly on the one historical period and the one philosophical synthesis which may be said to constitute their own private intellectual property.

This reliance on medieval modes of thought derives partially from the very real excellence of the Scholastic synthesis; partially from the spirit of the counter-Reformation, during which period Scholasticism proved itself an admirable instrument for repulsing the assaults of heresy; partially from the decline of Patristic and Biblical scholarship; and partially from the popular belief, still encountered among Catholics, that Renaissance humanism was entirely the expression of a pagan, earthly vision.[1] In American Catholic education the emphasis on medieval ideology, to the virtual exclusion of insights drawn from the Patristic, Renaissance, Englightenment, and Romantic periods, is more probably the result of such facts as these: first, that in the English-speaking world research in the Scriptures and in the Fathers has been until recently a preserve of Anglican and Lutheran scholarship—exception being made to such as the two Kenricks, to Father Spencer, in this country, and to Bishop MacEvily and the men of Maynooth in the British Isles; second, that liberal Protestantism has embraced the Renaissance and the Enlightenment as the source of its own development, and so has apparently consecrated these two periods to its own ends; third, that the domination of Catholic thought in America and England by the Congregation of the Propaganda, as both Newman and Gilmary Shea noted, tended to stifle all but the most pedestrian and ultraconservative views. As a result of all these factors, Catholics often ignored the Fathers, treated the Old Testament as a closed book, and acted as if they did not know of the existence of such men as Colet, Vives, Vittorino, Erasmus, Campion, and Allen, or, knowing vaguely of their existence, regarded most of them as being precursors or sympathetic to Protestantism.

In recent times those who advocate an educational emphasis on medieval culture have attempted to show that the intellectual synthesis of the Middle Ages embraced Biblical and Patristic themes. This is patent, but it offers all the more reason why the student of the present day should examine these themes in their original sources. It is equally patent that Scholasticism draws both for its philosophical theses and for its theological doctrine upon the Bible and the writings of the Fathers. But it is in Scholasticism's somewhat narrow and excessively problem-solving manner of reliance on these earlier fonts of Christian thought that one can recognize a number of deficiencies: deficiencies (as I have already said) purely of the pedagogical order, which need not be related in any way to theological science as such.

No one doubts that it is necessary for Scholastic theologians to utilize the Sacred Scriptures almost exclusively as a deposit of revelation, and thus primarily to see in them the final resort for resolving specific theological issues: this is the palmary and primary role of the Scriptures. But by the direct translation of this necessary theological method into the educational order, frequently the poetic urgency of the Fathers and the Bible are lost, as are also many themes, perhaps, of secondary doctrinal import, but unquestionably of great pedagogical worth; and it is precisely these themes and the poetic tone, the sense of mystery, of beauty, of interiority, and the appeal to all man's faculties, which the Scriptures and the Fathers radiate, that are lacking in contemporary Catholic education. In short, American Catholic higher learning has suffered, and is yet suffering, from a despotic and tyrannic domination by the reason over the other human faculties.

Any effective pedagogical method must take into account that air of mystery and awe which permeates the Old and New Testaments, and which stands in marked contrast to the siccative temper of many writings in the Scholastic tradition; it must take into account that extraordinary blending of Platonism with revealed truth in the Sapiential literature of the Old Testament: for here is a congruence of classical humanism and divine wisdom far more significant than that to be found in St. Thomas' use of Aristotle. And, in passing, it may be said that those educators who are seeking to animate the school by insights unique to the Catholic tradition—since much of this Wisdom literature is closed off to Protestants by their limitations on the Canon—could profitably look into this Old Testament interrelation of a man-centered and a God-centered ideology. Such educators might discover, among other things, that this exploration would increase their esteem for that other period in the Christian era, the Renaissance, when a man-centered and a God-centered world-view met.

An effective pedagogical method must also take

into account the import of the spirit of simplicity and childlike reverence present in the writings of the Fathers. Such a spirit must be recognized as of value because it is the expression, not of untrained and uncouth, primitive intelligence, but in many ways of the *faithful* man seeking to know, of the Christian scholar in his purest state. Because it is a "spirit," an air, an attitude, that is being discussed, it is impossible to define it precisely; but perhaps it can be grasped in the consideration of such an historical example as that offered by Ignatius Martyr silencing the clamor for documentary proofs, with his statement: "Christ is all the documentation I need." Or one recognizes it in Tertullian affirming: "The soul came before letters, speech came before books; ideas, before writing; and man himself, before the philosopher and poet." [2] If naïveté and piety go hand in hand, as Peter Wust suggested, and if piety toward one's forebears and toward one's Creator is a necessary disposition for accepting any traditionary discipline, then this spirit of the Fathers must find a place in a Catholic educational method.

The apologetic temper which prevails in Catholic education, and which has been intensified as a result of current criticism by various neo-nativist and secularist groups, makes of truth not, as it was for the Fathers, an object of contemplation, but rather an object of utilization. We are less interested in that truth which requires for its comprehension a slow and gradual ferment within all the faculties, and which is realized in a dawning sympathy, than in that which is readily certified and immediately usable as fodder for the reason. This is a practical age and this, a practical people: Catholics no less than others. But there is nothing practical or usable about a spirit, an attitude, or an air; one cannot convert the sympathetic, nor confute the critical, nor test one's opinions, nor prove one's beliefs, by having recourse to a temperament. What the Fathers offer us is not bound by the rules of logic; it is rather a floating power, an ethos, a religious disposition that slowly emerges on the understanding after the manner in which a fruitful symbol reveals itself. The Fathers read the Scriptures not in pursuit of useful texts, but rather in search of a religious tenor hovering behind, and supporting the written word. For them, the world of faith, as that of reason and nature, was not an object for experimentation to be exploited: it was a parable to be unveiled; the word of the Bible was a moral force, not the point of departure for a syllogism. Now all of this is alien to the modern mind.

Thus, without rejecting in any way the essential principles underlined by the medieval experiment, it will be necessary, if these principles are to be applied in the modern world, that they be taken out of their Scholastic setting and be reshaped by the school in accord with that spirit of interiority, of reverence, and of poetry which the Scriptures and the Fathers reflect.

Moreover, if one recognizes the doctrine of the Mystical Body of Christ as not only the most important theological notion resurrected by contemporary religious thought, but also as the informing element in Catholic life and worship for any age, then one must also recognize the fact that this doctrine received its most extensive historical development, not in the age of Scholasticism, but in the age of the Fathers, and in the seventeenth-century French school of spirituality. It is not surprising, then, that the late Emile Mersch, in his studies on the doctrine of the Mystical Body, passed over the medieval period with a relatively slight emphasis—save for the important teaching of the grace of headship—that stands in contrast to the long and detailed discussion he presented on other schools and other periods.

Similarly, if the liturgy is to animate the entire work of a Catholic school, there must be an intellectual concern, not only with rubric and ritual, or with a theological conception which stresses the Eucharist as a sacrament to be adored rather than as a sacrifice to be shared in; and for the development of this spirit of worship in the school, one may not rely exclusively on the ideals and practices of medieval Christendom, which often obscured the notion of communal participation, but one must draw also from the tradition of the primitive Church and the Fathers, and from those roots in nineteenth-century romanticism which reaffirmed in the arts the value of gesture and imagination and, in philosophy, the value of interiority and mystery.

To these two doctrinal notions must be added the Pauline teaching, so frequently overlooked, that Christian wisdom illumines the eyes of the heart, and that it has, therefore, an affective and subjective aspect to it. Christian wisdom and the Christian intellectual life make of truth, not merely something to be known, but something to be loved and lived. We are, as St. Paul said, "doers of the truth." [3]

None of this implies that Scholastic principles have little relevance to a comprehensive educational program; it simply says that their value is severely limited by the problem-solving tone—philosophically understandable, but nonetheless pedagogically indefensible —of many Scholastic works. With regard to Scholastic principles it is certain that they must inevitably play a major role in any Catholic educational theory; their importance, to take one example alone, in correcting the anti-intellectualism both of the Fathers and of the nineteenth-century fideists, cannot be overemphasized. It is not necessary, then, to go so far as the late Msgr. Russell: "Christ was constantly seeking to bring God close to us. Philosophy tends to make Him distant"; for such a statement might be revised more accurately to state that, not philosophy, but some philosophers tend to make God a remote object of human thought. Nor, on the other hand, need one go to the extreme of saying with Père Clérissac: "Christ is the true Peripatetic" [4] (unless, of course, one wants to declare that the Word is the truth in Platonism, or the truth in existentialism, since in Christ is all truth). For, it is largely in the non-Peripatetic tradition, in the Platonic and Augustinian tradition, that many insights, long neglected and of great pedagogical importance, are to be found. And these insights, as St. Thomas himself once observed, supplement the Aristotelian vision and form a more balanced synthesis.[5]

I

Since I have already pointed out above and in Chapter One a number of self-imposed limitations that the neo-medievalist is bound by when he organizes a curriculum, and since these limitations seldom affect courses other than theology and philosophy, the following section will be entirely devoted to expanding my earlier brief notes on the spirit of an educational method broader than that based exclusively on medieval premises.

For the development of an organic pedagogical method, in addition to the desiderata enumerated above, there must be a return to the primacy of contemplation and to the essence of the learning activity in the personal encounter of being with being. Much of the formation of our students is not at all intellectual because it is concerned primarily with the preambles to the exercise of intellect; it is often taken up almost entirely with the purely propadeutic, rational training of the mind, with the work of gathering, coordinating, and verifying data, and with the creation of symbolic instruments for measuring and circumscribing reality; such activity is "work" in the real sense of the word because it falls within the precinct of *ratio*, of the discursive, laboring faculties of man, rather than within the realm of *intellectus*, of his seeing and intuitive powers. Such activity is valuable; it is important; it is even indispensable; but it is not education.

Indeed, in many cases, because the school has been given over almost exclusively to this rational exercise, and because the mind of the student has been so absorbed over long periods of time with this discursive operation, quite often the results may be said to be the very opposite of education; the student is, not infrequently, left with such a scattered collection of data that his spirit is smothered and stifled, and so inhibited that it cannot recognize the configuring, the informing element in these data; it cannot do the one thing in which all its training should have culminated: it cannot universalize; it cannot exercise spirit; in short, it cannot face being. The "educated" man is then the mis-educated, the non-educated, and the poet well says:

> It may be that the ignorant man, alone,
> Has any chance to mate his life with life,
> That is the sensual, pearly spouse, the life
> That is fluent in even the wintriest bronze.[6]

That this rational exercise is not education is evident in the very root meaning of that word; for "education," as commencement speakers are so fond of showing, etymologically means "to draw out." And this drawing-out process implies the maturing and perfecting of the student's being so that it resonates in harmony with the being in the world about him. When the spirit in the student is awakened, when his conscious being comes to life through any profound contact with truth, goodness, beauty, so that this being, this spirit, goes out of his person, as it were, to embrace this being in the object—then, and only then, is there education. What orators at academic affairs rarely explain, in their gesture to philology, is how a rational discipline which has been concerned exclusively with "pouring in" may be called education. Such explanation is not proffered, because it doesn't exist. The process which in many of our schools we have dignified with the title, education, is educative only by good luck or happy accident.

I must insert here, as preface, that in what I am about to say, although the terms "method" and "mode of instruction" will be used, the point of the argument must be recognized as centering on the principles and ends of education—and this, simply because the methods flow from the ends. Certainly, throughout this discussion, I am presuming the type of intense training in grammar, in mathematics, and in science, which is necessary as a preparation for any educational venture. And, although these preparatory disciplines have often been neglected, their neglect has not gone unnoticed by serious educators, so that it does not seem necessary to repeat here what has already been said, and said with vigor and common sense elsewhere. I am presuming, also, that every field of learning has its own introductory notions, and that the more highly refined such a field may be, the more time will be consumed in teaching and inculcating them. The following observations, then, while they touch upon the means for broadening such notions, are aimed primarily not at the type of instruction necessary for a highly specialized proficiency in a particular subject, but to the end product of a general program of liberal studies, as such a program has been defined in the following terms:

With regard to the development of the human mind, neither the richest material facilities nor the richest equipment in methods, information, and erudition are the main point. The great thing is the awakening of the inner resources and creativity.[7]

Every man has within himself the sources of his own originality, of his own creativity, which he can exploit by more and more conforming his actions to his interior life. But first he must know what is the direction of the unique spirit which possesses him, that is, he must come to recognize consciously his very selfness. Since man can experience his selfness only when it is being exercised, only when his spirit is related to the spirit in the external world, he must put himself in contact with the being which is apart from him. The being in which he participates, and which makes him to be uniquely himself, must grow and be nourished and be exercised by contemplating the being which is externally manifest in the true, the good, and the beautiful.

This is the first stage of education, which is reached when the child, already possessed of some power of self-reflection, from the separation which he makes between himself and other persons while emerging into adolescence, comes to recognize vaguely his own apartness, his own uniqueness. This sense of personality, of selfness, is strengthened by the educator who initiates the adolescent, first, into the world of beauty;

second, into the world of moral good; and, third, into
the world of truth. Now without entering into any
detailed program for attaining this goal, or making
any artificial separation among these three transcendental properties of being, it may be said that it is
the beautiful which is most apt to excite youthful
interest, and which therefore must be emphasized
during these early formative years. To that end,
courses in music appreciation aimed, not at developing a highly sophisticated taste, but simply at awakening a mood of silent wonderment, cannot be too
highly praised. Similarly, studies in literature should
not be concerned primarily with historical data and
chronological movements, but with introducing the
adolescent into the world of ennobling empathic experience—as this has been brilliantly achieved in *The
Christian Impact* textbooks. In the area of the good,
the student should be taught not the traditional dogma, moral, and worship of the catechism, but rather
should be presented with these three segments of religious life through the medium of the personality
of Christ. Furthermore, the student should be in-
structed by teachers of a markedly upright and lofty
character—this, as I have said, is the reason why the
professed religious will always play a more important
role than the layman in secondary education. In the
realm of the true, the teacher cannot expect to introduce the adolescent to metaphysical abstractions. Following Newman's doctrine, as set forth in his University Sermon, "Personal Influence the Means of
Propagating Truth," the teacher will clarify to his
charges, by means of close association and friendly

intercourse, the nature of their adolescent confusions and bewilderment. The students may thus be brought to realize that their natural desire for originality and creativity can be satisfied, not by adopting the external symbols of individuality in oddities of dress and conduct, not by embracing the Bohemianism of the perennially angry young men, but simply by pursuing the insights and directives born of the evolution and maturing of their own sense of selfness.

On the university level, three simple illustrations may serve to illustrate this same ideal. The student may know, as a physicist, the nature of light; he may have reached the advanced stage of being able to opt for one or two varying or combining conceptions of that nature; and he may have measured the spectral changes as light is reflected and refracted through various media surrounding the great stars. But if after all this, his mind in the presence of, let us say, a beautiful sunset can enter upon no activity save to tinker with whatever new scientific problem the twilight scene suggests, if he can experience no delight in beauty, no bond with being, then he has not been educated. He may know as tyro-psychologist or sociologist all the facets of the human personality, the sublimity of its attainment and the perversions its daimonic character may leave it subject to; he may know by laboratory experiment its capacities and its failures, or by statistical survey, the external modes of its relation to other persons of a community. But if, after all this, he is not moved to a gesture of love in encountering a profoundly spiritual person, then he has not been educated.

Similarly, if a student of literature can enumerate every historical movement, every critical trend, every poetic school, and if he has read all the major works of his language and is familiar with the best thoughts of its best minds, can he be said to be educated when in the presence of a great poem, in reading—let us say—"Spectral Lovers," or "Eros Turannos," he is capable only of classifying the poem as typical of this or that tendency, or of dissecting it for its structure and imagery? And if he grasps the specific initiation theme in such fiction as *The Magic Mountain, The Bear,* or *The Heart of Darkness,* and yet, after such recognition, his own being is not educed to communicate with the being about him, so that he himself is not initiated into the mystery of reality, can he be said to have truly comprehended these novels, or to be truly educated?

It has been necessary to indulge in all this rhetoric to make it quite clear that the one aim of education, as that aim is being defined here, has nothing directly in common with any specialized training. And it is a sad commentary on how highly specialized even undergraduate education has become that the very positing of such questions as these above will be regarded as an expression of the crudest romanticism by those—among Catholics—who measure our inadequacies by the failure of our students to make a mark in business and economic life,[8] or by those others— among Catholics and non-Catholics alike—who had no interest in academic issues until Soviet successes became known, and who are now passionately devoted to organizing college programs in technology that will manufacture scientists and engineers in the best assembly-line fashion: this latter process, as illiberal as it is, being defined as "defending the *free* world" through education.

However, there are two objections to the ideal which I have introduced above, and which I will develop in the body of this chapter, that must be weighed; and, although I hope to answer these objections more fully as this discussion progresses, it is necessary now to sketch the general line such answers will follow.

First, it is said that the approach suggested in the preceding paragraphs, far from being progressive, tends instead to reject all the accomplishments of modern intellectual research and to erect as a scholastic standard something approximating that of the nineteenth-century English classical education. Now inasmuch as teaching and research in the arts, in natural science, and even in theology, have been stamped with a positivist character, and have been marked by a repudiation of all sense of wonderment, such an objection is well-founded. But far from conceiving the repudiation of that positivist spirit, which is as much an outgrowth of decadent Scholasticism as of the Enlightenment, to be retrogression, one may accept such a rejection as a step forward toward the reaffirmation of man's essential humanity and of his native bonds with the external world.[9] The student examining his own highly specialized and technical training, and comparing it with nineteenth-century schooling, the student saying to himself, "Look on

this picture and on that," may well want to throw off
the strait jacket of a narrow positivism and be buck-
led in a tweed outworn.

From the viewpoint of development of interest,
and of competence, that is, from the viewpoint of
what would be called, today, general education, the
nineteenth-century accomplishment is much closer
to any liberal ideal than what has been achieved after
all the visions and revisions of the last twenty years
of theorizing and reassessing in American education.
One does not have to look for the personification of
this ideal in the giants, Newman, Arnold, Jowett, for
it is represented as well by the wide humanistic
culture of such diverse figures as Stanley, Dr. Arnold, Church, Plumptre, Gladstone, Morley, Russell,
Shairp, Kingsley, and MacColl. Though not all
scholars, these men showed an extraordinary breadth
of concern and ability in many different fields; and
is it not indicative of the value of this schooling
in the classics that men such as Kingsley, Manning,
and Stanley had an awareness of the great social issues
of their day which was not to be encountered among
other clerics trained, for example, in that rigid non-
humanistic tradition Newman so scorned at the Propaganda? Without entering into any discussion of the
rectitude of doctrine, one must recognize in all those
impressive names I have marshalled above a range of
intelligent interest and ability in political, social,
educational, theological, and literary questions, rarely, if ever, encountered in our time.

A man who has himself been caricatured as a
nineteenth-century figure suggests one reason for this

extraordinary breadth of competence. T. S. Eliot, in an essay entitled "Modern Education and the Classics," wrote:

I do not ignore the great value which negative and obstructive forces can have. The longer the better schools and the older universities in this country (for they have pretty well given up the struggle in America) can maintain some standard of classical education, the better for those who look to the future with an active desire for reform and an intelligent acceptance of change.[10]

But classical education alone does not explain the range of interest shown in so many different fields by the scholars I have mentioned above. This classical training was shaped by that English spirit—a spirit which is necessary to us both because our universities are largely patterned on those of England and because of the Anglo-Saxon roots of our general cultural life—whose ideal of learning, as Christopher Dawson says, "was not rational analysis, but that direct intuition of reality by imaginative vision which unites the mind with its object in a kind of vital communication." [11] It is this spirit of wonderment with which I am occupied here, and which must be restored to its place in an educational work now frustrated by its positivist and rationalist tenor.

The second of the two objections raised against any such restoration rightly maintains that no teacher can by his own efforts bring about that direct communication with the object which has been defined above as the single end of general education; such a communication, such a marriage of subject and object in the mysterious climate of interiority, it is asserted, remains a pure intuition that no amount of training can guarantee. Again, as with the first objection, far from attempting to controvert this statement, I would embrace it as a truism. But what has been the flaw in much academic practice is that, on the valid ground that this intuition remains largely a gratuitous gift, comparable in some ways to an actual grace, many educators have over the years completely lost sight of its very existence as the unique goal toward which all their teaching should be directed. As a result, the original unity of wisdom, its natural simplicity flowing from the spiritual character it possesses, has been so shrouded by a multiplicity of material techniques, that education generally has disfigured the instinct of the intellect for union with being, by focusing the life of the mind on the verification of instrumental symbols and myths.

While it is true that no educational undertaking, no matter how well planned or organized, can guarantee this intellectual insight, yet extending the above comparison with the supernatural order, it may be said that just as sanctifying grace is the ordinary predisposition for actual grace, so, too, in the educational order, it is possible to create an environment, an atmosphere, which will dispose the mind for such intuitive vision.

The nurturing and development of this environment is eminently the work of the teacher who, by his own intense spirituality, acts as the transparent medium through which the student glimpses and grasps some transcendental property of being. The teacher is then the heart of any educational effort. Whatever may be the value of administrative policy, and of all that academic panoply of splendid libraries and laboratories, and of wealthy endowments, he remains the one dominant educational force within the school. And this unique responsibility demands of him that he be a spiritual man—that he be, in the ancient sense of the word, a *religious* man: a man who is empowered to "bind" together contingent and necessary, immediate and ultimate realities. He must be literally a man "inspired," a man who has been inspirited because he lives and breathes in that spiritual climate in which his every gesture and expression reflect his intellectual vision. Splendidly has Newman said all this in a much-neglected essay:

. . . its great instrument, or rather organ, has ever been that which nature prescribes in all education, the personal presence of a teacher, or, in theological language, Oral Tradition. It is the living voice, the breathing form, the expressive countenance, which preaches, which catechizes. Truth, a subtle, invisible, manifold spirit, is poured into the mind of the scholar by his eyes and ears, through his affections, imagination, and reason.[12]

This is the voice of the nineteenth century, the voice of tradition. What does the twentieth century offer in its stead? Courses "given" by closed-circuit television.

Unfortunately, if a multiplicity of aims and ends has obscured the nature of the educational act, it has obscured even more the nature of the teacher's role. As a result, on the one hand, teachers who are mere

technicians tend to overwhelm or strangle the student's spirit by the revelation of an infinitude of facts
and phenomena, which, because of the teachers' own
fractionary perspective, can find a pretext of unity
only in some purely logical or grammatical synthesis;
or, on the other hand, such teachers rely on superficial enthusiasm and excitement which merely travesty the tensely charged atmosphere that prevails in
those classrooms where a genuine intellectual experience is taking place.

To illustrate the work of the teacher in engender-
ing such a spiritual atmosphere or climate, I will
again make use of examples drawn from the arts. In
encountering any artifact, that is, in comprehending
the unique transcendental participation in being
which a particular art work embodies, one can rely
on no exclusively problem-solving technique that dissects the object of contemplation according to texture, pattern, meaning, because such reliance is to
make among the various elements a division which is
incapable of being resolved posteriorly. The artifact,
as Debussy insisted, admits of no separation among
its parts because it is a configuration, the constituents
of which are organically synthesized in an existential
tension, and hence they can be contemplated only in
their natural unity.

For example, in comprehending a poem, to seek to
understand, first, the verbal communicative element
in it, without at the very same time, in the very same
process, and by the very same act, grasping the total
structure of the work is, as it were, to kill this beautiful object by separating its body from its soul. One

may further say that then to seek to resurrect this body and soul is in a sense to arrogate to one's critical faculties a kind of divine power. When man with his limited and restricted capacity for grasping being, when the critic with his limited and restricted capacity for contemplating beauty, takes a poem and dissects it by reducing its verbal elements to such categories as pattern, texture, continuity, and by reducing its literal meaning to its "basic English" equivalent, then such a critic has made it impossible to recognize the poem as it is in its original existential oneness. The poem is not merely a union of idea and music, just as man is not merely a union of body and soul, but a third thing transcending its composites. When a critic does make this separation, this dissection, his appreciation of the poem is already conditioned by the insertion of his own critical machinery between himself and the art work. He now views the poem, not as it was born in indivisible unity from the intuition of the poet, but rather he views it through the medium of his own manufactured instruments; and, having treated the poem as a kind of Cartesian body-spirit, what he finally contemplates is not the poem itself, but its cadaver.

Man embraces the total significance of an art work as he embraces the total person of his beloved. When a man comprehends the spiritual character of his beloved, he does not do so at the end of a detailed analytic process; rather he simply possesses the person of the beloved, in all its goodness and beauty, in one synoptic intuition. Such an intuition will, of course, be the result of a long period of contemplation. But this is precisely where all methodologies of appreciation, all yogisms, all systems for comprehending being fail: they seek too much too rapidly. They assault the art work, and, so to speak, plunge grasping, probing, clutching instruments into it, to pluck out, as it were, its living soul—as if there were any mechanical process, any technique, for an act of love. All poets have testified: "Nor can foot feel being shod."

> O sweet spontaneous
> earth how often have
> the
> doting
>
>   fingers of
> prurient philosophers pinched
> and
> poked
>
> thee
> ,has the naughty thumb
> of science prodded
> thy
>
> beauty [13]

This argument, then, is not directed against any employment of the various batteries of critical technique, but against that exclusive self-reliant employment which is conceived in a spirit of greedy plunder rather than in a spirit of contemplative repose.

It may be said that one must be in love with the art object as one must be in love with any spiritual reality, and then, and only then, will the fullness of spirit radiate out from that object. All properties of being tend to diffuse themselves. Beauty tends of its nature to go out of itself, and man possessing being in a conscious way tends to go out of himself and encounter this beauty, embrace this beauty, and share his being, his inner personal beauty, with the beauty of the object. In this moment of mutual sharing, the object is no longer "object"—that which is projected outside the self—for object and subject, without losing their separate identities, are interfused. Hence, in the terminology of Marcel, the relation of subject and object is one of mystery. Mystery is any relation to being which impinges upon and absorbs one's very self; it is a relation the meaning of which cannot be adequately reduced to external terms. Mystery demands union. Problem, which is any relation in which subject and object remain detached and divorced, implies permanent separation. Now, in the light of these distinctions, a critic can neither say that he is going to study an art work objectively, nor, paradoxically, can he talk meaningfully of the objective "meaning" of the art work. The critic who regards the poem as a problem to be solved, as an object to be analyzed, never touches the inner core of the poetic work; forgetting that what the genius of the artist has joined together, man cannot separate, such a critic can merely manipulate the various living elements of the poem, and devote himself to embalming its corpse in some prose description or paraphrase.

It is probably because of the modern craze for universal knowledge and because of the influx of so many untrained students into the colleges and universities that it has been deemed necessary to devise readily applicable methods for the easy comprehension of the arts. Schools which seem concerned with information rather than formation have shown themselves intent on providing all students with the right recipes and "gimmicks" to be applied to every artistic monument they may come across: such schools could as well teach courses on the art of love or on the art of praying. Of course, since man is not an angel, and cannot know by simple and immediate intuition, technique should play its small part in the educational effort—as, for example, a knowledge of scansion and metre is desirable for students of poetry. But training in technique ought not to be confused with education.

It is universally accepted by spiritual writers that the various "methods of mental prayer," authored by such masters as St. Ignatius or M. Olier, do not guarantee contemplation; there can be no such guarantee, and this, not only because contemplation entails a supernatural grace, but because the purpose of these methods is merely to prepare, to condition the mind for praying. On the contrary, what is often taught in our schools as critical methodology is not regarded as a device for familiarizing the student with the peripheries of poetry and the arts; what is taught is *the* way for "understanding poetry"—significantly that phrase is used in the title of at least three college textbooks of literature. Methods of mental prayer fulfill the same function in the realm of contemplation that the kind of extra-curricular training, provided by

many schools, in dancing and in the social graces, fulfills in the order of human love: a very minor preparatory role in no way essentially linked to the object
toward which such technique may be directed. Yet
the rationalist methods that are taught in many
schools for the "understanding" of art works are similar to a shamanistic training in mystical contemplation, or to popular pagan techniques for what is
called "love making."

There are five aspects of spirit, all analogically related, to which man can be bound in an interior
union: God, who is absolute spirit; man, who participates consciously in spirit; and truth, goodness, and
beauty which, as properties of being, manifest spirit.
Now a bond with any of these cannot be the direct
result of some activity in the order of technique, in
the order of matter, because spirit has a natural affin-
ity with spirit alone, and not with any artificial material nexus that man may construct to force this
bond. Thus it is the God whose absolute spirituality
is His nature that man loves; it is not any abstract
theological definition nor any barren verbal conception—though these may have their great value—to
which man is related. Similarly, when a person loves
another person, in the temporal order, it is not the
exterior traits, the sum of all the qualities, that are
loved, but the spiritual person himself in all his ontological richness. So, too, in the comprehension of a
profound truth. For the more profound a truth is, the
more it shares in spirit, and the less capable it is of
being completely exhausted by the technical instruments of logic. Hence the apprehension of first prin-

ciples cannot be the product of deduction: not simply because these principles themselves provide the
basis for deduction, but because they are immediately
seized in that natural juncture of being with being
which engenders meaning. The same holds true in
the contemplation of a beautiful thing: a radiant sunset, when the world is about to take its rest and all is
transmuted, when descending twilight preludes the
suspension of labor, and darkness clothes man and
nature in the garments of sleep. And so, too, in reading such lines as:

> Nox erat et terras animalia fessa per omnis
> alituum pecudumque genus sopor altus habebat [14]

> Lo giorno se n'andava e l'aere bruno
> Toglieva gli animai che sono in terra
> Da le fatiche loro . . .[15]

> The day gan failen, and the derke night,
> That reveth bestes from hir besinesse . . .[16]

> . . . Twilight gray
> Had in her sober livery all things clad;
> Silence accompanied for Beast and Bird
> They to their grassy couch, these to their Nests
> were slunk.[17]

Similarly, when hearing the introduction to Franck's
D Minor Symphony, and this same theme as it acts as
a link between Liszt's *Les Preludes* and Wagner's
later variations on it: in every case, one is present before an epiphany of beauty that stirs one's inner life,

and awakens one's conscious being to surge and thrust and finally embrace this beauty. And with regard to the above examples, which have not been chosen at random, it may be said that one is in the presence of that continuity which exists even thematically throughout the universe of beauty, and which hints across the aeons at the primordial oneness of contingent being with Being.

Now can one say that there is some recipe for these acts of love, for the juncture of being with being, that the above examples evoke? One cannot dare in the presence of this truth, goodness, or beauty to take out his contrived apparatus of criticism and, with the scalpel of some methodology, tear the heart out of these transcendentals. There is no perfect instrument to relate participated being to being, just as there was no instrument in the first relation of essential being to contingent being in the divine act of implanting a soul in the first man. One can merely face the particular configuration of being he is contemplating, and in this confrontation of an organic whole, open himself to the existential yearnings of being for union with itself.

One recognizes, when examining his reaction to all the examples I have mentioned above, an element that cannot be verbalized; for one makes in any relation with being or its properties an ontological response, the original utterance of which is stripped bare by later efforts to bring it into the logical order. What, then, must the teacher do in attempting to arouse his students to an awareness of this transcendental aspect in things? The question is a fundamental

one, and the one which we set ourselves to answer at
the beginning of this section. Certainly the teacher
must not dispense with all canons of criticism, examination, and verification, and substitute for them a
vague emotionalism; and certainly, too, he must not
be driven to stammer like the mystic in a vain attempt at expressing the ineffable.

Without setting aside the traditional instruments
of measuring and analyzing some facet of his particular discipline, the teacher must realize the inadequacy
of these instruments in bringing about a genuine
communion with the object, and he must realize that
any exclusively technical method, however subtle and
refined, cannot produce this mysterious union of being with being. He must realize further that no
matter how desirable on democratic or egalitarian
grounds it may be to develop a technique that will
reduce the arcana of the spiritual sciences to a popular understanding, such a desideratum remains—
through technique alone—unattainable because of
the disproportion between a material instrument and
the spiritual ends toward which it is directed.

The teacher, the spiritual man par excellence, may
depend initially on analysis, but he must rely finally,
for this ultimate educational achievement, on a
highly personalized reflection over the body of truth
or beauty being considered. In this way his own spiritual insight becomes the instrument for awakening a
consciousness of their being within his students;
which consciousness, when it is awakened, is then
capable of responding to the being in all reality. The
instrument for the educational act is not material,

but spiritual; not method or technique, but the personal reflection of the teacher. Such a highly personalized and poetic reflection will be necessarily diffuse and repetitious, for, while the mystery of being cannot be perfectly exhausted by logical instruments alone, it can be encompassed and thus *gradually and organically* assimilated by rhetoric. And this rhetorical expression will be, in turn, metaphoric rather than descriptive. Description tells what a thing does; metaphor conveys what a thing is; descriptive analysis is concerned with the products of a thing, and with the effects flowing from its conjunction with other things; description, then, is concerned primarily with a thing being *such,* that is, with *agere.* Rhetorical metaphor is concerned with creating a format of ambient symbols and parables which, in its dependance on all facets of life and experience, in its reliance on a *Gestalt* of images drawn from all elements in the universe, generates a revelation of the thing itself: of the things *being* such: the encounter with *esse.*

Descriptive language is language derived from a material instrument employed upon the object; it is the language of those who hold the object, as it were, at arm's length, who are anxious to keep the object remote and detached. The result of such a disengaged examination, when it culminates in nothing higher, is to objectivize the person himself—a condition one recognizes in some scientists who, however talented and professionally adept they may be, appear, as persons, stunted and dwarfed. Yet even descriptive language, the language of science and of most phi-

losophers, may transcend its own limitations and may
culminate in the language of metaphor, in the language of love. For such is the power of the language
that even the most prosaic and pedestrian utterance
reaches beyond its crudity to touch the skirts of
beauty. And that poet who has taken metaphor for
his theme, as well as for his medium, has said:

> It is better that, as scholars,
> They should think hard in the dark cuffs
> Of voluminous cloaks,
> And shave their heads and bodies.
>
> It might well be that their mistress
> Is no gaunt fugitive phantom.
> She might, after all, be a wanton,
> Abundantly beautiful, eager,
>
> Fecund,
> From whose being by starlight, on the sea coast
> The innermost good of their seeking
> Might come in the simplest of speech.
>
> It is a good light, then, for those
> That know the ultimate Plato,
> Tranquilizing with this jewel
> The torments of confusion.[18]

That relation to the object whereby one "ingath-
ers" all subordinate, "objective" knowledge so that
such knowledge is no longer a mere collocation of
data, a mere assemblage of facts, but is literally "oneself" and is grasped as one grasps one's own selfness—

that relation, in the strict sense of the phrase, "beggars description." For description implies a circuit, a movement around the object: as the expression "to *describe* a circle" indicates. Description is the language of exteriority; and the more it is exclusively employed, the more it tends to exteriorize the person. But metaphor is the language of interiority; it is the language of the communion of being with being; that is, it is the language of mystery: of love. Description is the language of "apartness," of problem. Metaphor is the supreme communication because it is expressive of union, not of separation; it presupposes description, but goes beyond it; metaphor, then, does not contradict description, but supplements and perfects it. In the terms of Newman and Blondel, and of Gabriel Marcel, metaphoric language takes the notional and makes it the real; it takes the problem and makes it mystery; it moves from primary reflection to secondary reflection.

Because metaphor is the language of love (whether one thinks of the rudest expressions—e.g., "sweet," "honey"—or the purest poetry) it is also the language of spontaneity. The choice of word is not premeditated; the structure of words is not prearranged; but neither are they left to hazard, to indetermination. Metaphoric language is dictated by the teacher's encounter and union with the object being contemplated. Certainly, one prepares specific remarks and comments, and certainly, too, one's descriptions are prepared. But at that moment when, in the presence of the object, one is moved to speech by its beauty or by the depths of truth it discloses, at that moment when takes place the marriage of subject and object, and when occurs the educational act itself, at that moment, the teacher is an *enthusiast:* he is moved, as it were, from on high; he is inspired, and he speaks the language of inspiration, the language of metaphor.

It is when the mind of the teacher is in full activity that those insights born of the "ingathering," born of the union with the object, become vocal. For this reason, the Lutheran bishop, Nathan Söderblom, has observed of the first great teacher ". . . to Socrates the Daimonion was something that fell upon him when exercising his vocation, not something attainable by a methodic schooling and training of the mind." [19] There is no method for such intuition and for such expression:

> One's grand flights, one's Sunday baths,
> One's tootings at the weddings of the soul
> Occur as they occur.[20]

Yet one can *condition* himself to verbalize these "grand flights." To use again an illustration from the life of prayer: according to spiritual writers, the best preparation for contemplation, for the prayer of simplicity—for "the weddings of the soul"—is not the proximate directing of the mind to God, but the habitual awareness of God's presence. So, too, the best preparation for this metaphoric expression will not be one's immediate attention to the object of contemplation—though this is indispensable as a prelude—but an extensive knowledge, an habitual consciousness of as wide a field of human endeavor as one can encompass. If the intellect is, as the philosophers say, "in a certain way every thing," then the educator must have as broad a knowledge as possible, so that there will be resident within him a universe of images and symbols that will be evoked at the moment when the object playing upon his mind is suddenly seized in its totality. Just as the theologian will illuminate his doctrine by principles drawn from philosophy, from the contemplation of nature and of art, and just as the scientist will bring the notions of physics, mathematics, and chemistry in convergence on the point he is elucidating, so, too, the great teacher must throw his ideas into another and another calculus of language, in order that the object he is revealing may become more and more evident: until the planes of each succeeding expression he uses gradually take shape and the polygon of his utterance more and more approximates the circle of the object. The inscribed polygon will never identify itself with the circle; the object will never be completely encompassed: but man the knower will know as perfectly as his imperfect faculties allow.

II

In concluding this discussion, it is necessary to repeat that the above strictures on analytic, dissective methods are not intended to apply to those preliminaries of the act of education which play a large role, and rightly take up so much time, in secondary schooling and in the initial stages of university formation; nor

are these strictures intended to apply to the preparation of the student's mind for a specialized knowledge
of a particular field. But it must be repeated, also,
that these preliminaries should not be regarded as
merely a step toward a higher analysis, which higher
analysis then gives way to a more nearly ultimate
analysis, and so on, *ad infinitum*. These preliminaries, if they are to constitute part of a general program of humane and liberal studies, and not merely
be an element of specialized professional training,
must be expressly oriented toward that higher synoptic insight which I have discussed above.

This brings the topic of this chapter full circle and
back to the original point of departure: the imperative need for introducing other insights into the pedagogical order than those drawn from the medieval
world-view. For, as already noted, it is in an exclusive
dependence on Scholastic methodology that the real
dissociation of sensibility in American Catholic education is most apparent.

Many aspects of Scholastic thought have been criticized as narrowly essentialist by contemporary thinkers; whether this is a valid criticism philosophically is
a question for the philosophers themselves to answer
as best they may. But I would think it undeniable
that pedagogically such a criticism has considerable
validity. The assumption often embraced by educators, in the name of Scholasticism, of the prime
objectivity of truth determined by logical instruments
alone; the notion of a *summa* of knowledge, as in the
medieval encyclopedias, "treasuries," "gardens," and
theological constructions; the notion of a world large-

ly devoid of natural mystery; the world, as Wallace Stevens said, of "the man of glass who in a million diamonds sums us up"—all of these are suppositions bound too closely to an historical period in which the pursuit of truth was often equated with the exploration of a universe of remote, detached, objective essences that were seemingly conceived as immutable, inalterable, and complete. But, on the other hand, it must be acknowledged that they are suppositions undeniably relevant to the man of our age, for they have yielded their store of truths; but unquestionably, too, these are often disturbing and discontenting truths. They leave much unsaid.

No one questions the great unity which prevailed in the Middle Ages; and all the oft-repeated phrases, so eagerly exploited by Catholic apologists about the cathedrals, the *Summa Theologica,* and the *Commedia* expressing in different media this unity, may remain inscribed in the textbooks. No one questions the assertion that Dante was a theologian and that St. Thomas was a poet. But may one not examine the character of this unity? May one not point out that Dante's theology is as frigidly impersonal as his vision of hell, and that St. Thomas' poetry is little more than another adaptation of the Victorine sequences? Is not, then, this unity somewhat monolithic, not only by reason of its imitativeness, but even more by reason of its detachment from concrete realities and its indifference to the plight of the individual? In hierarchizing medieval society, did not the Schoolmen, while recognizing the worth of the person in their philosophical and theological treatises, often ignore this worth in the practical order, and thus frequently leave the individual person—that individual person whom today, with all due respect, we may call the common man—prey to every social force, every disordered superstition, every flourishing Catharist cult, and by this same practical ignorance of the worth of the individual sometimes make it difficult for him to respond to the gifts his Faith showered upon him? We may admire Émile Mâle's panegyric of cathedral worship:

Man confined within his social class, within a trade, his forces dispersed and frittered away in the work and life of every day, recovered here a sense of unity and regained equilibrium and harmony. The crowd, assembled on great feast days, felt itself an organic whole, the mystical body of Christ, Whose soul mingled with its soul. The faithful were humanity, the Cathedral was the world, and the spirit of God simultaneously filled man and all creation.[21]

But after admiring this harmonious scene, we may well question whether liturgical worship alone can provide that wide range for man's leisure activities which is so necessary if man is to be truly free. M. Maritain has called medieval culture a "sacral" culture; whether the title is apposite is not so important as that for the present purpose it may serve to point up at least one aspect of the medieval spirit: the frequent relegation of temporal problems to the realm of the profane, with sometimes a consequent indifference to the very existence of such problems.

I have said that the truths which the Schoolmen

enunciated, while by definition, truths, yet are disturbing because they leave much unsaid by reason of their hyperobjectivity. For example, one might examine those four Last Ends, which medieval literature and art so often illustrated, and think of Dante dispassionately narrating the horrors of his medieval hell, and, in a moment of pique, contributing to the torments by plucking out a sinner's hair, and one may ask whether hell was not something so familiar to this medieval mind that its pains were simply *facts* to be catalogued and classified, and its torment merely that into which one inserted whatever immortal soul may have given offense. Or again, one thinks of the theologian noting that few men achieve excellence in anything, that beatitude is excellence, and on the basis of a syllogism and some limited hermeneutics consigning a majority of mankind to the eternal flames.

Now Dante may have been writing an allegory, a didactic tale, a trope, but he was also writing a poem, an object of interest complete in itself, and from this latter point of view, the only thing in contemporary literature approximating the passage in Dante, to which I alluded above—read as a statement alone— would probably be certain fictional accounts of Gestapo practice or certain murder mysteries written as "entertainments." To the medieval theologian's syllogism above, one may contrast Newman's wrestlings with the problem of eternal punishment and the brilliant theological clarification he developed.[22] The Catholic of no period in history denies theological truth, and there is no question here of such denial.

Certainly, Newman's observations on the eternity of
hell are not indicative of less Faith than is evident
in the Schoolmen; they are indicative rather of a
different sensibility, of a great Faith supported by a
great sensibility. It is not *what* the medieval mind
enunciated that is disturbing, but the manner of
enunciation; it is the tone of the voice, not the utterance.

III

The importance of "Christian culture" as an integrating principle of the curriculum has recently
been underlined by Christopher Dawson. This is not
the place to discuss the pedagogical merits of the
study of "Christian culture," but it *is* the place to
point out that if this culture embraces the period,
roughly, from the dissolution of the empire in the
West to the fall of Constantinople, that is, the period
conventionally defined as the Middle Ages, then one
is going to have to treat of such things as that suppression of individual conscience which Acton discussed in his essay, "The Beginnings of the Modern
State." [23] One is going to have to note with Fanfani
in *Catholicism, Protestantism, and Capitalism,* and
with Auerbach in *Mimesis,* that medieval society, frequently ignoring the worth of the individual as such,
often recognized his merit only in virtue of the office
he held or the work he did—hence, the significance of
costume as a badge of distinction.

One is, therefore, going to have to revise such
sweeping assertions as Dorothy Sayers, along with

other neo-medievalists, indulged in when she said of
Western painting that attention is seen to be focused
successively upon the: (a) pre-humanist period: the
body as symbol and vehicle of spirit (about fifteen
centuries) : (b) post-humanist period: (1) bodies in
themselves; (2) bodies as emotive stimuli . . .[24] A
little historical revision is necessary here because,
while medieval theology did recognize the sacredness
of the body, just as medieval philosophy may be said
to have recognized the sacredness of the person, this
recognition affected only slightly the practical order.
And in a discussion on art, we are not talking about
theological and philosophical dicta, but about historical realities, about concrete cultural manifestations.
For this reason we cannot confine ourselves merely to
Scholastic principles. In painting and sculpture, one
might suggest that, when the shrouding of the human
figure did not come about through ecclesiastical pressures or social puritanism or esthetic requirements,
it resulted from so mundane a matter as the simple
need for identifying the subjects painted or sculptured. Miss Sayers tells us that to "the Christian centuries the flesh was holy"—and indeed it was, at least
in the theological manuals—and that this was the
reason for veiling its "awful majesty." That, is a
pious illation. One might further suggest, as a hy-
pothesis at least as explanatory as Miss Sayers', that
it was precisely in the unveiling of the body, in the
discovery of the nude form by the humanists that
one may find the flesh regarded as the "symbol and
vehicle of spirit." The nude figure, when not used
merely as design or pattern (as in Egyptian art), may

be said to represent man in his intrinsic dignity, man as a being of merit in his own right under God, and entirely apart from his status in society; it represents man as man, not man clothed as king, priest, knight, nun, or serf. It is no mere accident of history that the nude emerged in Aegean art, flourished in the Greek, and was reborn in the humanist era, and that whatever notions we have of democratic life we owe largely to these three periods. M. Maritain has said, "Democracy carries in a fragile vessel the terrestrial hope, I would say the biological hope of humanity."[25] There are those who have some reservation about democracy, but even they cannot doubt that it is based on some concept of the dignity of the person. It is, then, not mere historical accident that all totalitarianisms, whether sacred or secular, have interdicted the nude form. Just as democracy has led to abuses, so, too, the depiction of the nude body; but as the men of the Middle Ages would remind us, *abusus non tollit usum*.

Furthermore, in the development of a program for the schools in "Christian culture," one is going to have to take into account the popular culture reflected in the Goliardic songs, and in the vulgar literature surveyed, among others, by Curtius in his *European Literature and the Latin Middle Ages*. One will also have to take note of the aberrations that flourished in a good part of the era of "Christian culture," and which are exemplified in the paintings and sculptured works on the "Dance of Death" theme, in the flagellant mobs, in the ecclesiastical frauds and forgeries, in the Inquisition, in the burning of heretics. If one looks out of the West for this "Christian culture," one may examine Byzantium, and meet what Soloviev excoriated as a non-Christian culture, in *Russia and the Universal Church*. And if one looks to the period before the fifth century, one will find a considerable expansion of what can be called theological culture, but less that can be called "Christian culture," in the sense of an intellectual and social order that reflected the Christian spirit in its politics, its literature, and its art.

If one is going to point out the relevance of medieval thought to contemporary political practice, one will have to observe with Ewart Lewis that "the idea that some sort of claim to freedom was inherent in human nature flickered through medieval theory, but it remained ambiguous and undeveloped." One is going to have to recognize with E. M. Sait in *Political Institutions* that the democratic character of the Dominican priories was less influential on political thought than the progress of the communes. And one will probably conclude that, among the common people, real estate development, not philosophical principles nor ecclesiastical guidance, engendered the longing for freedom.[26]

I do not mention all these authors in support of a thesis of my own making; the thesis flows from the facts which they have disclosed. And in almost every case, these are authors who are Catholic or who are sympathetic to the cultural achievement which has often attended a vital Catholicism. It would have been easier to cite Karl Vossler or Coulton, but one would have then had to disengage the fact from the bias.[27] The thesis which the facts give birth to, is that there often was a fissure, a separation between the lofty and admirable *credenda* of theology and the *agenda* of temporal affairs. One may call it what he will: a separation of theory and practice, of the sacred and the profane, of the objective and the subjective, of the system and the element, of the community and the person; but it is a separation that must be acknowledged, and that leads one to wonder whether the term "Christian culture" is the best description for historical phenomena which are composed of so many non-Christian forces.

When Catholics talk and write about Renaissance culture, they do not hesitate to treat of its defects, of its disordered tendencies. When Catholics talk and write about contemporary culture, they often devote more attention and more effort to lamenting its sins than praising its virtues. But when Catholics talk and write about Western culture from the period of the introduction of Christianity to that of the discovery of America, they generally treat of the great achievement of bringing order out of barbarian chaos, of the rise of the cathedral schools and the universities, of Scholasticism—and these should certainly be emphasized. If that were all that had to be emphasized, one might well describe such a culture as "Christian"; unfortunately, it is not all. Acton has written of a certain historical school, the heirs of which are still active in the twentieth century:

The mission of that school was to make distant times, and especially the Middle Ages, then most distant of all, intelligible and acceptable to a society issuing from the eighteenth century. There were difficulties in the way; and among others this, that, in the first fervour of the Crusades, the men who took the Cross, after receiving communion, heartily devoted the day to the extermination of Jews. To judge them by a fixed standard, to call them sacrilegious fanatics or furious hypocrites, was to yield a gratuitous victory to Voltaire. It became a rule of policy to praise the spirit when you could not defend the deed.[28]

Strachey called Acton, "that almost hysterical reviler of priestcraft and persecution"; [29] yet Acton represented moral law, while Strachey stood for the ethic of Bloomsbury; Acton wrote history, while Strachey wrote caricature. Does anyone believe that evil can be too much reviled? We are told to remember Dachau and Buchenwald as the fruits of modern secularized culture; and so we should. But we ought not to forget the extermination of the Albigenses, the persecutions of the Jews, and the Crusades. I am not ignoring the anti-social character of the Catharist sects, anymore than a Roman historian would have ignored what he thought to be the anti-social character of Christianity; I simply point out that these various persecutions were evil and were recognized as such by some theologians and philosophers. But this recognition by theologians as well as by the authorized interpreters of Christ's teaching, the bishops, often had little effect in the practical order.

If "Christian culture" were comprised in doctrinal definitions or even in the teachings of theologians, no one would object to the phrase Christian or Catholic culture; but a culture has to do with historical actualities, with political, social, and intellectual realities; accepting that truism, and accepting also the fissure, the dissociation, if you will, that existed between Christian teaching and the practice of Christians, one may doubt the appositeness of the phrase "Christian culture."

I am not, then, questioning Mr. Dawson's assertion that, "Medieval Christendom is the outstanding example in history of the application of Faith to life"; because if we are talking about Faith (upper case) and mean supernatural faith, then, I suppose, it is the only example. I merely question whether this period or any other period composed of such disparate forces can be termed a period of "Christian culture," and I would pose the question on the same grounds that I imagine a nineteenth-century student might question the attribution of the title "Catholic" or "Christian" Majesty to the kings of Spain or France; but whereas this attribution was only a kind of *sehnsucht*, "Christian culture," we are told, represents a fact, an existent.

In an article in *The Catholic World* (Dec., 1957) Sister Marie Corde McNichols, R.S.M., raised a similar objection to the use of this phrase "Christian culture." In a reply to this article, Mr. Dawson wrote:

. . . she is fundamentally opposed to the concept of Christian culture in itself and questions whether such a culture "ever has existed or could possibly exist." Yet for the last eighty years the teachings of the social encyclicals have been expressly concerned with this very issue. Again and again the Popes have insisted on the social mission of the Church as the inspirer and promoter of Christian culture and they have even pointed to the case of medieval Europe as an outstanding example of this creative process. "There was a time," wrote Leo XIII, "when states were governed by the principles of Gospel teaching. Then it was that the power and divine virtue of Christian wisdom had diffused itself throughout the laws, institutions and morals of the people permeating all ranks and relations of society." [30]

However, this is an historical question, and cannot be resolved by the teachings of authority. And without trying to compose any twentieth-century *sic et non,* I do not see why this, and the other encyclicals Mr. Dawson quotes from, may not be paired with the following statement by Pius XII:

But even the culture of the Middle Ages cannot be characterized as *the* Catholic culture. . . . The Catholic Church is not identified with any one culture: her essence forbids it. She is ready, however, to enter into relations with all cultures. She recognizes and leaves to subsist whatever in those cultures is not opposed to nature. To each, however, she brings in addition the truth and the grace of Jesus Christ.[31]

From this are we to assume that Catholic culture and Christian culture are different?

The interpretation to be put upon the papal texts, which Mr. Dawson has quoted, is that, as a desideratum, as an ideal to be striven after, "Christian culture" has a reality; it has the reality of a thesis. As a fact, as a concrete existent, it will be realized only when the teaching of Christ has penetrated completely the fabric of society, which would be, I submit, when all things are drawn under the headship of Christ, when the great "recapitulation" of St. Paul is completed, that is, on the eve of the Parousia. One may point out the great merits of cultural phenomena inspired by Christian doctrine, as Mr. Dawson has so sympathetically and so masterfully pointed them out in the second volume of his Gifford Lectures; [32] and one may point out, with Lord Acton, the aberrations in medieval society. But between these two worthy historical exercises one is stranded when he seeks to identify this society and this culture with Christian culture *qua* Christian culture.

Cardinal Newman addressed himself to this question of "Christian culture" in *The Idea of a University,* when he spoke of the duties of the Church toward literature. Now "literature," as Newman is using the word, does not mean merely *belles-lettres,* nor even simply the written records of a particular nation or period; "literature," in his context, meant all the expressions and manifestations of the human spirit. It meant, then, what we today would call "culture." Newman gave "literature" that wider meaning because he was seeking in this lecture to define the relation of the Church to the work of a university, that is, the relation of ecclesiastical authority to the two main divisions within a university, the faculty of science and the faculty of letters. And so he wrote:

Literature is to man in some sort what autobiography is to the individual; it is his Life and Remains. Moreover, he is this sentient, intelligent, creative, and operative being, quite independent of any extraordinary aid from Heaven, or any definite religious belief; and *as such,* as he is in himself, does literature represent him; it is the Life and Remains of the *natural* man, innocent or guilty. I do not mean to say that it is impossible in its very notion that Literature should be tinctured by a religious spirit; Hebrew Literature as far as it can be called Literature, certainly is simply theological, and has a character imprinted on it which is above nature; but I am speaking of what is to be expected without any extraordinary dispensation; and I say that, in matter of fact, as Science is the reflection of Nature, so is Literature also—the one, of Nature physical, the other, of Nature moral and social. Circumstances, such as locality, period, language, seem to make little or no difference in the character of Literature, as such; on the whole, all Literatures are one; they are the voices of the natural man.[33]

Now, substituting the word "culture" for the word "literature," it will be possible to determine Newman's attitude toward the notion of "Christian culture."

I wish this were all that had to be said to the disadvantage of Culture; but while Nature physical remains fixed in its laws, Nature moral and social has a will of its own, is self-governed, and never remains any long while in that state from which it started. Man will never continue in a mere state of innocence; he is sure to sin, and this whether he be heathen or Christian. Christianity has thrown gleams of light on him and his Culture; but as it has not converted him, but only certain choice specimens of him, so it has not changed the characters of his mind or of his history; his Culture is either what it was, or worse than what it was, in proportion as there has been abuse of knowledge granted and a rejection of truth. On the whole, then, I think it will be found, and ever found, as a matter of course, that Culture, as such, no matter of what nation, is the science or history, partly and at best of the natural man, partly of man in rebellion.

. . . I say, from the nature of the case, if Culture is to be made a study of human nature, you cannot have a Christian Culture. It is a contradiction in terms to attempt a sinless culture of sinful man. You may gather together something very great and high, something higher than any Culture ever was; and when you have done so, you will find that it is not Culture at all.

Such is man; put him aside, keep him before you; but, whatever you do, do not take him for what he is not, for something more divine and sacred, for man regenerate. Nay, beware of showing God's grace and its work at such disadvantage as to make the few whom it has thoroughly influenced compete in intellect with the vast multitude who either have it not, or use it ill.[34]

Mr. Dawson said in his correspondence in *The Catholic World* that "the concept Christian culture is far wider than that of the Middle Ages." The "concept" certainly is; it is as wide as one wishes to make it. One may define one's historical concepts to fit one's views, but the problem arises in aligning the conception with the historic fact. When Mr. Dawson talks about "Christian culture," he is not talking about an ideal "concept"; he is talking about a specific intellectual and social structure in a given historical setting. So precise is this specification that it is sometimes difficult to avoid the impression that what is called "Christian culture" is regarded as a kind of ponderable, tangible body of ideas, indeed, as a lump of knowledge. Mr. Dawson continued: "No Catholic would deny the defects of modern Western culture or its heavy responsibilities for the plight in which the world finds itself today. But this has nothing to do with Christian culture." One may not be bothered by the judgment, though it is difficult to realize why the defects of modern Western culture did not spring from the defects of "Christian culture," as the Renaissance sprang from the Middle Ages, and the *Aufklärung* from the Renaissance. Or is it possible that "Christian culture" begot no defects? If so, it will be impossible to attribute the notion "Christian culture" to any social organism which did not subscribe fully to Roman Catholicism, and such an attribution will leave one theoretically with little more than medieval Western European culture—if with that —to study, while equating Catholicism with that culture. But this is not what I am inquiring about. The quotation with its contrast between "modern Western culture" and "Christian culture" suggests that "Christian culture" *qua* culture is historically a thing of the past.

Mr. Dawson has said that the concept of Christian culture is "not only potentially and ideally, but actually and historically," far wider than the Middle Ages. However, as noted above, we are not talking about

Christian culture as an *ideal concept*, since historical data would then be irrelevant. When Mr. Dawson proposes a course of studies in "Christian culture," he is talking about that culture as an historical entity, not as a metaphysical schema. This Christian culture "has nothing to do" with modern Western culture, and is "far" wider than medieval culture. It is here that I find it difficult to avoid the impression that "Christian culture" is conceived as a kind of measurable lump of knowledge. To account for the fact that "Christian culture" is far wider than medieval culture, then "Christian culture" presumably embraces a number of elements and factors certainly not Roman Catholic in inspiration, but yet Christian in character. Mr. Dawson would perhaps not agree, but, in these terms, would not American culture qualify as "Christian culture"? I ask the question rather baldly, and I use American culture merely as one of many possible illustrations from what may be termed "modern Western culture." M. Maritain has written of the Founding Fathers of the American Republic:

. . . their philosophy of life and their political philosophy, their notion of Natural Law and of human rights, were permeated with concepts worked out by Christian reason and backed up by unshakable religious feeling.[35]

And he has written also of the "Christian meaning" of America's social and political existence. Is not, then, American culture as illustrative of Christian culture as, let us say, the culture of the Eastern Empire after Justinian?

I do not see how one can avoid this dilemma: if one is going to study the concept of "Christian culture" "ideally and potentially," then such a study is going to center on theological and philosophical data that do not depend in any way on historical contingencies; and this study, I might add, is now being pursued in Catholic colleges in courses in social and political philosophy. If one is going to study "Christian culture" "actually and historically," then one will be faced with an impossible problem of definition: what is the place of the Christian elements in the Renaissance, in the Enlightenment, in American culture? Are these aspects of "Christian culture"? What of the Christian elements in that "modern Western culture" which by definition "has nothing to do with Christian culture"? The only resolution for this dilemma would be to limit programs in "Christian culture" to the study of the direct social and intellectual radiation of Roman Catholicism. But this field is also now being covered in the curriculum; only it is not called "Course of Studies in Christian Culture": rather mundanely, it is called Church History.

The confusion in talking about "Christian culture" arises, first, out of applying the attribute *Christian* to any human undertaking not directly sanctioned by revealed truth or religious authority. It arises, second, out of an ambiguous use of the term *culture,* so that the word is used in the same expression as genus and as species: we simply cannot talk of "modern Western culture" and "Christian culture" and mean the same thing by the word "culture." The problem, then, is a semantic one.[36] One is free to use words as he pleases, and to define their meaning as seems most apt. There are those who have found sense in the expression "Christian science," and who have put this coinage into currency; and we all talk sensibly about the "*holy* Roman Empire"— such practice doesn't quite make us nominalists, but neither does it usually make for fruitful dialogue. One might then suggest that, instead of referring to "Programs in Christian Culture," we follow the example of the poet, and refer to "Programs for the Study of Christian Culture with Notes Toward the Definition of That Culture."

Turning now to the pedagogical issues involved in a "Christian Culture Program," it will be best to start again with an examination of Mr. Dawson's own statement in *Medieval Studies:* ". . . what is needed, it seems to me, is a comprehensive course of studies which would deal with Christian culture in the same integrative and objective way in which the humanist educators dealt with Classical culture." Excluding the semantic difficulties raised by the term "Christian culture," there is an educational question that must be raised. The assumption underlying the statement is that Classical culture has objectively less relevance to the man of our time than "Christian culture." This is a tenable assumption, for certainly any body of ideas and practices inspired by theological wisdom is more important and of greater value than any purely human construction. But in this issue, we are interested not in the intrinsic superiority of divinely guaranteed truths over fallible natural intellectual achievements; what is of interest here is the pedagogical advantage in a course of studies that would be centered upon "Christian culture." Since the humanist educators made Classical culture the basis of their education and, as Mr. Dawson observes, the principle of integration for it, then we are, in accord with these explicit notions, to take in the twentieth century "Christian culture" as this basis and this principle of integration. On theoretical grounds— since we have only four years for collegiate education —no one is opposed to graduate programs or specialized courses in what may loosely be called "Christian culture." But from Mr. Dawson's words, we may agree at the beginning, that he is suggesting we make "Christian culture" the foundation and the integrating element for college education as such.

The argument which follows will be drawn along the lines that, as grace presupposes nature, so, in a sense, the study of "Christian culture" presupposes the type of training and knowledge that the study of Classical culture provides. There is, I suggest, a parallel between the efforts of Mr. Dawson in favor of "Christian culture" and the efforts of medieval thinkers to subordinate the liberal arts to the new disciplines of Scholastic thought. I have already cited Newman's words on this topic (Chapter One, Section IV); one may cite also the frequent medieval disputations on the theme of the "victory of theology over the arts"; and finally there may be cited the example of John of Salisbury whom Mr. Dawson in his Gifford Lectures has called a "medieval humanist and a student of the classics." Yet even John of Salisbury, for all his efforts to maintain the place of the traditional arts in the university, and for all his classical lore, suffered from the same myopia that invariably afflicts those who exalt the sacred at the expense of the profane, and exalt grace at the expense of nature. Thus this "student of the classics," like Bernard of Chartres, and like Fulgentius, approached the ancient literature as an exercise in virtue.[37] John of Salisbury took Vergil as merely a moral teacher, and read the *Aeneid* as a parable of life, as an ethical work to be lived, not as an artifact to be contemplated. Fulgentius is even more interesting, since he saw in the *Georgics* and the *Eclogues* philosophical doctrines so profound as to be unfathomable. These are not just illustrations of the allegorizing and didactic bent of the medieval mind; they are, I think, permanent lessons to be learned from any subordination of those intellectual disciplines furnished by the classics to some vaguely pious higher vision. A critic may read the *Aeneid* in the light of his own Christian sensibility— as Theodor Haecker has shown—but this presumes that he *know* Vergil, that what he is reading *is* Vergil. It presumes, in a sense, that his classical training form the basis of his religious culture.

Did not the nineteenth-century educators seek to make science the integrating factor in the curriculum, to make science usurp the place of the classics, and did not this result in the type of utilitarian and formless education that Newman so vigorously opposed, and that we in the twentieth century are now suffering from? There is a close similarity in the texts to which I referred from the medieval writers and the following observation of Herbert Spencer: "That science necessarily underlies the fine arts, becomes manifest *a priori*. . . ." And like the Schoolmen subordinating Vergil to their peculiar ethical vision, Spencer subordinates Myron to his:

But sculptors unfamiliar with the theory of equilibrium, not uncommonly so represent this attitude, that the line of direction falls midway between the feet. Ignorance of the law of momentum leads to analogous blunders; as witness the admired Discobolus, which, as it is posed, must inevitably fall forward the moment the quoit is delivered.[38]

When the classics lose their place in an educational work, then quite often every authoritarian, omnicompetent, *soi-disant* higher wisdom or science has a field day—the results are evident above.

There are more direct historical grounds for doubting that "what is needed is a comprehensive course of studies which would deal with Christian culture in the same integrative and objective way in which the humanist educators dealt with Classical culture." And these grounds are provided by the history of the humanistic education in the Renaissance. For the humanists, Classical culture did not exist as an historical corpus of knowledge to be studied for the permanent value—in terms of literary and philosophical truths—it would have throughout one's life; it was not the knowledge itself that was so important as it was the disciplines required to secure this knowledge, and the direction in which it led. On this the humanists are quite clear.[39] Vives wrote:

Let it be firmly fixed in the boys' minds that what they are going to receive at school is the culture of the mind, i.e., of our better and immortal part; that this culture has been handed down from God to the human race, as the greatest gift of His fatherly indulgence, and that it could not have been given from any other source, and that assuredly this is the pursuit and way in following which, they may please God, and attain to Him in Whom is their highest happiness. In this way they will love such culture of the mind and recognize it as necessary for them, and reverence and adore it as sacred and sent down from heaven.

This then is the fruit of all studies; this is the goal. Having acquired our knowledge, we must turn it to usefulness, and employ it for the common good. Whence follow immortal reward not in money, not in present favour, or pleasure, which are fleeting and momentary.

Erasmus wrote:

For this, knowledge is inculcated: for this, philosophy; for this, eloquence: that we may know Christ, that we may praise His glory. This is the scope of eloquence and the sum of learning.

Vergerius wrote:

For the man who has surrendered himself absolutely to the attractions of letters or of speculative thought follows, perhaps, a self-regarding end and is useless as a citizen or as a prince.

I quote all these passages because they show that among the humanists, the study of the classics was regarded as a preparation for all higher studies including theology, and that it was regarded as providing the type of intellectual training necessary for any cultivation of the mind. We are told that, "to Erasmus the sincere study of Letters had for its end the deepening of man's hold upon realities." For Vives "scholarship is not the end of life; it is the glorious means whereby a man renders himself the most effective human agent in promoting the real ends of piety and the search for truth."

These are not the expressions of a base utilitarianism; they do not subserve any higher principle, though they recognize the existence of a higher principle and are in conformity with it. As such, the ideal of the humanist educators has been called "training for the Christian citizenship." [40] This ideal is pragmatic only in the sense that any intellectual culture is pragmatic, that any intellectual discipline pursued for its own sake will have consequences in the practical order. Humanist education, however, was not based on any *simpliste* theory of transfer of training or of formal discipline. The study of language was seen as a means to an end, and that end was classical literature; the study of classical literature was seen as a means to an end, and that end was the sharpening and refining of the powers of the intellect. Classical culture was studied in the humanist schools, not as a body of truths of pre-eminent value *per se,* but as a body of truths indispensable in the formation of the young mind. One cannot, then, ad-

vocate making "Christian culture" the integrative
principle in education without flying in the face of
the best Renaissance and the best contemporary
practice. This practice is important because it is not
based on the judgment of a few "professional classicists"—to the pedagogical tradition a "professional
classicist" would be as much an anomaly as a "professional saint" would be to the theological tradition
—but on what Newman has called the "instinct of
civilization and the common sense of society."

The simple question to be considered is, how best to
strengthen, refine, and enrich the intellectual powers; the
perusal of the poets, historians, and philosophers of
Greece and Rome will accomplish this purpose, as long
experience has shown; but that study of the experimental
sciences will do the like, is proved to us as yet by no experience whatever.[41]

What Newman says about the study of experimental
science may be applied as well to the study of "Christian culture."

What is needed, then, is not a program in "Christian culture" to replace the dying classics, but a new
renaissance of Classical culture itself. The classics
were wounded by the very theory that attempted to
revive them: the theory that the study of language
provided a "formal discipline" similar to that allegedly rendered by mathematics. But this was not a
theory supported by the Renaissance humanists. Erasmus wrote: "Language, indeed, is not an end in itself . . ."; Bruni d'Arezzo wrote: "Proficiency in lit-

erary form, not accompanied by broad acquaintance with facts and truths, is a barren attainment." [42] Given the obvious truisms that parsing Vergil is not the way to grow in appreciation of the poet, and that purely grammatical studies oriented toward themselves have little value for general education; and given the fact underlined above that the classics *do* provide the best instruments for shaping the young mind—given these truisms and this fact, it may be suggested that what is needed in American Catholic education is a comprehensive program of studies in the classics read in translation. Beyond a limited knowledge of the languages themselves—a knowledge which is necessary—a program of this nature could improve upon the goals attained by Renaissance humanist education.[43] The precise form such a course of studies should take is a topic for discussion; but that it ought to be broader than what is customarily embraced by surveys of "world literature," and that it ought to cut across departmental lines so that the works may be examined in their historical settings: these do not seem to me topics for debate. They are necessities dictated by the nature of education itself. Such a program might well be based on the profound observations of an eminent philosopher:

Classics can only be defended on the ground that within that period, and sharing that period with other subjects, it can produce a necessary enrichment of intellectual character more quickly than any alternative discipline directed to the same object. In classics we endeavor by a thorough study of language to develop the mind in the regions of logic, philosophy, history, and of aesthetic apprehension of literary beauty. The learning of the languages—Latin or Greek—is a subsidiary means for the furtherance of this ulterior object.[44]

IV

It has been suggested in the preceding two sections that pedagogical schemata founded on an exclusively Scholastic or medieval world-view often suffer from a kind of "dissociation of sensibility." Now, there are within the Scholastic system itself, and particularly in the notion of connatural knowledge, the principles for rectifying this dissociation; but it is a fact that this rectification had never been systematically undertaken until the present historical period, and that it has been undertaken now only at the instigation of alien philosophical schools. As a result it has not yet affected the educational order.

On the other hand, there is a large body of thought that illumines the mystery of man, the mystery of the world, and the twofold mystery of man's relation to that world, which does not yet seem to have been discovered by many educators; and all these facets of "the mysterious universe" have been explored within the Catholic tradition, certainly by the Schoolmen, but just as certainly, and often in greater detail, by the Fathers, by the Renaissance humanists, by Pascal, by Newman and Scheeben, by von Hügel, Blondel, and Marcel.

That we are presented with two sides of the same coin in this pedagogical antithesis of essentialist and existentialist is evident, as it is equally evident that if we are preoccupied with one side to the exclusion of the other, we will have only a counterfeit education. And if I have emphasized, in the preceding sections, those themes which may be called existentialist—in the large sense of that abused word—this emphasis is not the result of disdain for complementary assumptions, but simply because such themes have been so long overlooked in American Catholic education. For, just as what I have said above, concerning the synoptic, personalized reflection of the existential method, may occasionally degenerate, in the actual work of teaching, to a barrage of emotionally overloaded, intellectually barren, verbiage, so, too, the essentialist method often succumbs—as history testifies it did in the late Middle Ages—to what has been accurately described as "gerund grinding" and "logic chopping." And in the same manner, an exorbitant concentration on the existentialist approaches to learning may result in the sacrifice of "truth" to "poetry," whereas an exaggerated stress on essentialist notions may result in an oversimplification that strips away mystery and, by that fact, also distorts truth.

One may be optimistic about the gradual unifying of these two views, for such a work of unification is everywhere being attempted in all areas of knowledge. In philosophy it is seen in the *rapprochement* which has been effected by Marcel, Blondel, and by Maritain between various personalist themes and the traditional metaphysics of the School; in theology it is apparent in the reaffirmation of the place of the

Fathers in the continuum of Christian thought, and in the emphasis on a liturgical theology ordained to worship and to the *kerygma*; in science one recognizes this unification in von Weizsäcker's plea for a spirit of contemplative wonder and awe even in the study of physics, and in the poetic, religio-scientific synthesis of Teilhard de Chardin; in literature it is apparent in the reassessment of Milton—lately supported by Mr. Eliot himself—whose diffusiveness finds its stylistic analogues in Kierkegaard, and in the recognition that the "metaphysicals" achieved a style, abstract and objective, which is basically essentialist; in the representative arts this unification is apparent in the resolution of the architectural dichotomy of function and decoration, and in the growing realization that the great painters of our time are not all loyal imitators of Cézanne's abstract and essentialist style, but are also those accomplished masters, like Chagall, who have blended essentialist concern for linear form and design with the existentialist interest in lyricism and poetic values.

These illustrations are not intended to be either exhaustive or definitive; they are merely an adumbration of what is, I believe, an undeviating tendency of modern thought.[45] In the educational order, too, it is not a question of an either/or foundation, of one exclusively Thomist or Augustinian, exclusively medieval or modern; it is a question rather of developing that long overdue synthesis which, rooted in the classics, will draw for its content as well as for its methodology upon all aspects of the Christian intellectual tradition.

I have discussed the unique position of the Catholic educator with regard to the continuum of Western intellectual life, when he accepts this continuum in its totality. From Biblical insights, from Patristic wisdom, from the medieval achievement, from Renaissance humanism, from the origin of humane *Aufklärung* themes in Victorio, Bellarmine, and Las Casas, from the rebirth of the spirit of interiority in de Lamennais and Newman—from all intellectual history the Christian may rightly draw for his educational enterprise; and this enterprise, based on the classical disciplines, will inevitably be successful. Moreover, the Christian educator may rely on this intellectual heritage with the assurance and the conviction that it is his rightful patrimony—and to a large extent, his alone.

On the contrary, the educator who does not adhere to the Christian tradition may pick and choose among these various elements that constitute it, or may from the superior vantage point of an agnostic relativism, examine them all without committing himself to any; yet he must do so, in a very real sense, as an intruder among the household goods of the Catholic. Nor can such an educator, on practical grounds alone, embrace these elements as his own intellectual property, for they have been translated through the ages by the medium of a religious attitude and a religious organism which he rejects; and on theoretical grounds, his purely academic engagement with this tradition can never possess the spiritual and moral force of that Christian commitment to it which has been expressed in Justin the Philosopher's declaration that "the truths which men in all lands have truly spoken belong to us Christians," or which has been summarized in Tertullian's statement, "Caesar belongs to us Christians more than to you, because he has been appointed by our God."

But in an even deeper sense, one may say that the mission of the Catholic educator is unique. For—again, as the Fathers say [46]—"the Christian is to the world what the soul is to the body," and it is to the nature of this unique, animating, and informing work that I now turn.

THE MISSION OF
CATHOLIC SCHOLARSHIP

THERE HAS APPEARED, WITHIN THE PAST FEW YEARS, a number of studies on Catholic higher education, marked in general by a legitimately critical spirit and by a sincere desire to contribute to the improvement of Catholic scholarship and Catholic learning. Some of these studies, however, often leave one with the impression that the same criteria that determine judgments on non-Catholic educators and on non-Catholic colleges have been applied to our own teachers and to our own schools. There is something to be said in defense of this application—as I have noted in Chapter One—so long as it does not lead one to equate the work of the Catholic school with that of its secular counterparts. Yet it seems that some educators have become so accustomed to denominational

232

colleges of all possible confessions that unknowingly they often assume that each sect ought to support schools of its own persuasion merely in order to safeguard the religious formation of its youth. The limitations in this view, which is frequently seen as one of those indefinitely multiplying ramifications of the "American Way," are patent when related to the Catholic college or university which exists, not primarily as a moral preservative, but as an instrument for the deeper comprehension and transmission of truth—a comprehension and transmission that can be achieved in their fullness *only* by the Catholic scholar.

It is necessary to add here that the Catholic secondary school, as I see it, has not an intellectual, but a moral mission. Given the tensions of adolescence and the confusions of puberty, so indiscriminately anatomized in our popular literature, and so well analyzed by Joyce and Gill, and so well depicted by such artists as Munch and Hodler, it seems justifiable to maintain that the purpose of the high school is not immediately enlightenment of the reason, for the young mind can only be blinded by being exposed prematurely to the radiance of truth, but ethical direction, religious discipline, and affective and emotional guidance; all of these will lead ultimately to that contemplation of truth and beauty which can be successfully undertaken only when the passions, as Aristotle said, have been brought under the political direction of the will.

It would be tragic for the secondary schoolteacher to repeat the pathetic experiment of Baron Friedrich von Hügel who, as a religious philosopher, is without peer in the twentieth century, but who, as a pedagogue, was sadly deficient, at least as evidenced by his attempt to introduce his immature daughter to religious and historical truths that her tender emotional condition could not support. Her consequent spiritual collapse offers a melancholy reminder of the dangers of entering upon the intellectual engagement before the completion of a long and serious moral novitiate.[1] During the course of such a "novitiate," the development of the reason will not be neglected, but the accent will be on moral culture, on the training of instinctual and emotional drives; for, in the high school, we are, in a certain sense, at what Whitehead called the second level of education: the plane of discipline.

Of course, such a cultivation of the moral powers will entail an intellectual effort, but this effort will not have as its immediate end—from the viewpoint of the teacher—the contemplation of truth for itself; rather it will be concerned—again, from the instructor's point of view—with the effect of this contemplative act on the moral improvement of the student. In accord with Dietrich von Hildebrand's profound analysis of the development of personality it must be emphasized that the end the teacher has in view differs from that of the student; for the latter, in marveling at truth, goodness, or beauty, should not be intent on self-improvement, but simply on the spiritual delight of such contemplative activity. Only then will his contemplation have a truly formative effect on his whole personality.

But while the proper end of the secondary school is the formation of character through the contemplative act, the proper end of the Catholic university is the contemplation of truth for its own sake. From Gerbert's defense of philosophy as its own end, in the tenth century, to Maritain's *Education at the Crossroads,* our educational tradition has envisioned the university as primarily, and essentially, intellectual. However, to say this is not to say enough, for we are speaking here of the *Catholic* university—and in this case the adjective, far from being the enemy of the noun, is rather its necessary complement. For this intellectual function of the Catholic university is fulfilled by a "new man" who has been, as St. Paul says, renewed in the spirit of his mind. This means that, other things being equal, the Catholic scholar, the consecrated intelligence in act, should, if he is aware of the presence of the Holy Spirit and His gifts, see more deeply, more truly, and more broadly than his non-Catholic colleague. And this superior vision will arise, not only from a knowledge of the Christian fact and its theological corollaries, but also from an interior consecration of the intelligence.

The first insight to be examined, in attempting to understand the nature of this "consecration," is derived from the doctrine of the character in the sacraments. This doctrine, which played so great a part in the sacramental theology of earlier ages, has been obscured in the writings of many theologians of the counter-Reformation period and of the nineteenth century. And so, anyone studying the nature of the character in such writings (e.g., the *Theologia Wirce-burgensis*, which was intended as a complete *cursus theologicus*) will come away from them with a great deal of information useful in apologetics, but with very little knowledge clarifying the structure and function of the sacramental seal in the life of the Christian. Apologetics is a useful weapon in battle; but when apologetics assumes the mission of theological science as such, so that more concern is shown with defending the Faith against the onslaughts of those outside the Church than is shown for elucidating it to those within, one may say in all justice that theologians have contributed in their own way and in accord with their own lights and duties to a temporary suspension of one of the secondary functions of the *Ecclesia docens*. The faithful seeking the bread of doctrine are handed the stone of apologetics, and no matter how valuable this latter may be in assaulting the strongholds of heresy, it is not very nourishing to a hungry soul. "Christ feeds the hunger of our intellectual starvation," wrote Niceta of Remesiana.[2]

Now that the necessarily defensive work of the counter-Reformation has been completed, theology can turn itself from manning the ramparts to the task of nourishing the citizens of the Christian City. And in the execution of this task one of the most fruitful teachings is undoubtedly that of St. Thomas on the sacramental character.

The character which was for St. Paul a mark of designation, branding the Christian as the property of Christ, that character which was for the Fathers the seal of God's indissoluble marriage with the soul, so that baptism, confirmation, and orders could be received but once: this character is recognized by St. Thomas as the mark which configures us to Christ as priest (S.T. III, 63, 3, ad 2). The Angelic Doctor, with some of the Fathers, saw in the anointing with holy chrism in confirmation, not merely a symbol of the strengthening of the soul for the battles against Satan, but a kind of priestly and royal ordination along the lines of the Catholic epistle: "But you are a chosen race, a royal priesthood, a holy nation" (I Peter 2:9). For St. Thomas, holy orders gives a power to confer and administer the sacraments; baptism gives a power to receive the other sacraments; while confirmation strengthens the Christian to receive the sacraments fittingly and to profess Christ publicly. And since the sacramental character configures the Christian to Christ as priest, and since the priesthood of Christ includes his offices as king and prophet as well, it may be said that the character configures the Christian to the whole Christ, to Christ as priest, prophet, and king.

With the Fathers, one may then regard baptism as making the Christian the subject of Christ the king; confirmation, in turn, allows Christians to share in the prophetic, teaching mission of Christ by making them *ex officio* witnesses to Christ who is truth; and holy orders give a power to teach and to govern the Christian people, to share, that is, directly and in a higher way in the priesthood of Christ; hence, the bishop who has the fullness of holy orders is by office the chief priest of his church, its chief teacher, and its chief ruler. Furthermore, the theologians maintain that each of the three characters is distinct, though each is related to the other; so that just as confirmation increases one's role in the Church and therefore is of greater dignity than baptism, so, too, orders confers a greater dignity and a greater responsibility on its recipients. This interrelation has been briefly summarized by Bellarmine:

To agents pertain the sacrament of orders, because by it a man receives power to confer and administer the sacraments. Baptism pertains to receivers, because by it the power validly to receive the other sacraments is conferred. . . . Confirmation pertains to agents and receivers, because by it is conferred the power fittingly to receive other sacraments and to defend actively the faith of Christ, *ex officio,* as a soldier.[3]

It is to the active role conferred by confirmation that we now turn. The testimonial of his faith that the Christian makes in virtue of confirmation is a public profession, for confirmation, as St. Thomas says, concerns not primarily the private good of the individual, as does baptism, but rather the good of the whole Church; it is in a very real sense a "social" sacrament (*S.T.* III, 72, 5c). This profession by the confirmed Christian has traditionally been described in terms drawn from military life. Now such an image is both comprehensive and precise in its application to the members of that Church which is properly called "militant," and whose sanctification depends on victory over the forces of evil in the world and over Satan himself. But the witnessing to Christian truth, to which one is committed by his character as a confirmed, is primarily a social work; and since the struggle with the powers of darkness is largely a personal and interior battle—though not for that reason without its profound social effects on the body of Christ—it cannot be fully described in the strict sense as entailing a "public profession." The field of battle, then, for which confirmation strengthens one is more accurately defined in terms of the world itself.

Here one faces the fundamental paradox in Christianity, and its unique structure as an incarnational faith, which distinguishes the teachings of Christ as set apart from those of the Old Law. The Christian cult does not repudiate the world, as did all ancient spiritual religions, for the Christian recognizes this world as the work of God—"And God saw that it was good" (Genesis 1:31). And he realizes that "God does not regret his gifts" (Romans 11:29). The Christian does not reject the world, for Christ said, "I pray not that you take them out of the world, but that you keep them from evil" (John 17:15). The Christian does not fear the world, for Christ said, "Fear not, I have overcome the world" (John 16:33). Yet even though he knows that the world was created good, and that it has been even more marvelously restored by Christ's redemptive work, he does not immerse himself in it by his own activity, for he recognizes not only the truth in the above teachings of our Lord, but also the significance of the injunction, "Love not the world, nor the things of the world." [4] And finally, the Christian accepts the truth that Christ by His passion and resurrection has conquered the prince of this world, that "when life and death fought a duel," Life conquered. But this conquest, this struggle, must be continued and extended by the individual Christian, who as a member of Christ makes up "that which was lacking to the passion" of his Saviour. He fulfills this mission of completing the work of Christ, through the power of Christ, by embracing in his personal life the cross, which was the instrument of conquering Satan, and in his social and public life, by continuing to struggle against the prince of this world.

But since the Christian is configured by baptism and confirmation to Christ the priest, to Christ who has overcome the world and so has wrested it from Satan's domination, he now views the world not primarily—as the non-Christian must regard it—as an alien land to be conquered, but he sees it as Christ sees it: as part of God's primeval patrimony which must be returned to its original Overlord, to the creating and redeeming Father. Without forgetting that Satan is the prince of this world, the Christian knows that he is a defeated prince—though a prince who has not yet "unconditionally surrendered"—and that, as a result, Satan's conquered kingdom, even though it has not yet submitted entirely to the *pax Christiana*, may be viewed by the soldier of Christ as no longer enemy territory, but as a province of his own captain, his own chief, his own head: Christ.[5] The soldier of Christ must continue this victorious conquest under the leadership of Christ, for the prince of darkness has yet some power in his rebellious kingdom, in the kingdom of night. But led by the Prince of Light, the soldiers of light, who have been enrolled in the army of light by that illumination which is baptism, no longer think of the world as the kingdom of night, for, as the Fathers say: "The sons of light look upon the night as day." [6] And in this we find some resolution of the Christian paradox: rather than envisioning his task as simply that of battling the world and struggling against the natural structure of things in the world, the confirmed Christian accepts this structure as the original stamp of ownership with which God has marked his property: "Since the creation of the world, his invisible perfections, his eternal power and divinity, have been made visible to the intelligence, in his works" (Romans 1:20). By fidelity to this structure, the Christian reasserts God's original claim over the world; he restores it to that Christ to whom all things belong, and in whom and by whom they belong to the Father. This is the only resolution of the tension, which has been alluded to throughout this work, between the "this-world" and the "other-world" poles of Christian life.

A comprehensive metaphor to explain the Christian's relation to the world might be drawn from the history of the late Roman Empire. Rome had ruled over the civilized world and had imposed the *pax Romana* on it; after the barbarian invasions, it was taken from its Roman masters and subjected to the rule of the various tribes from the East (the Fall); but not even two hundred years of Vandal and Gothic rule could erase the vestiges of Roman culture from North Africa and Italy (as the millennia of Satan's rule could not destroy God's activity in the world); when Justinian sent his general, Belesarius, to Africa and Italy, the Vandal and Gothic leaders were decisively overcome in battle (Redemption), and the emperor once again ruled over those lands. There was then set in motion the vast organization of governors, tax collectors, judges, and legates who completed the work of Belesarius and carried out in the name of the emperor the implementing of the *pax Romana;* these officials had as their task, not pillage and destruction, but restoration; for although these lands were in one sense enemy territory, yet by prior claim they were the rightful domain of the empire. (Such is the mission of the Christian in the present moment of history: to restore the world to its original ownership.) Finally, after a period of a few years, during which the natives of Italy and Africa would have proved themselves worthy of Roman citizenship, and the various imperial administrators would have completed their work of restoration, the ancient privileges of Italy and Africa were renewed; the natives were no longer provincials, but received their full rights as citizens of the empire (Parousia). (We are those "administrators," "each of us working according to the activity which is proper to us," "who have received the seal for the day of redemption," "who play the role of ambassadors" of our Emperor, who "open the eyes of the pagans in order that they may pass from shadows to light, from the power of Satan to that of God.") [7]

Two conclusions directly relevant to the intellectual life of the Christian "ambassador" may be drawn from the above metaphor: first, the Christian recognizes in creation its longing to "share in the glorious liberty of the children of God"; and so he comports himself with reverence in the face of the legitimate tendencies of modern culture, seeing in them their hidden "vocation" to the supernatural. Second, the Christian, in his work of "recapitulating all things in Christ," speaks "the language of truth and of reason," that is, he employs all his natural gifts and talents in the service of his Lord.[8]

While acknowledging the accuracy of the military image to describe the work of the confirmed Christian, I think it is evident that this figure does not exclude other conceptions of the Christian's relation to the world. Moreover, an exaggeration of this image may sometimes engender an attitude of enmity toward the world, toward the natural structure of things, so that the mission of the Christian is not seen as that of sanctifying the legitimate aspirations of human life and thought, but of contradicting them. Two other errors derive from an overemphasis on the military role of the confirmed. First, on a level which can only be called *simpliste*, the militant Christian may be led to assume an air of pugnacity, a kind of chip-on-the-shoulder spirit, when faced with non-Catholic or Protestant achievements; and the Christian effort becomes merely a defensive undertaking, a kind of holding action; and on the same plane, this defensive work may often be defined in terms of a physical struggle. Thus one may read in a comprehensive and even sophisticated theological work that

. . . the pontifical zouaves who struggled to defend the papal states, at the time of their invasion by Piedmont,

have fulfilled magnificently their obligation as confirmed. . . . And the heads of government who remained
passive at the time of this invasion have betrayed their
character.[9]

The second misconception to which the military
image sometimes gives rise is that the office of the confirmed Christian is generally assumed to be, in the
intellectual sphere, that simply of an apologist or
polemicist. The laity may, as Newman remarked,
"most gracefully" fulfill this important role; but that
does not mean this is the only intellectual apostolate
open to the layman—as I will show in Section III
below.

Moreover, because of the factious spirit that disputation and polemic often breed, it will be necessary
for the layman who does undertake any apologetic
to have a knowledge of doctrine which is much
broader than that of the "official catechisms." [10]
Without a solid foundation in dogma, the lay apologist tends to accept this or that religious assumption,
not on the sound basis of theological insight, but on
the grounds of prejudice, expedience, or emotion.
It was the extreme and partisan views of William
George Ward (whose theological culture, though brilliant, was narrow) and of Louis Veuillot (who was,
compared to Ward, merely a religious journalist) that
led Archbishop Ullathorne at the time of the Vatican
Council to talk about forcing lay theologians to "follow, rather than to lead" in doctrinal discussions.[11]
The layman, as Newman suggests, might well take
the philosophy of religion as his special field, but this

study, as is apparent in von Hügel or in Wilfrid Ward, entails a profound knowledge of theology. As another layman, whose work is not without its religious significance, has said:

. . . we are not considering what will suit an untutored savage or an illiterate peasant woman who would never come to an end of the *Imitation* or the *Serious Call*. Her religion may be enough for heaven, without other study. Not so with a man living in the world, in constant friction with adversaries, in constant contemplation of religious changes, sensible of the power which is exerted by strange doctrines over minds more perfect, characters that are stronger, lives that are purer than his own. He is bound to know the reason why. First, because, if he does not, his faith runs a risk of sudden ruin. Secondly, for a reason which I cannot explain without saying what you may think bad psychology or bad dogma—I think that faith implies sincerity, that it is a gift that does not dwell in dishonest minds. To be sincere a man must battle with the causes of error that beset every mind. He must pour constant streams of electric light into the deep recesses where prejudice dwells, and passion, hasty judgments and wilful blindness deem themselves unseen.[12]

I

If, as St. Thomas says, in a beautiful parallel, the character consecrates the created trinity of spirit, intellect, and will to the uncreated Trinity of Father, Son, and Holy Ghost (*S.T.* III, 63, 1c), then one may define this consecration as embracing something more than is immediately apparent in the image of a mili-

tary commission. The reason for such wider definition is not that the Church militant will pass away
while the character will perdure, but simply that an
army does more than wage war, that soldiers do more
than combat. For, just as it may be said that in modern warfare there are many who do not engage directly in battle, but are devoted to the equally
important strategic or provisioning works and who,
at the termination of the war, are obliged to carry
out the civilizing mission of their ruler, so, too, in
the warfare and in the restorative task of the Church,
the field of the confirmed Christian is not to be confined to a purely apologetic or defensive profession of
faith.

The military figure is one which has been exploited by the whole of the Christian tradition, even
to the present day when Catholic Actionists receive
the title "militants"; hence, it is an image which cannot be regarded as merely an empty metaphoric expression, proper to but one past age of the Church.
This figure, as the Carmelites of Salamanca showed
by their many comparisons of confirmed Christians
to the soldiers of the Catholic King, draws its significance from its relation to the royal office of Christ;
and this royal office, in turn, derives from Christ's
mission as high priest. But certainly a king does more
than wage war; he governs; he directs; he judges;
and he even teaches his people. And it is under this
last heading that the kingly office touches upon the
prophetic office, and concomitantly touches upon the
character of confirmation as related to the intellectual life. For good reason does Billuart observe that

St. Thomas in his treatment of confirmation "does not say that the character is ordained to the divine worship, but to those things which pertain to the divine worship." Thus, while the sacrament of confirmation is ordained to the divine worship inasmuch as it strengthens one's capacities to share in the sacramental life of the Church, it is ordained "to those things which pertain to the divine worship," inasmuch as Christians are empowered by the character to bear witness publicly to Christ. And this they do not only in a negative and purely defensive way, but positively, first, by teaching—when so mandated by authority—the truths of Christianity, and, second, by allowing the radiance of Christianity to be made manifest in all their works.[13]

That confirmation is a "social" sacrament has led some to limit the scope of the layman's testimony to such immediately civic activities as projects concerned with economic, political, and industrial life. Without denying the great importance of these various undertakings, such a limitation, if made a matter of principle, would be a serious error; for teaching and research in all areas of human achievement have also their social consequences. Furthermore, since confirmation is the sacrament of adult Christianity, and since this adulthood is to be understood, not only with reference to the maturing of the Christian's spiritual life, but also in the sense that by confirmation the Body of Christ increases and grows to its full stature, then the character may be seen as directly related to what St. Paul calls the great "recapitulation in Christ," the cosmic restoration of all things in and under the captaincy of Christ. In this restoration, in this maturing of the Mystical Body, the Christian intellectual has a major role, for it is not merely social institutions which must be ordained to the service of the God-man, but the whole realm of human culture and human activity.

The relation of the character of confirmation to the intellectual life has been clarified in a short study by Msgr. Soubigou,[14] who has noted that the sacramental seal is engraved on the intelligence in order to confer on it a consecrated nature by which "it exercises its cultural activities in conjunction with those of Christ" (p. 27). Such a teaching may serve to explain why there have been those who have applied the following passage from St. Paul to literary men: "Some he has made apostles, others prophets, others evangelists, some pastors, some *teachers,* for the perfection of the Christians, for the task of building up the body of Christ" (Ephesians 4:11). The teachers here, according to some readings, are not the teachers of religious truth only, but teachers of humane arts and letters as well.[15] St. Paul, of course, is writing of the charisms which were evident in the early Church, but his words have a meaning to Christians of all ages, for the charisms are not gifts confined to one period in the history of Christianity. And since they are ordained to the manifestation of spiritual doctrine, as St. Thomas shows (*S.T.* III, 7, 7c), they too, like the character of confirmation, may be said to have a social significance. For this reason they have a definite bearing on the work of Catholic Action and on the apostolate *in all its forms.*

If one may see in the character of confirmation that which configures the Christian to Christ the high priest, and if one may see in all that Christ did a relation to his priestly office, may one not rightly conclude that all Christian activity is, in a real sense, consecrated to Christ? Such a conclusion is based on the premise that Christ, who became like to man in all save sin, entered into human works and human enterprises in order to sanctify them, to the end that whatever His members would do, they would do for Him. Thus, the Christian exercises his cultural apostolate not simply by a formal act of intention, nor specifically by the general economy of grace, but by being configured to Christ through the sacramental character. Grace is, of course, the first cause of meritorious works, but the sacramental character is the immediate principle whereby these works are achieved in conformity with the one High Priest. All the salutary actions of the Christian have been sanctified by Christ who, as St. Irenaeus said,

. . . came to save all through Himself; all, that is, who are reborn in God: babies and children, and boys and young people and adults. Thus He came through all ages, and became an infant for infants; a child for children, so sanctifying those of this age, and being for them also a model of filial love, of justice, and of docility; a youth for youths, setting an example for them, and so sanctifying them for God. So, too, He became an adult for adults that He might be a perfect master for them, not only through the preaching of doctrine, but also by having the same age.[16]

This is a teaching which bears upon all the undertakings of the Christian, and, hence, in the present context, it is particularly relevant to the intellectual life. This relevance is apparent when one recalls that Christ acquired knowledge, and, as the Gospel mentions in a number of places, marveled at the wonders in man and nature that He was contemplating. One notes, in passing, that the word used to express this act of wonderment is that word by which Plato described the beginning and the culmination of the contemplative act. It may then be said, with no irreverence, and in accord with Catholic doctrine on the communication of idiom, that in these various texts it is the Son of God who is spoken of as philosophizing. Similarly, since it is the Person of the Son of God and never His human nature alone that is referred to when the Gospel declares, "Jesus marveled," one may apply the text of St. Irenaeus above to this "wonderment" of Christ, and illustrate how all salutary philosophical efforts of the Christian are thus consecrated to the God-man. This is not, certainly, to suggest that the natural activities of the Christian are in and by themselves supernaturalized. First, it is to say with Cardinal de Bérulle:

We must consider the infinity which is communicated to these mysteries [the actions of Christ] by the infinite Person who performs them in His human nature. We must weigh, as it were, the perpetuity of these mysteries. They took place under circumstances in the past, yet they continue and are present and perpetual in a new manner. They are past in execution, but present by their virtue.[17]

Second, it is to say with St. John Eudes:

Thou, Christ, didst merit and acquire, by the power of thy holy actions, a special grace for all our acts, to enable us to perform them meritoriously. Hence we can and must do everything devoutly; otherwise we nullify and waste the graces thou hast acquired for us in the performance of similar actions.[18]

And, third, it is to assert that such activity ought not to be labeled "profane," if this term is understood as a pejorative, for it is an activity which was dignified by the God-man Himself, and which is carried on in the present time by Christians who are themselves configured to the one Priest and Prophet, and who are conscious of their mission as living temples of God. How can the work of the temple be characterized as simply profane?

It might be said in criticism that there is in what has been outlined above, concerning the cultural activity of the Christian, a confusion of the two orders of nature and supernature. This would be a serious charge were it well-founded; but that it is not well-founded can be shown by a brief summary. What has been maintained is that, given the sacramental obligation of witnessing to Christian truth, even in literary and scientific studies; and given the "special grace," of which St. John Eudes and St. Irenaeus have written, that enables the Christian to undertake even philosophical researches in conformity with Christ;

and finally, given the duty of asserting Christ's headship, and of recapitulating *all* in Him—then, given these spiritual principles, one may rightly affirm that such "profane" exercises are both sanctified and sanctifying when engaged in by the convinced Christian intellectual.

Throughout the above discussion, I have failed to emphasize the role of what is called the "right intention," not because this notion is of little importance, but because I have presumed as a first principle in any treatment of the intellectual life of Christians that these various cultural activities will be pursued by one who is fully conscious of his character as a redeemed man. The notion of the "right intention" is, then, absorbed and included in the total orientation of the Christian effort toward the final restoration of all things in Christ. While the formal renewal of this intention may be valuable on psychological grounds, it is not a necessity; [19] moreover, for the convinced Christian—and it is with such a Christian that this discussion has been concerned—this frequent renewal may have the unfortunate consequence of diverting the mind from complete absorption in the literary, scientific, or philosophical research being carried on, and, as a result, may unconsciously lead the scholar to minimize the importance of the work itself, and to justify its alleged unimportance and its presumed insignificance by some appliqué religious motive.

The Christian scholar must act toward reality as God acts in moving creatures toward His ends; that is, he must act in conformity with the nature of

things. Too great an emphasis on the "right intention," as a formal act, among Christians of a mature
spirituality tends to develop a moral climate in which
the work being done is seen as an inferior good to
which one can devote one's efforts only halfheartedly.
Research and teaching suffer, then, from a kind of
split standard, so that what is embraced with one
hand is spurned with the other.

This schizoid standard blinds one to the fact that
it is not to a man's intelligence alone, not to a man's
faculties alone, that we attribute his achievements.
We do not say that the intelligence of St. Thomas has
achieved a great theological study; we do not say that
the creative imagination of Dante has achieved a
great poetic work; for these faculties are the faculties
of somebody, and this "somebody" is a Christian person. And as Canon Masure has said when speaking of
the hypostatic union, "should not the person put his
mark upon his nature and somehow reveal himself
by means of it?" [20] Do we not then say, and rightly,
that it is this Christian man, St. Thomas, this Christian man, Dante, who has achieved this particular
work? And may we not say that these works reveal the
Christian character of their authors? This is surely
one sense of the prayer of the dawn Mass at Christmas:

Grant, we beseech Thee, O Lord, that we who have been
enlightened by the new light of the incarnation of the
Word, may reflect *in our works* that light which has been
kindled in our minds by Faith.

Furthermore, the vocation of the Christian scholar
is not primarily to a life of cloistered contemplation,

but to the life of research and teaching, to the life of "the contemplative in action"; and this research and teaching are not entered upon merely from the laudable motive of exploring reality, nor from the motive, often suggested to the Christian, of diverting the mind and recreating the faculties so that he may return refreshed to the life of prayer; nor, again, because one must muddle through, as best one can, this vale of tears; rather the contemplative in action, he whose vocation it is to be a witness to Christ in the full activity of the world, explores reality in humanistic and scientific research that he may configure these areas of knowledge to his own intelligence, and so configure them to Christ.

Thus the Christian scholar contributes in his way—"each one working according to the activity which is proper to him"—to the great recapitulation in which all things shall be restored under the "captaincy" of Christ. Such a restoration demands, not the external application of religious principles to the natural structure of things, but the organic penetration and comprehension of reality; it demands a genuine understanding of reality as it is in itself, for only by this means can it be truly configured to the intelligence, and thus configured to Christ. And this is not an easy task, nor one which can dispense with any effective instruments of scientific research. The prince of this world, as well as sloth, lethargy, and indifference, oppose this restoration of all things in Christ; but it is because this task is difficult and because it is dangerous that it requires the confirmed Christian for its fulfillment. And it is precisely because the

world has remained under the domination of the
power of darkness that only the confirmed soldier of
Christ, who has received that illumination which the
Fathers called baptism, is empowered to wrest the
universe and its elements from the prince of darkness,
and to assuage its anguished "groaning and travail-
ing," by returning it to Him who is named, not only
the Light of man, but the Light of the World.

II

When one applies to the university the preceding
sketch of the confirmed Christian scholar, of his teaching mission, and of his role as a student seeking to re-
capitulate all in Christ, it becomes evident that such
a university takes its authentically Catholic character
and significance, not merely from its recognition of
the limitations that theological science may impose
on the inferior sciences, nor merely from its acceptance of revealed doctrine, nor finally from its submission to the decrees of the Holy See, but rather
from a deeper and a broader comprehension of all
reality, whether natural or supernatural. Such a comprehension is aided, certainly, by the various truths
which theological science may enunciate, but it is
aided even more by that Christian ethos of the intellectual life in which the illuminating function of
Faith is manifest, not in a more precise natural knowledge, but in a kind of inner climate, in a deep, interior movement creating a totally new relation of
the subject to the object.[21] Thus, the Christian of
whom John of the Cross has written will certainly

engage in any intellectual work with an attitude differing from that of the non-Christian who sees in himself and in the world only material forces. John of the Cross declared:

For since God grants her [the soul] the favour of attaining to being deiform and united in the Most Holy Trinity, wherein she becomes God by participation, how is it a thing incredible that she should perform her work of understanding, knowledge and love in the Trinity, together with It, like the Trinity Itself, by a mode of participation, which God effects in the soul herself.[22]

It must be borne in mind throughout this discussion that the greater comprehension of reality, referred to above, does not imply that the Catholic *qua* Catholic has a knowledge broader than that of non-Catholic scholars in literary or scientific matters, or that the supernatural gifts engender an infused wisdom in the natural order. This would be an over-simplifying error, for one must not confuse the two orders, or so mingle them that the distinction between them, on the practical or on the theoretical plane, is denied or ignored. However, if it is important to maintain this distinction, it is equally important to maintain that the various natural and supernatural forces come into play, not in any isolated and empty abstraction, but in a particular human person. And this conjunction, this intersection, as it were, of two worlds, produces in this individual person, who is aware of his destiny, an intellectual demeanor, an intellectual comportment which differs from that of the man who has rejected or who has not consciously accepted the supernatural gifts. It has been a great misfortune that, in the necessary emphasis on what man achieves by nature and what he achieves through grace, there has been a consequent lack of stress on the moral and intellectual ethos in which the individual Christian lives and acts.[23]

The Christian may learn from revelation a number of truths otherwise inaccessible to him, and these truths will certainly have a bearing on the inferior arts and sciences. This is the fundamental principle on which Cardinal Newman defends the role of theology in a university, in his nine Dublin discourses; but although it is a sound principle, yet it is one which, to a great degree, could be embraced by non-Christians who, believing themselves to lack a balanced worldview, might well make use of the body of Catholic doctrine, and even of the decrees of the Holy See, as a kind of point of departure for their own teaching and research. Indeed, it seems probable that this is the practical attitude of a large number of educators who see in Catholic theology, and in the insights it provides, a system of thought to which they give only provisional assent, while directing this thought— sometimes with a vigor which should shame Catholics —toward their own ends. It is not, then, entirely inconceivable that one might have a university, staffed by such educators, which would fulfill almost all the requisites of Newman's definition, and yet in its tenor be largely non-Catholic.

Such educators are not to be condemned as hypocritical, for they are merely acting on the relativistic bias in the learned world as a whole; and while they may have hit upon Catholic theological science as the best theoretical foundation for their work merely from a pragmatic motive, yet in their own way they are witnesses to Christian truth. Moreover, as history has often shown, this interest in Catholic theology may be the medium through which they are introduced into the faith; and what Père Hugon has said of groups such as the Benedictines of Caldey may be applied, *mutatis mutandis*, to these educators:

As to souls of good will, Providence has certain means to enlighten them, and to lead them to the normal economy of the sacraments. . . . These persons had already received eminent graces, come directly from the Eternal Pontiff; but once the preliminary work is done, God introduces them into Catholicism, as if to make them realize that if the preparation can be completed out of the Church, the ultimate coronation must take place in the one true Church and by the sacraments.[24]

But the point to be stressed now is that, even if one acknowledges that a theologian without faith, like Bernanos' Cénabre, is no theologian at all, such an educational enterprise, though undertaken by non-Christians, could satisfy in its broad lines the ideal of a Catholic university which many educators now uphold.

But as I have been insisting throughout this section, there is another and a more important factor which marks a university as Catholic, and which distinguishes it from all other universities. This is what I have above called the Catholic ethos, or the Catholic intellectual demeanor. Here it is, I repeat, not a question of a Catholic *gnosis* that, in a mechanical or automatic fashion, would proffer more nearly adequate "answers" to the questions posed by developments in the arts and sciences; rather it is an attitude of mind, an intellectual comportment, which is derived, first, from the conscious realization of one's dignity as a confirmed witness to Christ who is truth; second, from one's personal awareness of his mission, as one configured to the Head of all creation, to be an agent in penetrating all reality, and thus to bring it under the "captaincy" of Christ; and, third, from a refusal, as M. Gilson has said of Augustinianism, "systematically to blind reason by closing one's eyes to what faith shows." [25]

This attitude of mind engenders a disposition toward the pursuit of truth which the non-Christian cannot display, and which finds expression in a number of what may be called "scholarly virtues." Of these "virtues," I will sketch only three. First, this attitude develops a sense of acceptance, of openness, with regard to what is *given* in the world of nature. The convinced Christian is the most detached of observers of real phenomena because he accepts things as they are. Recognizing in the universe a world which has a structure of its own, he is safeguarded against imposing his personal and private, artificial pattern upon it; and so he views the world as, one may say, God views it. For just as God moves creatures according to their natures, and even moves man, whose nature is to be free, without destroying freedom, so, too, the Christian scholar respects the intrinsic nature of things and does not seek to constrain or subvert that nature for his own purposes, even when they may appear laudable or religious.

Second, this intellectual demeanor engenders an attitude of reverence for the world of created things; and this is a reverence, not merely for their inner constitution, but for their materiality as such. This reverence will be evident in the work of all Christian intellectuals, as Teilhard de Chardin has shown in his essay, "Le Coeur de la Matière," but it may be best illustrated by the achievement of the Christian artist. The Christian artist, living in a sacramental society, will fashion his materials with a profound appreciation of their natural plastic values, and with a sense of their inner worth, that necessarily transcend the purely negative respect, and confute the open contempt for the medium, displayed by many non-Christian artists. The latter, through a kind of rational hypertrophy, often regard the material constituent as a debasing adjunct of the art work, and hence take refuge in such abortive experiments as the purist geometrism of Mondriaan, or the arid abstractionism of Morris. The Christian artist, opposed to all Manichean asceticism, may be said to prefer "more matter and less art"; and he makes this preference on grounds that are at once religious and esthetic. Informed by the spirit of Christian reverence, he will know by religious instinct how to preserve himself and his work against all Apollonian temptations.

Third, this intellectual comportment creates an attitude of sympathy for the legitimate undertakings of all scholars, Christian as well as non-Christian. The Catholic intellectual, striving within the community of the faithful toward one common goal, acquires a charitable sympathy for the efforts of his co-workers, and this sympathy destroys that bitter competitive passion which leads one in the pursuit of success to master only his narrow speciality and so to lose sight of the common body of liberal knowledge. This sympathy extends to non-Christian scholars because the Catholic knows them to be potential members of the Body of Christ, and because he knows their works to be potentially subject to the headship of Christ.

Now the two sources of Christian sympathy, which I have just mentioned, are derived from the Catholic's *knowledge* of theological truths; but without in any way ignoring the importance of such knowledge, I would like to confine myself in this discussion to the sources of this sympathy in what might be termed the "instinctive Christian consciousness." From the viewpoint of Christian experience, this sympathy may be related to the supernatural gift of knowledge. The effect of this gift on the Christian is, in brief, to show him how created things minister to his supernatural destiny. No broader definition is necessary here because other than the recognition of its presence, it is not with the nature, but with the consequences, of the gift that I am concerned. St. Thomas, following St. Augustine, associates the gift of knowledge with the beatitude, "Blessed are they that weep" (*S.T.* II^a-II^{ae}, 9, 2), on the grounds that this gift empowers one to see more deeply the traces of God in the universe,

and thus awakens in the Christian an anguished longing for union with Him.

The recognition [of these traces] of the presence of God
in creation, powerless to give Him to us, however much
they may reflect Him, comes from the gift of knowledge.
It makes us know God sufficiently to be attached to Him,
without revealing Him completely. This corresponds to
the first night of the soul.[26]

Now just as the gift of knowledge is analogous to
the natural intellectual virtue of knowledge, so too
are the tears of "[those] that weep" analogous to that
blind despair which has harrowed the minds of men
since the beginning of self-reflection, and which has
come to be recognized in our age as the very anguish
of existence. Who better than the Christian—the conscious subject of the gifts of the Holy Ghost—can sympathize with this suffering, as Cardinal Newman
sympathized with that *anima naturaliter Christiana*
who recognized "tears in things"? or as Newman's
great contemporary, Scheeben, recognized in these
tears a kind of hidden "vocation" to the supernatural?
Who better than the Christian can sympathize in our
day with those souls driven by this anguish to the
wall of despair or to the erection of monuments of
stoic pride? And finally, who better than the Christian can aid such souls, by appreciating the great
value in their works and the secret longing they reflect for some union with the absolute?

There are a number of other "scholarly virtues"
which the Catholic intellectual demeanor engenders,

and these have been discussed in Dietrich von Hilde-brand's masterful essay, "Catholicism and Unprejudiced Knowledge."

Returning now to the nature of a Catholic university, one may say, in the light of the preceding, that such a university has as mission: first, as Newman testified, to supplement and to rectify other sciences by truths of the theological order; second, as Scheeben has pointed out, "inasmuch as faith is concerned with rational truths . . . to guide reason in its domain, by showing it in what direction it must seek the truth"; [27] third, to bear witness to the radiant message of Christianity, not only in matters pertaining to the supernatural order, but also in the realm of the arts and sciences; fourth, to explore all reality in conformity with the spirit of Christ, who as man acquired knowledge; fifth, to enter into all salutary areas of human activity and human learning to draw them under the headship of Christ; and sixth, to constitute a community of research and teaching in which the best methods and techniques will serve scholars and students who are aware of their Christian dignity and who, being aware of it, regard all reality and the rightful creations of all men's minds with the uniquely Christian attitudes of reverence, objectivity, and sympathy. It is this organically interrelated structure of ideals and attitudes, along with the truths we learn from theological science, which it is the duty of the Catholic university and college to cultivate, to foster, and to teach.

All of this has been said so incisively and so profoundly by Dietrich von Hildebrand that I will close this Section with his observations:

The Catholic may never artificially divest himself, even in the use of his natural reason, of the attitude which the *lumen supranaturale* imparts to him; on the contrary, for the sake precisely of really unprejudiced, objective knowledge and genuinely scientific work, the Catholic cannot follow too much the guiding influence of Revelation in the formation of his fundamental attitude, cannot be too Catholic. Catholic universities are therefore necessary for the sake of truly adequate objective knowledge, not by any means merely for the protection of the religious convictions of the students. They are needed as the institutions where Catholic thinkers and men of science, supported by a truly Catholic environment, informed in their attitude by the spirit of Christ and of His Church, shall be enabled by a really unbiased, truly liberated and enlightened intelligence to penetrate adequately to reality and to achieve by organized teamwork that *universitas* which is nowadays so urgently needed.[28]

III

Before discussing a number of abuses to which the above conception of the mission of the Catholic university and of the Catholic scholar may be subject, it is necessary to enter the following disclaimer.

A few essays have appeared in the Catholic press during the past decade which have claimed that the real deficiencies in Catholic education lay in the fact that it was really not *Catholic* enough: a claim, as noted above, with which all sincere educators must agree; for, indeed, the work of achieving a truly Catholic university, like the personal task of the scholar in achieving a completely Catholic comportment in the face of reality, is an undertaking that can never be fully accomplished. But these articles to which I refer specified that what was wrong with Catholic colleges and universities was that they had cultivated "pagan learning" and employed "pagan methods" of research. Now, inasmuch as "all truth belongs to us Christians," and inasmuch as the Catholic scholar is obliged, both by his intellectual commitment and by his vocation as a witness, to embrace all good things, this was a type of criticism of no value whatever. When these same articles then suggested that this highly desired infusion of more "genuinely Catholic knowledge" would take the form of eliminating "pagan" courses and introducing what are known as "Catholic" courses, it became apparent that here was a real mingling and oversimplification of the orders of nature and supernature.

Indeed so widespread is this type of oversimplification that quite generally one can assume that when certain critics complain about the paganization of Catholic schools, they do not mean that there is a failure to teach all aspects of knowledge, in the light of Christian wisdom, with the highest competence, and with the best methods—they mean simply that there is too much humanism and not enough catechism. I would regret it, then, if the observations in the preceding section on the nature and ends of Catholic higher learning were to be so misconstrued as to provide a handle to the argument of those whose own knowledge of the catechism seems slight, and who appear, on principle, opposed to the cultivation of the intellect.

Because the Catholic scholar is the conscious subject of the various forces which I have discussed above, it would be a serious error to envision his role as that of inquisitor to the universe or belligerent *defensor fidei;* his first loyalty is to truth as he sees it. He must, then, avoid the two extremes of an excessive reliance on dogmatic principles and a prideful disdain for the sincere efforts of non-Christian thinkers. And these extremes must be avoided not out of any sense of superiority, but rather out of the sincerest humility, as by one who realizes that he carries a heavier burden and has therefore a deeper responsibility to the truth.

In the following paragraphs, I would like to offer some historical illustrations of the failure to accept this burden.

This deeper responsibility may be readily observed as antithetical to that narrow bias one recognizes in certain works of the past three decades dedicated to proving—almost on *a priori* grounds—such things as the Catholicism of Shakespeare or the poetic pre-eminence of Joyce Kilmer. When a Catholic critic can publicly announce, in a nationally circulated magazine, his regrets at the failure to include Father Tabb in the *Oxford Anthology of American Verse,* or when a Catholic university can award a doctorate in literature for a dissertation which discovers Shakespeare's Catholicism in the poet's alleged belief in the immortality of the soul, in the indissolubility of marriage, and in the evil of suicide and adultery, is it not apparent that a misty apologetics has systematically blinded critical sense, and that rather than seeing things as they are, one is seeing them as he imagines they ought to be?

It is certainly justifiable for a Catholic scholar to examine such subjects as directly pertain to his own religious tradition, provided that he has no apologetic preconceptions, and that he is willing to accept whatever facts his research may disclose. But this implies that the best critical apparatus be employed, and that it be employed honestly and objectively—as it has, for example, in the case of Shakespeare, in Father Grunwald's dissertation, in Canon Looten's imaginative study, in Father Thurston's essays, or in Gerard de Groot's *The Shakespeares and "The Old Faith."* Nor should one regard those particular Shakespeare studies which have been authored by priests as expressions of that narrow interest many Catholics, and more particularly the clergy, sometimes display toward peripheral sectarian themes. Rather than being a reflection of what has been called the "ghetto mentality," these various studies fulfill one of the secondary ends of Catholic scholarship and of the Catholic university.

Because the Church Militant is a visible society which necessarily influences, one way or another, temporal affairs, it is to be expected that Catholic scholars in all fields will explore these influences out of a legitimate sense of family pride, and that they will undertake this exploration even though these exclusively confessional issues are often of little more than intra-mural interest. And if, on the one hand, this justifiable preoccupation with "family" matters leads one to the type of a-critical pietism represented, for example, in this country by the late Msgr. Semper on *l'amour courtois,* or in Europe by the late Père Mandonnet on the *Vita Nuova,* this does not justify condemning the preoccupation as such; for, on the other hand, one may see the benefits flowing from this same sense of family loyalty in—to take another example from Dante studies—such a work as M. Gilson's *Dante and Philosophy.* Thus there is no reason why what has often been mistaken for the ghetto mentality should not, when rightly understood, deepen one's interest in a specific field, and provide one with stronger motives for examining it.

An ardent spirit of devotion to the Church as a temporal society is in accord with the work and the objectives of a Catholic university, and this spirit ought never to be identified with the ghetto mentality. The latter, which *is* the product of sectarian prejudice, amounts to an obsession with things that are merely nominally or materially Roman Catholic; it is really that pride of the Pharisees which is, by definition, the antithesis of the universality of the Catholic vision and of the truly Catholic university. All displays of this exaggerated confessional loyalty embarrass the sincere Christian; and when they do not offend truth itself, generally they offend critical sensibility, good judgment, or good taste. Faced with such offenses, one can only applaud Abbé Bremond's characterization of "yet another" anthology of *Catho-*

lic Poetry as "a dismal cemetery where I have counted five hundred tombs." [29]

The failure to grasp the true mission of Catholic scholarship, and the objective attitude that mission implies, was apparent in a number of articles which appeared at the time of the Goethe bicentennial in 1949.[30] These articles made it only too obvious that there has taken root among some American Catholics a strange proclivity for hurling hasty anathemas at thinkers of different world-views. This tendency leads its victims to misinterpret an author's life and works, to bring them into conformity with some predetermined thesis: the thesis generally taking the form of refuting a particular writer, not on the grounds of intellectual error, but on the basis of his failure to accept certain Roman Catholic doctrines. For example, one may read in certain Catholic treatments of Goethe published a decade ago that the poet "represented the pride by which the angels fell, and the same pride which saw Germany's dark collapse under the Nazis. . . ." The German people, says the critic I am quoting, followed Goethe "as sheep follow a shepherd." Now these are judgments with which no objective student, so far as I know, has expressed agreement. Goethe, it is true, did influence a number of the intellectuals and savants of his day, but there was never, then or since, any general popular adherence to his thought or his person, that one could refer to in the same way that one might speak, for instance, of the vulgar cult of Nietzsche.[31] Even *Werther* was not so much an influence as it was the confirmation of an already existing literary and social trend.

Goethe had alienated the masses by his opposition to the revolution, and he had offended the rising *littérateurs* by his ardent classicism. Indeed, so definitely did Goethe divorce himself from popular life that it is more common and more reasonable to err in the opposite direction by regarding the poet, not as a shepherd leading Prussian sheep, but as an escapist cut off from all contact with practical affairs.

This student of Goethe, whom I have been indicting, had a unique interpretation of Dean Stanley's remark that Newman would not have entered the Church if he had known German. This, we are told, was said "with Goethe's German-philosophy background in mind." Unfortunately, there is nothing in Dean Stanley's writings or in those of Mark Pattison, who transmitted the remark, which can be said to justify even remotely this interpretation; [32] and there are, as a matter of fact, passages in Newman which would serve to disprove it.

One consequence, then, of this lack of objectivity is the distortion of historical fact: a distortion which, certainly, does not result from any yearning to deceive, but rather from a desire to be, in a sense, more Catholic than Catholicism. And this zeal, though ostensibly born of Christian principles and of good intention, usually leads by reason of its extravagance to two additional errors of judgment. First, it equates the philosophical assumptions negatively supported by faith with the very spirit of Catholicism. Thus— again in the example of Goethe—while the personal philosophy which the poet constructed may not have been in conformity with Scholasticism, it was rarely in total or even in occasional disconformity with the principles of Christianty; [33] and yet notwithstanding this, these ultra-Catholic critics to whom I refer have put the poet in the ranks of such notorious anti-Catholics and antitheists as a Thomas Paine or a Proudhon.

The second error consists in minimizing the reality of grace. It may seem self-contradictory to accuse writers of a deeply Christian purpose of overlooking grace, though, in fact, this ignoring of the supernatural, as the history of theological controversy testifies, may be taken as one of the typical characteristics of the religious zealot. Goethe—or for that matter, those other thinkers who have been the targets of the ultra-Catholic barbs, such as Valéry, George Eliot, Emerson, or Thomas Mann—could not have developed a totally adequate picture of the mysteries of man and nature, of God and creation: he lacked the necessary equipment. One wonders if what he did achieve is therefore always to be demeaned. Though remarkably gifted by nature, Goethe had not received the ultimate gift, the gift of faith; and for this, he has been decried and pilloried by critics who, with all their verbal vigor, seem themselves to have lost sight of some of the implications of their theology.

There are many Olympian figures whose personal lives tend to alienate or even to disgust the Christian critic, and whose genius is not readily subject to being idolized or hero-worshiped; and it is these figures, often remote and haughty, whose works are generally difficult to assess sympathetically. It would not be necessary, for example, to read *Lotte in Weimar* to

discover that egotism and self-complacency were Goe-
thean traits, any more than it would be necessary to
read *Wife to Mr. Milton* to discover that the Miltonic
temper was often vindictive, splenetic, and arrogant.
But it is precisely in the study of such singular per-
sonalities as Goethe and Milton—or, for that matter,
of St. Jerome, or Savonarola—that the attitudes of
sympathy and objectivity, which have been extolled
above as the instinctive virtues of the Christian scholar, should be most apparant. Yet, unconsciously one
seeks to examine the man's work in terms of the man,
or, what is worse, in terms of one's subjective opinion
of the man. To condemn Goethe or Wagner as artists
on political or moral grounds, as I believe Theodor
Haecker did, or again, to depreciate the poetic
achievement of Milton because of his violent Puritanism, as I believe Belloc did, is in both cases to
fall into this unconscious error of judgment. It is, as
Lord Acton said, "stumbling at the ass's bridge, for
scientific thought begins with the separation between
the idea and its exponent." [34]

This is not to say that one may not favor, on
the grounds of purely personal prejudice, perhaps
Chaucer over Langland, or Hopkins over Arnold, or
Donne over Milton; such prejudice, one way or the
other, is largely unavoidable. What the above paragraphs do say is simply that one must keep this personal bias from obtruding in critical studies, and
leading to assessments in purely esthetic questions.
When, for example, one looks back on the type of
examination to which Milton's personal life was subjected, after Mr. Eliot had disfranchised the poet, and

when one recalls the subsequent adulation of Donne —romantically worshiped as the penitent rogue with whom everyone who wasn't dissociated had so much in common—one has the impression that much of what passed for critical esteem of the metaphysicals was founded on nonpoetic, nonesthetic bases. But again, this is not to suggest that one should not on the grounds of private enthusiasm for this or that writer's character examine his works; on the contrary, it will often be found that one's interest in a particular author, not only as artist or thinker, but as man, will induce one to pursue the necessary research on his achievements with all the more diligence and devotion. This has certainly been true of a number of excellent critics: one thinks of E. K. Rand on Vergil, of Gerald Walsh on Dante, of Samuel Eliot Bassett on Homer, of James H. Hanford on Milton. But it would be a grievous sin against the "scholarly virtues" to carry personal predilection to the extreme where another poet or philosopher or scientist is convicted of bad poetry, bad philosophy, or bad science, not on poetic, philosophic, or scientific evidence, but merely because he has fallen short of some extraneous standard.

No Catholic scholar is obliged to study the works of a man whose character and/or religious beliefs seem in some way or in many ways reprehensible; but having once undertaken such a study, the Catholic scholar, above all other scholars, should be able to exercise proper caution to avoid passing ethical judgments on esthetic or metaphysical issues; and this, because the attitudes of sympathy and objectivity are dictated to him by supernatural as well as by natural motives. If one cannot exercise this caution, if one cannot awaken this sympathy, if one finds one's personal tastes so alien to a particular figure's life or work that critical judgment may be blinded or obscured, then one ought—after the example of Wilfrid Ward declining to write Acton's biography—to abandon this line of research in favor of more arable fields.

An even greater restraint is imposed on the Catholic scholar when it is a question of analyzing studies which are maliciously inimical to Christian truth. Rather than violently censuring such works, as if by heaping abuse on them one could obviate their error, they should be welcomed by the student as providing an opportunity to set forth the Christian vision in all its clarity. Moreover, when one assaults with empty tirades the position of his opponents—even his prejudiced opponents—one creates among objective and sincere scholars the impression that emotion is being substituted for intelligence, and incompetence is seeking to disguise itself in rhetorical bluster. Far more consonant with his mission would it be for the Catholic student to animate himself with that passion for truth which led Lord Acton to see in the attacks of Strauss and Renan a providential instrument for bringing Catholicism to examine its historical conscience and to explicate its apologetic more fully. A truly admirable example of this creative Catholic attitude in our own time is Père de Lubac's study of one of the most frankly virulent antitheists of the last century, Pierre Joseph Proudhon.

I have discussed above the attitudes of the Catholic scholar, first, to what Goethe himself called "the Great Pagan," that is, to the invincibly ignorant, magnanimous non-Christian; second, to the non-Christian thinker who, through culpable blindness and malice, attacks the Catholic ideal. It is necessary now to consider the Christian attitude toward the delicate situation raised by apostasy. Here, too, one must be on guard against invoking the clichés of dogmatism or the frigid and pseudo-objective simplifications of certain catechetical works. The recent studies on Luther by Lortz, Congar, and Karl Adam, with their correction of a number of traditional prejudices, should indicate how difficult it is for man to assume the prerogative of "searching the reins and the heart," and furthermore should suggest the imprudence and the injustice of trotting out, without sufficient documentation, the customary accusations of pride, ambition, and duplicity to explain away every defection from the visible Church.

When Fernand Hayward, writing of the Vatican Council, says of Dr. Döllinger: "The leader of the opposition in Germany was a university professor of great learning, but also of excessive pride," does not one immediately mistrust the judgment which with its facile handbook phrases seems to absolve its author from all historical seriousness? When Hayward goes on to state—and contradicts the word of Pius IX in so doing—that Döllinger's opposition to the Council resulted from disappointment at not being invited, one is tempted to cry out with Newman to Kingsley, "Why, man, you are writing a romance!"

Or when the apostasy of de Lamennais—whose simplicity of character is attested to by the shrewd judgment of Disraeli, and whose service to religion is attested to by Newman—is summarily dismissed as the result of pride and duplicity, is there not a great danger of abdicating critical intelligence in the name of a spurious theological assumption? [35] Neither dogmatic bias, as evidenced by the examples above, nor a false liberalism, as apparent in Petre on Tyrrell or Dimnet on Loisy, can govern the determination of such issues. Only an absolute fidelity to historical truth, as seen in the light of Christian reverence, sympathy, and objectivity can be one's guide.

That spiritual arrogance which, rightly or wrongly, Gide attributed to Claudel seems to have afflicted Catholic philosophers even more seriously than scholars in other fields. There are two reasons for this: one which may be called philosophical, and the other, historical. First, because Scholastic philosophy, as M. Gilson has often pointed out, is in many ways an outgrowth of theology, it is to be expected that some of the certitude of religious doctrine will carry over to philosophical assumptions. When this influence reaches the proportions of the following statement, in what purported to be a serious work, one is touching upon the historical reason for such a phenomenon. In *The Philosophy of the Bible*—a title as confusing as the book itself—published in 1876, the Archbishop of Halifax wrote of "philosophic quacks, such as Hegel, Kant, Darwin, and *id genus omne.* . . . Spinoza who gave such a proof of mental aberration that a schoolboy who would be guilty of similar contradictions would most surely be doomed to lose his first holiday. . . ." [36] *"Id omne genus . . .":* seven years before these words were written, the only voice in the English Catholic world capable of speaking out with vigor and moderation against this "metaphysical ultramontanism" had declared of another *genus* of philosophers:

Our theological philosophers are like the old nurses who wrap the unhappy infant in swaddling bands or boards— put a lot of blankets over him—and shut the windows that not a breath of fresh air may come to his skin as if he were not healthy enough to bear wind and water in due measure. They move in a groove, and will not tolerate anyone who does not move in the same. . . . I come more and more to see than I did, what an *irritabile genus* Catholic philosophers are. . . .[37]

The historical reason for that arrogant vehemence which Newman decried is that in the nineteenth century the last infirmity of the noble mind—symbolized in Turgenev's Bazarov and Dostoevski's Stavrogin— reached epidemic proportions; and when this pride, taking the form of scientific Messianism in Spencer, Comte, and Marx, was encountered by the Scholastic philosophers, they reacted as did Piux IX when the secular arm of nineteenth-century ideology captured Rome: they walled themselves within the Scholastic castle, appearing on the battlements only to hurl vitriolic denunciations at modern thought. (From the vantage of this parallel, one might suggest that the commission given by Leo XIII to Msgr. Mercier had an historical significance comparable to that of the Vatican treaty of 1929.)

This self-immurement led to an even greater reliance on revelation and to an overwhelming contempt for non-Christian philosophers. This spirit of reaction against modern thought—understandable in its genesis, but inexcusable in its extension and duration—reflected in the Jesuit Lorenzelli's classification of all philosophy since the seventeenth century as corrupt, and in Cornoldi's characterization of modern thought as "the pathology of human reason," ultimately was responsible for smothering those specifically Catholic attitudes of reverence, objectivity, and sympathy which should have endowed the Catholic scholar with a more comprehensive view of reality. Rarely are philosophers subjected so thoroughly to the relentless logic of their own canonized maxims: *corruptio optimi pessima* is the only heading for this sad chapter of intellectual history.

Unfortunately, one cannot close off the movement of history the way one may close the books which relate it; there is a footnote to be added to this melancholy narrative. The Church is a communion; it moves as a body, as a whole, and if there was intellectual pride among many men of the Church in the nineteenth century, there was also social pride. It was the one same affliction which blinded Christian thinkers to the significance of the experiments of Saint-Simon, Fourier, and Marx that also engendered what Pius XI called the "scandal of the nineteenth century," and that mockery of intellectual freedom which Newman assaulted.

There was true private judgment in the primitive and medieval schools—there are no schools now, no private judgment (in the religious sense of the phrase), no freedom, that is, of opinion. That is, no exercise of the intellect. No, the system goes on by the tradition of the intellect of former times.[38]

Considering this interrelation of intellectual myopia and social indifference on the part of many nineteenth-century Catholics, it is not surprising that the same man who did so much to prod and spur the Catholic social conscience was also one of the strongest forces, before his fall, for a Catholic intellectual revival. How different might not the history of the Church, the history of nineteenth-century religious thought, and the history of American Catholic higher education have been, had de Lamennais founded—fifty years before its actual realization—the Catholic University of America! [39]

IV

It ought not to be necessary to apologize for taking so much space to explain the abuses to which the ideal of Catholic scholarship and of the Catholic university may succumb, for often the best way of determining what a thing is, is to show what it is not. Moreover, the abuses that I have discussed above have been exemplified in the men and events of an historical period, the disordered heritage of which is largely responsible for the present confusion in American Catholic education.

I would like, in concluding, even at the risk of possible misinterpretation, to mention three individual studies which seem to reflect in all its reverence, objectivity, and sympathy, that ideal which I have sketched above for Catholic scholarship. In the Lowell Lectures on Dante by Gerald Walsh, S.J., in Teilhard de Chardin's synthesis, *Le Phénomène humain,* and in Emmanuel Mounier's works on personalism, one may find, I believe, a level of Christian understanding, dependent certainly on theological theses, but in its totality rooted rather in a comprehensive insight, explicable only as the fruit of a conscious realization of the import of one's sacred character as a witness to Christian truth. Other illustrations of this insight may come to mind, but I have intentionally confined myself here to these three men, a humanist, a scientist, and a social philosopher, who, while our contemporaries, have since passed to their ultimate insight, to that insight we call Beatific.

Perhaps to mention particular persons is to court misunderstanding, because it is frequently difficult or impossible to determine what derives from natural talent and what derives from the perfection of natural talent by the Christian intellectual demeanor. Moreover, it cannot be too much emphasized that this comprehensive insight, born of the consciousness of one's redeemed character, will be evident, not primarily in the resolution and understanding of specific problems, but in the ethos of one's whole intellectual life where one's Christ-orientation will be manifest as a kind of inner climate, as a profound interior movement, creating a more reverent, objective, and sympathetic relation between the subject and the object.

NOTES

1 The Knapp-Greenbaum study has been subjected to minor revisions by J. H. Holland, *Science,* September 6, 1957.

2 Cf. the observations on adaptation by the eminent Jesuit canonist, J. Creusen, in *Review for Religious,* March, 1949.

3 The citations are, respectively: *Poetics,* 1451b 5; *The Idea of a University,* "Christianity and Letters," edited by Daniel O'Connell, S.J., Chicago, 1927, p. 276. All further citations will be from this edition.

4 The citations are, respectively: *The Higher Learning in America,* New Haven, 1936, p. 99; *The Chicago Maroon,* April 4, 1952.

5 Cf. "The Philosophy of Growth," in *N.E.A. Journal,* January, 1948, and the treatment of the "philosophy of discipline"; also, the "philosophy of industrial-auto mechanics," in *Industrial Arts and Vocational Education,* April, 1958. Citations could be multiplied almost indefinitely.

6 Cf. "Shortages in the Curriculum," in *N.E.A. Journal,* May, 1948: "As an educational objective, learning how to have fun came into the school curriculum rather late and met a reserved welcome. It was hard to fit with a set of aims, proceedings, and standards. Now across the land there are outstanding examples of school programs which produce fun and which teach ways of developing one's fun activities. . . . No one field has anything like a monopoly on the obligation to help children and young people learn how to have fun. All aspects of the curriculum have valuable resources for it."

7 For Newman, cf. "Knowledge Viewed in Relation to Learning," pp. 163 ff.; for the University of London, cf. *University College, London*, London, 1929, Chapter 12, on "University Reform."

8 One may apply to the Benedictine educators what St. Benedict's Rule says of the abbot: "Let him so adjust and adapt himself to every one—to the one by gentleness of speech, to another by reproofs, and to still another by entreaties, to each one according to his bent and understanding—that he not only suffer no loss in his flock, but may rejoice in the increase of a worthy fold." *Rule of St. Benedict*, Chapter 2.

9 Cf. Francis McMahon, *A Catholic Looks at the World*, New York, 1943, pp. 303 ff.; of particular relevance here are Sister Madeleva's criticisms of inadequate theological preparation for teaching Sisters in *Proceedings of the Forty-Sixth Convention of the N.C.E.A.*, 1948; Dom Virgil Michel's educational work is discussed at length in the dissertation on him by Paul Marx, O.S.B., Collegeville, Minnesota, 1957, and in Mortimer Adler's contribution to the memorial issue of *Orate Fratres*, 1938; Leo R. Ward, C.S.C., *Blueprint for a Catholic University*, St. Louis, 1949.

10 Berdyaev, whose early writings, with their anticipation of "a new Middle Ages," were highly praised by Catholic critics, speaks of the Enlightenment as "the temporal punishment of the Renaissance" (*The End of Our Time*, New York, 1933, p. 31). The description is understandable in the light of Berdyaev's definition of democracy as "an assertion of a right to error and falsehood, a political relativism, a sophistry" (*Ibid.*, p. 54). It may be true that Locke and the philosophers of the Enlightenment embraced a theory of democracy and private property which was largely individualistic (cf. H. Johnson, *The New Scholasticism*, April, 1950), as it may also be true that more comprehensive principles are to be found in the Schoolmen. But from an historical standpoint, it must be acknowledged that these principles received only slight application in the Middle Ages (cf. Ewart Lewis, *The American Political Science Review*, June, 1956); and, in fact, the men of the Enlightenment, whatever their errors, made this application, as Maritain and Sturzo have admitted (cf. *Christianity and Democracy*, New York, 1945, p. 40; *Church and State*, New York, 1939, p. 307). Concerning the equally important issue of slavery, the benefits of the philosophy of the Enlightenment are underlined in Latourette's *A History of the Expansion of Christianity*, New York, 1941, Vol. IV, p. 158. One might also contrast the traditional Catholic attitude of de Lamennais (*Essay on Indifference in Matters of Religion*, London, 1895, Vol. I, p. 249) with that of Wilberforce and the other Evangelicals toward this question.

[11] "Christianity and Letters," p. 279.

[12] *Ibid.*, p. 276.

[13] *Newman: His Life and Spirituality,* New York, 1958, p. 310.

[14] *Humanism and Theology,* Milwaukee, 1943, p. 73.

[15] *De Ratione Studii,* text in W. H. Woodward, *Desiderius Erasmus Concerning the Aim and Method of Education,* Cambridge, 1904, p. 164.

[16] *Forty-First Yearbook,* Bloomington, Illinois, 1942.

[17] *Ibid.*, p. 269.

[18] *Ibid.*, p. 270.

[19] "Christianity and Letters," p. 275.

[20] *Forty-First Yearbook,* p. 275.

[21] "Duties of the Church Towards Knowledge," p. 251.

[22] Two additional factors must be mentioned because they have generally gone unnoticed in the current discussion on Catholics and the higher learning: first, the difference between the Protestant and the Catholic attitude with regard to temporal achievement, which is developed in the classic studies by Weber and Tawney, and discussed in detail by Newman in *Anglican Difficulties;* second, the very real persecution and the intellectual contempt to which American Catholics were subjected in the nineteenth century.

[23] Newman to J. C. Shairp, December 18, 1870, in *Principal Shairp and His Friends,* London, 1888, p. 286.

[24] Father D'Arcy has some stimulating observations in his "Comment on Philosophical Systems" (*Thought,* June, 1950); cf. also Gaston Fessard in *Recherches de Science Religieuse* (Juin, 1949) on Père Marc's *Psychologie réflexive* which "has proposed the notion of a system open not only to the progress of human truth and philosophical thought, but also to the idea of a possible plurality of systems, each in its own way rendering homage to the unique Truth." On the pedagogical level, the important work of the Franciscan Sisters of Milwaukee, in their textbook series *The Christian Impact,* must be taken into consideration in any assessment of Dietrich von Hildebrand's educational position.

[25] No one doubts that the Aristotelian-Scholastic synthesis does have much to say in esthetics, as this has been said, for example, in the Mellon Lectures of Professors Maritain and Gilson; but I am talking about the tenor of much Scholastic criticism, about the attitude which it often reflects: the attitude, for instance, exemplified in the recently translated de Wulf, *Art and Beauty,* or in Arthur Little's *The Nature of Art* (I have discussed these two works in *Renascence,* Spring, 1952). This attitude may also account for that failure of the Aristotelian-Scholastic critics to

come to grips with the poetic object itself, which Yvor Winters examined in *The Hudson Review* (Autumn, 1956).

26 Margaret Townsend O'Brien in *The New Scholasticism* (October, 1946). Faced with such omnivorous philosophism, one can only be amused at recalling that an eminent humanist (Abbé Dimnet) attributed the achievement of an eminent philosopher (M. Maritain) to his literary ability, not to his metaphysical acuity (*My New World*, New York, 1937, p. 129); one recalls also the words of Wallace Stevens, ". . . in spite of M. Jacques Maritain we do not want to be metaphysicians" (*The Necessary Angel*, New York, 1951, p. 59).

27 *Unpublished Letters of Matthew Arnold*, New Haven, 1923, p. 17.

28 Philipp Frank in *Conflicts of Power in Modern Culture*, New York, 1947, p. 168; Teilhard de Chardin in *Nouvelles Lettres de Voyage*, Paris, 1957, p. 180.

29 *Anglican Difficulties*, London, 1901, Vol. II, p. 25. Newman was speaking not as an Anglican but as an Englishman when he criticized "Romanist" theology: "It arranges, adjusts, explains, exhausts every part of the Divine Economy. It may be said to leave no region unexplored, no heights unattempted, rounding off its doctrines with a neatness and finish which is destructive of many of the most noble and most salutary exercises of mind in the individual Christian. That feeling of awe and piety which the mysteriousness of the Gospel should excite fades away under this fictitious illumination which is poured over the entire Dispensation. Criticism, we know, is commonly considered fatal to poetic fervour and imagination; and in like manner this technical religion destroys the delicacy and reverence of the Christian mind" (*Lectures on the Prophetical Office of the Church*, London, 1837, pp. 108–109). One is reminded of the words of the intensely English and intensely Roman Catholic Dean Colet to Erasmus: "Why do you preach Aquinas to me? For if he had not had much arrogance, he would not have defined everything so boldly and proudly" (E. W. Hunt, *Colet and His Theology*, London, 1956, p. 9).

30 *De Studiis et Literis*, text in W. H. Woodward, *Vittorino da Feltre and Other Humanist Educators*, Cambridge, 1921, p. 123.

31 *Pilgrim of the Absolute*, edited by Raïssa Maritain, New York, 1947, p. 75.

TWO:

AT THE SOURCES

1 The texts are, respectively: Basil Moreau, *Our Light and Our Way*, Milwaukee, 1936, p. 147; *Recueil de différents petits traités*, Paris, 1932, p. 106; *True Devotion to the Blessed Virgin*, Bayshore, New York, 1946, p. 57.

2 The shadow of the Monophysites hovers over the French school, and there is a close parallel between the negative attitude of its theologians to the humanity of Christ and the disdain shown by its great pedagogues, notably St. de La Salle, to the humanistic disciplines.

3 *The Thomist*, April, 1949.

4 *Letters and Shorter Works*, New York, 1947, p. 103.

5 *The Spiritual Teaching of Father Louis Lallemant*, Westminster, Maryland, 1946, p. 66. Such a teaching as that of Père Lallemant is neutralized by St. Thomas, *Contra Gentiles*, II, 3: "It is obviously false to assert the opinion of those who said that whatever we think about creatures has no bearing on the truths of faith, so long as we think rightly about God." Cf. St. Teresa (*Life*, trans. by David Lewis, Westminster, Maryland, 1948, Chapter 13, p. 103): ". . . it is of great consequence that the director should be prudent—I mean, of sound understanding—and a man of experience. If, in addition to this, he is a learned man, it is a very great matter. . . ." St. Teresa is famously insistent on this point: cf. *Ibid.*, Chapter 5; *Spiritual Relations*, Chapter 3. Père Lallemant's teaching may be compared with that of other manuals: cf. P. Lejeune, *An Introduction to the Mystical Life*, London, 1924, p. 299: "But true learning, that which in a soul is joined to Christian simplicity, far from being an obstacle to an elevated form of prayer, is, on the contrary, an excellent preparation for it."

6 *Le Milieu Divin*, Paris, 1957, pp. 37–38.

7 *Transformation in Christ*, New York, 1948, p. 184.

8 Cf. Robert Rumilly, *Le Frère Marie-Victorin et son Temps*, Montreal, 1949, pp. 45, 412; Nicolas Corte, *La Vie et l'âme de Teilhard de Chardin*, Paris, 1957, p. 25. I have treated of this intellectual and religious tension in Marie-Victorin (in *Journal of Arts and Letters*, Autumn, 1949) and in Teilhard de Chardin (in *The Commonweal*, April 13, 1958).

9 St. Louis, 1937, pp. 431–432.

10 *Lectures on the Prophetical Office of the Church*, p. 121.

11 *The Way of Perfection,* trans. by Alice Alexander, Westminster, Maryland, 1946, p. 87.

12 p. 299.

13 *The Christian Vision,* ed. by Mary Ellen Evans, Westminster, Maryland, 1956, p. xiv.

14 The exaggerations in Vacant have also been corrected by the excellent essay in the encyclopedia *Catholicisme,* Paris, 1948; the editor, Abbé Jacquemet, notes that "the reaction against 'Americanism' retarded the creation of Catholic Action."

15 *The Church and Modern Society,* Chicago, 1896, pp. 63, 81, 88.

16 *The Satin Slipper,* trans. by John O'Connor, New York, 1936, p. 136.

17 Ward, *Life of John Henry Cardinal Newman,* London, 1912, Vol. II, 180.

18 *Ibid.*

19 For this reason, Newman himself said of Father Hecker: "I have ever felt that there was a sort of unity in our lives, that we had both begun a work of the same kind." Quoted in *The Catholic Encyclopedia,* "Hecker."

20 Ward, *op cit.,* I, 584.

21 New York, 1936, p. 216.

22 *Goethe the Poet,* Cambridge, 1949, p. 285.

23 *The Jesuit Code of Liberal Education,* Milwaukee, 1938, p. 136.

24 And there is in Ignatius' writings a sense of the value of natural achievement and humane learning. Cf. his letter to the college of Coimbra in Daniel H. Bartoli, S.J., *History of St. Ignatius de Loyola,* New York, n.d., Vol. II, pp. 249 ff.

25 *St. Jean-Baptiste de La Salle,* Paris, 1944, p. 191.

26 *Essays on Education,* New York, 1911, pp. 7, 154. But the "law" of spirit is the inverse of this law of matter, for spirit tends toward unity.

27 For Dom Graf, *The Homiletic and Pastoral Review,* June, 1951; the French committee reported its findings in *Supplément de la Vie Spirituelle,* Fév., 1950. Cf. also the correspondence published in *Orate Fratres,* June and July, 1950; the extracts which follow are by a teacher, by the editor of *Orate Fratres,* and by a novice master. (1) "All of us realize the tragic need for implanting the liturgy in the minds of the young people in our schools; but faith comes by hearing, and how are the students to hear these ideas unless the teachers themselves are familiar with them? It is not enough that religious teachers take this or that course in 'Liturgy'; it is much more important that they live the prayer of the Church in their own communities—and where is the religious teaching community of Sisters or Brothers that is even attempting

this?" (2) Concerning the spiritual ennui of some religious: "In not a few of these cases, a certain sense of disillusionment with the religious life arises, not immediately perhaps, but after about eight or ten years of profession, centering around the fact that it does not provide an organically constructed and spiritually satisfying prayer-life." (3) "I refer particularly to the Divine Office: *Orate Fratres* has made a start in breaking down the wall of ignorant prejudices which some temperaments hold and dig out of constitutions which are not yet fifty years old." Notwithstanding the important contributions being made by *Worship*, and by such publications as *The Sister Formation Series* of Fordham University Press, the observations made above are still applicable to the present situation.

28 In the fine arts, the women's colleges are far superior to the men's which, with the notable exceptions of St. Ambrose and St. John's University, in most cases do not offer even introductory courses; the large urban universities are particularly deficient in this field, and their faculties might well sit at the feet of the religious women of Studio Angelico or Studio San Damiano, or take courses from Sister Mary of the Compassion, O.P., and Sister Esther, S.P.

29 *Desiderius Erasmus Concerning the Aim and Method of Education*, p. 204.

30 "God preserve us from convents where notions of honor rule! He Himself will never be greatly honored therein." St. Teresa, *Way of Perfection*, p. 228.

31 Dec. 16, 1950.

32 *Way of Perfection*, p. 9.

33 *France Pagan?*, London, 1949, pp. 109–110.

34 *Journal of Arts and Letters*, Autumn, 1949.

35 *Anglican Difficulties*, p. 269.

36 For Régamey: "The Present State of Religious Art," *Journal of Arts and Letters*, Summer, 1949; Jacques Maritain, "The Ways of Faith," *The Commonweal*, November 4, 1949.

37 *Vraie et fausse réforme dans l'église*, Paris, 1950, p. 542.

38 St. Bernard writes bitterly (Sermon 24, on the Canticle, *P.L.*, 183, 960) of those who acquire learning in order to sell it for money or glory. One feels that this just wrath is an element of the Saint's struggle against simony.

39 Ward, *op. cit.*, I, 381.

40 *Ibid.*, II, 196.

41 *Supplément de La Vie Spirituelle*, Août, 1949.

42 T. Mozley, *Reminiscences, Chiefly of Oriel College and the Oxford Movement*, London, 1882, Vol. I, p. 87; concerning Kittredge

and other "eccentrics," cf. Gilbert Highet, *The Art of Teaching*, New York, pp. 240 ff.

43 This value is perhaps underlined by St. Teresa's remark ". . . I was exceedingly troubled, because I trembled for his salvation, seeing that he had been superior for twenty years." *Life*, p. 387.

44 *Oxford Essays*, contributed by Members of the University, London, 1858, p. 266.

45 *Memoirs*, London, 1885, p. 96.

46 Dwight Culler (*The Imperial Intellect*, New Haven, 1955, pp. 116–118) has attempted to show the continuity in Newman's educational ideal between his Oxford period and his rectorship of the Catholic University of Ireland. I do not think his interpretative judgment can stand in the face of the written indictment of Tractarian education which Froude, Pattison, and Goldwin Smith made. Certainly *The Idea*, as Frederic Rogers noted (*Letters of Frederic Lord Blachford*, London, 1896, p. 247), is "derived from Oxford" experiences, since Newman had no other academic background to draw upon. Professor Culler's argument that Newman's own tuition was successful is largely irrelevant because Newman had no pupils during the period of the movement itself. Equally irrelevant is it to point out that while Newman's attitude may have been anti-rationalist, it was not anti-intellectual; for no one accuses the Tractarians of being simply anti-intellectual, but rather of confining their intellectual interests exclusively to theology. Of Newman's own college at the height of the movement, a contemporary witness has written: "The old tradition, which had obtained even amongst the undergraduates of Oriel who were content with the pass schools—that the cultivation of the intellect was at least one main object of life at the university— still lingered in the college—but only as a tradition" (Thomas Hughes, *James Fraser, Second Bishop of Manchester: A Memoir*, London, 1887, p. 23). Newman's position in the contest over the Sanskrit Professorship, and the general Puseyite attitude at the time of the election of Keble's successor as Professor of Poetry, point up the narrowness of the Tractarian educational ideal, and the truth of Faber's observation in 1835 that the university was in a state of "religious dislocation" (*Life and Letters of F. W. Faber*, London, 1869, p. 36). I would further suggest that it was the theological exclusivism of Tractarian education which disabled the university and left it open to the inroads of that Liberalism which Newman so feared. "The fact is that the Oxford Movement carried Oxford Liberalism in its womb. . . ." (*Goldwin Smith's Correspondence*, London, n.d., p. 268). It is no mere historical accident that it was not at Oxford, the citadel of An-

glicanism, that English theology made its first counterattack against the German criticism; Westcott, Hort, and Lightfoot were all Cambridge men. The obtrusion of a narrow theological party-spirit is pointed up by Samuel Wilberforce (*Life*, London, 1880, Vol. I, pp. 129–130), and in *Selected Essays and Papers of R. C. Christie*, London, 1902, p. xiv.

47 "Christianity and Scientific Investigation," p. 447.

48 Ward, *op. cit.*, I, 355.

1 Ward, *Life*, I, 323.

2 Rev. Richard Ginder, *Our Sunday Visitor*, April 13, 1958.

3 Cf. *The Wilfrid Wards and the Transition*, New York, 1934, p. 11.

4 Ward, *op. cit.*, II, 127.

5 André Rétif, Paris, 1950, Preface.

6 "Respect for the dignity of the priest has always been one of the characteristic attitudes of the Christian community; however, laymen also have their rights, and the priest, on his part, must respect them." Pope Pius XII, Address to the Second Congress of the Lay Apostolate, *Documentation Catholique*, November 10, 1957.

7 Ward, *op. cit.*, II, 296.

8 *Dogmatik*, Freiburg, 1948, Sect. 14, p. 99.

9 Shane Leslie, *Henry Edward Manning*, New York, 1921, p. 295.

10 The citations are, respectively: John O'Shea, *The Two Kenricks*, Philadelphia, 1909, p. 333; F. J. Zwierlein, *The Life and Letters of Bishop McQuaid*, Louvain, 1926, Vol. II, p. 48.

11 Cuthbert Butler, O.S.B., *The Vatican Council*, London, 1930, p. 29.

12 Cf. Scheeben, *loc. cit.*, ". . . the authority of the teaching body and of its doctrine is never merely a development or a reflection of the strength of the testimony; this testimony is not the only way, nor even the immediate and regular way, whereby the teaching body orients itself to the doctrine which it proclaims. Recourse to the profession of that faith which already exists within the Church-taught, is never more than a secondary means."

13 *Essays Ancient and Modern*, New York, 1936, p. 174.

14 *The Mechanical Bride*, New York, 1951, p. 44.

15 *Desiderius Erasmus Concerning the Aim and Method of Education*, p. 204.

FOUR:

DOING THE TRUTH

1 Cf. the violent attack on humanist education in *The New Renaissance of the Spirit*, New York, 1949, pp. 141 ff.

2 The texts are, respectively: St. Ignatius of Antioch, *Ad Philadelphensis*, P.G., V, 834; Tertullian, *De Testimonio animae*, v, P.L., II, 616.

3 The expression *veritatem facientes* has been the stumbling block of all those who are inclined to see in the Christian message only a truth to be grasped rationally; thus the phrase has been read as *veritatem studentes, veritatem sectantes, veritatem loquentes,* and *veritatem servantes.* Cf. Estius in *Epist. D. Pauli*, Paris, 1859.

4 For Msgr. Russell: *Orate Fratres*, January, 1949; for Père Clérissac: *The Mystery of the Church*, New York, 1937, p. 24.

5 *Opusc. var., De Substantiis separatis*, 14, cap. 3.

6 Wallace Stevens, "The Sense of the Sleight-of-Hand Man."

7 *Education at the Crossroads*, New Haven, 1943, p. 43.

8 In addition to the texts already cited (Chapter One, note 22) on the difference between the Protestant and the Catholic ethic, cf., from the specifically educational standpoint, Abraham Flexner, *Universities: American, English, German*, New York, 1930, p. 164: "Modern business does not satisfy the criteria of a profession; it is shrewd, energetic, and clever, rather than intellectual in character; it aims—and under our present social organization must aim—at its own advantage, rather than at any noble purpose within itself." And also Norman Foerster, *The Future of the Liberal College*, New York, 1938, p. 78: "Many of our large universities, both public and private—the dinosaurs of higher education—appear to have invited nothing less than retrogression toward barbarism. More and more they have dispensed a training which is fundamentally primitivistic, a training for ruthless competition in the modern jungle." Rather than bemoaning the failure of Catholic schools to train students for success in business and economic life, this failure ought to be cause for congratulation, and that on educational as well as on theological grounds. But I think it is possible to exaggerate the Calvinist roots of America's general orientation toward practical achievement and the ever-receding "new heaven and new earth." This orientation results not only from religious factors, but from such sociological conditions created by the reclamation of the West, and—one may say without getting involved in partisan controversies—from the influence of

the frontier. Such conditions affect every American, and must be recognized as being significant even in the cultural life of Catholics. They constitute the skeleton of that "Americanism" which was never condemned, and which affirmed the acceptance, not the rejection, of ineluctable historical contingencies, and the sanctification, not the frustration, of the work of the world.

9 Otto Karrer, *The Religions of Mankind*, New York, 1936, p. 122: "We men of today, whose organ of ratiocination is highly developed, no longer possess this gift, or at most only a few isolated individuals retain it. We have 'specialized the intellect.' We take everything to pieces with the understanding, analyze and dissect everything, and therefore never reach the essence of things. We obtain superficial impressions."

10 *Essays Ancient and Modern*, p. 172.

11 *Progress and Religion*, London, 1929, p. 26.

12 "What Is a University?", p. 471.

13 e.e. Cummings, "La Guerre."

14 *Aeneid* viii. 26, 27; Cf. iii. 147; iv. 522, 523.

15 *Inferno*, II, 1–3.

16 "Parlement of Foules," 85–86.

17 *Paradise Lost*, IV, 598–602.

18 Wallace Stevens, "Homunculus et la Belle Étoile."

19 *The Living God*, London, 1933, p. 238.

20 Wallace Stevens, "The Sense of the Sleight-of-Hand Man."

21 *Religious Art*, New York, 1949, pp. 96–97.

22 Of eternal punishment, Newman wrote: "I have tried in various ways to make that truth less terrible to the reason." *Apologia*, p. 38. (In later editions, Newman wrote, ". . . less terrible to the imagination.") For the various "ways," cf. Ward, *Life*, I, 246, and the appendix to *The Grammar of Assent*.

23 Cf. his essay on the Renaissance in *Lectures on Modern History*, London, 1920, p. 73: "For the men of the first generation of the Renaissance craving for self-help and the complete training of the faculties, eager to escape from the fixed types of medieval manhood, minted by authority, and taught to distrust conscience, when it was their own, and to trust it only in others, Seneca was an oracle."

24 Introduction to her translation of the *Purgatorio*, London, 1955, p. 24.

25 *Man and the State*, Chicago, 1951, p. 60.

26 Cf. Ewart Lewis, *The American Political Science Review*, June, 1956; B. Lyon, *The American Historical Review*, October, 1957.

27 I have not cited those lists of vices to be found in Langland or in

Bernard of Cluny's *De Contemptu Mundi,* because it is difficult to determine the prevalence of these various evils. I have avoided, also, citing Lea or Coulton because their works may be in part cancelled out by Haskins, Taylor, and, to a lesser degree, Gasquet; similarly one can counter the partisan extremes of Walsh's characterization of the thirteenth as "the greatest of centuries" with the equally partisan assertion of Rattray Taylor that "it is hardly too much to say that medieval Europe came to resemble a vast insane asylum." Particular value is to be placed on the judgments of Curtius and Auerbach because their method of phenomenological analysis of specific cultural expressions seems best adapted to grasping the spirit of an age.

28 "Inaugural Lecture," in *Lectures on Modern History,* p. 24.

29 *Eminent Victorians,* New York, 1938, p. 100. There is certainly nothing "hysterical" about Acton's dictum: "The inflexible integrity of the moral code is, to me, the secret of the authority, of the dignity, of the utility of history." *Essays on Freedom and Power,* Boston, 1948, p. 365.

30 Feb., 1958.

31 Text in *The Pope Speaks,* Autumn, 1955, p. 213. There is an excellent commentary on all the recent papal pronouncements on Christianity and Culture in Karlheinz Schmidthüs, *Von der Einheit der Welt,* Freiburg, 1957, pp. 139–147.

32 Notwithstanding the splendor of Mr. Dawson's panorama of the Middle Ages, one may yet be inclined to agree with M. Maritain that they are less admirable in reality than "in the refined memories of history." *Essays in Order,* New York, 1931, p. 23.

33 "Duties of the Church Towards Knowledge," pp. 247–248.

34 *Ibid.,* 248–249.

35 *Journal of Arts and Letters,* Spring, 1952.

36 The semantic confusion over the place of "Christian culture" in the curriculum recalls the polemic waged during the decade after the war over the question of "theology versus religion" in the college program. The advocates of "religion," led by Msgrs. Russell and Cooper, were regarded as proponents of some vague, moralistic, doctrinally enfeebled course of studies, whereas what they were actually suggesting was a more kerygmatic, a less contentious and less rationalistic treatment. In opposition to the proponents of "religion" was a group of Dominicans, inspired by the work of Father Farrell, who, in favoring "theology," left the observer with the mistaken impression that somehow Msgr. Russell's approach involved something less than theology. "Religion" became a pejorative term in academic circles; "theology" was the only course a self-respecting institution could offer its

students. But oddly enough, teaching "theology" usually meant
teaching *A Companion to the Summa;* these "theologians" having
forgotten Newman's words: "All theological definitions come
short of concrete life. Science is not devotion or literature. If the
Fathers are not cold, and the Schoolmen are, this is because the
former write in their own persons, and the latter as logicians or
disputants" (*Lectures on the Doctrine of Justification,* London,
1874, p. 31 n.).

37 Cf. *Polycraticus,* VIII, 24, trans. by Joseph B. Pike, Minneapolis,
1938, pp. 402–404. And a number of other texts in the biased but
factually accurate work by Domenico Comparetti, *Vergil in the
Middle Ages,* London, 1895, pp. 108, 112.

38 *Essays on Education,* pp. 32–33.

39 The five citations which follow are, respectively: *De Tradendis
Disciplinis,* trans. in Foster Watson, *Vives on Education,* Cambridge, 1913, pp. 87, 283; *Desiderius Erasmus Concerning the Aim
and Method of Education,* p. 59; *Vittorino da Feltre,* p. 110;
Desiderius Erasmus, loc. cit., Watson, *op. cit.,* p. lxiv.

40 Cf. *Vittorino da Feltre,* p. 242. All of the texts above are corrobo-
rated by an important recent work by George Ganss, S.J., *St. Ignatius' Idea of a Jesuit University,* Milwaukee, 1956.

41 "Christianity and Letters," p. 278.

42 The citations are, respectively: *Desiderius Erasmus,* p. 199; *Vittorino da Feltre,* p. 132.

43 No one questions the value of studying language for the discipline
of the mind or the type of cultural enrichment such study alone
provides, just as no one questions the immeasurable inferiority
of translations to the originals. But the fact remains that unless
secondary education is directed along the lines followed by the
British public school—a reform which seems to me both undesirable and unrealizable—utilitarian necessities that cannot be completely ignored would demand that the living languages be given
the nod over Greek or Latin.

44 Alfred North Whitehead, *The Aims of Education and other
Essays,* London, 1936, p. 96.

45 Cf. Msgr. Bruno de Solages, "Progrès modernes dans la Connais-
sance de l'Humanité," which treats of this tendency in the fields
of political economy, sociology, demography, and geography
(*Chronique,* Institut Catholique de Toulouse, No. 1, 1956). This is
a rectorial address which complements Msgr. de Solages' earlier
address on the work of Teilhard de Chardin ("La Pensée
chrétienne face à l'Evolution," *Bulletin de Littérature Ecclésias-
tique,* No. 4, 1947).

46 The three Patristic texts are, respectively: *Second Apology, P.G.,*

8, 466; *Apology,* cap. 33, *P.L.,* I, 448; *Letter to Diognetus, P.G.,* 2, 175.

FIVE:

THE MISSION OF
CATHOLIC SCHOLARSHIP

1 Cf. Michael de la Bedoyere, *The Life of Baron von Hügel,* London, 1952, p. 101.

2 "On the Various Names," *P.L.,* 52, 865. *Famen scientiae* is an alternate reading to *famen gentium;* I do not know the textual basis for the variant, but it seems to me to fit the context better.

3 *Cursus Theologicus,* Paris, 1828, XVI, 134.

4 All of these texts must be read in their ensemble, for Christ also said, "I have not come to condemn the world, but to save it" (John 12:47); and Christ and the Church are in union *in order that* the world may know that Christ has been sent by the Father (John 17:23).

5 I use the word "captain," because it has an English meaning broader than that of "chief"—which also expresses Christ's headship—and because it is apposite to the military role of the confirmed.

6 "The Usefulness of Hymns," attributed to Niceta of Remesiana.

7 The texts are, respectively: Eph. 4:16; Eph. 4:30; 2 Cor. 5:20; Acts 26:18.

8 The texts are, respectively: Rom. 8:20; Eph. 1:10; Acts 26:25.

9 F. Cuttaz, *Notre Pentecôte,* Paris, 1935, pp. 100–101.

10 Newman, "Elementary Studies," *Idea,* p. 386.

11 Butler, *Vatican Council,* Vol. I, p. 216.

12 *Letters of Lord Acton to Mary Gladstone,* London, 1913, p. 134.

13 Thus Blessed Alcuin wrote of the imposition of hands, in what probably constituted part of the sacrament of confirmation, that it strengthened the soul "in order that the Christian might preach to others" (*Epist.* 40, *P.L.,* 100, 292). This is a much more extensive formula than those which are too definitely military in tenor: e.g., John of St. Thomas, disp. 25, art. 6 (*Cursus theol.,* Paris, 1886, Vol. IX, p. 381), "for the profession of faith in the presence of tyrants."

14 *Ames de Lumière,* Paris, 1949.

15 Though the common interpretation of this text is to view the pastoral and teaching offices as one, à Lapide in his commentary on this passage notes that it has been applied to those "who teach in schools of letters." This is not a forced reading, if one takes

into consideration that the charisms are not confined to clergy and hierarchy, but may be given to any Christian for the manifestation of Christ's teaching in whatever field he is engaged.

16 *Adversus Haereses*, II, 4, *P.G.*, 7, 783.

17 E. Mersch, *The Whole Christ*, Milwaukee, 1936, pp. 536–537.

18 *Meditations on Various Subjects*, New York, 1947, p. 24.

19 John Grou, S.J., *Manual for Interior Souls*, Westminster, Maryland, 1956, p. 154. "The general intention of always pleasing God, and always doing His will is quite sufficient. . . . The general intention of doing the will of God . . . has the advantage of taking off our thoughts from ourselves."

20 *The Christian Sacrifice*, New York, 1943, p. 90.

21 Abbé Anger, *The Doctrine of the Mystical Body of Christ*, New York, 1931, p. 269: "Thanks to that inner sense of the Mystical Body, a sense which can be refined to a sensitive delicacy, the thoughts, outlooks, feelings, tastes, dislikes, tendencies—in fact, all that goes to make up that manifold complexity known as personality—take on a very special and distinct Catholic character."

22 *Works*, trans. by E. Allison Peers, Westminster, Maryland, 1953, Vol. II, p. 176.

23 Friedrich Jurgensmeier, *The Mystical Body of Christ*, New York, 1955, p. 101: "Sacramental character must not be regarded as a mere form of life or vital energy; it is rather that quality which stamps and shapes the members so that they become similar to the structure of the Head and are no longer alien to the Body, but become so homogeneous to it that they are capable of absorbing the life of the Head and of living in conformity with Him. Through this resemblance in structure, it is possible for the members to become one with the Head and to establish a state of harmony between their inner lives and their external actions."

24 *Les Sacréments dans la Vie Spirituelle*, Paris, 1935, p. 31.

25 *Introduction à l'étude de Saint Augustin*, Paris, 1929, p. 301.

26 A. Gardeil, O.P., *Le Saint Esprit dans la Vie Chrétienne*, Paris, 1934, p. 125.

27 *Dogmatik*, Sect. 52, p. 430.

28 *The New Tower of Babel*, New York, 1953, pp. 156–157.

29 Henry Hogarth, *Henri Bremond*, London, 1950, p. 150.

30 "The Goethe Bicentennial," *America*, July 30, 1949; "Goethe, the Pride of German Culture," *The Catholic World*, August, 1949.

31 Georg Brandes, *Wolfgang Goethe*, New York, 1925, Vol. II, pp. 474–475.

32 Stanley had reference to Strauss, Bauer, and Feuerbach; there is no reason for introducing Goethe into that triumvirate.

33 Cf. the possibly too optimistic study by Léon Emery, *Sagesse de Goethe*, Lyon, 1956.

34 *Letters to Mary Gladstone*, p. 164.

35 For Hayward: *The Vatican Council*, Dublin, 1951, p. 49. The historic fact is presented in Butler, *op. cit.*, I, 89. For Disraeli on de Lamennais: *Lord Beaconsfield's Correspondence with His Sister*, London, 1886, p. 208. Newman's attitude toward de Lamennais underwent a considerable change from his bitter Anglican essay, "The Fall of de Lamennais," *Essays Critical and Historical*, I, to his later remarks on the achievement of de Lamennais. Cf. Ward, *Life*, I, 484; and Newman's letter to Matthew Arnold in *Unpublished Letters of Matthew Arnold*, New Haven, 1923, p. 60.

36 Texts in Joseph Perrier, *The Revival of Scholastic Philosophy in the Nineteenth Century*, New York, 1909, pp. 246-247.

37 Ward, *op. cit.*, II, 254.

38 *Ibid.*, I, 588.

39 For de Lamennais and the intellectual revival, see Edgar Hocedez, S.J., *Histoire de la Théologie comme Science au XIXe Siècle*, Brussels, Vol. I, pp. 88, 123; for de Lamennais and the projected Catholic University, see Charles Sylvain, *Grégoire XVI*, Paris, 1889, p. 198.

INDEX OF NAMES